ICE TO ATHELSTAN

The
Emergence
of
England

ICE TO ATHELSTAN

The Emergence of England

A 10,000 year journey from the Last Ice Age
to England's first Crowned King

CHARLES BOUNDY

Copyright © 2024 Charles Boundy

The moral right of the author has been asserted.

Apart from any fair dealing for the purposes of research or private study, or criticism or review, as permitted under the Copyright, Designs and Patents Act 1988, this publication may only be reproduced, stored or transmitted, in any form or by any means, with the prior permission in writing of the publishers, or in the case of reprographic reproduction in accordance with the terms of licences issued by the Copyright Licensing Agency. Enquiries concerning reproduction outside those terms should be sent to the publishers.

Troubador Publishing Ltd
Unit E2 Airfield Business Park
Harrison Road, Market Harborough
Leicestershire LE16 7UL
Tel: 0116 279 2299
Email: books@troubador.co.uk
Web: www.troubador.co.uk

ISBN 978 1 83628 066 8

British Library Cataloguing in Publication Data.
A catalogue record for this book is available from the British Library.

Printed and bound by CPI Group (UK) Ltd, Croydon, CR0 4YY
Typeset in 10pt Minion Pro by Troubador Publishing Ltd, Leicester, UK

To Hazie – and our own evolving family

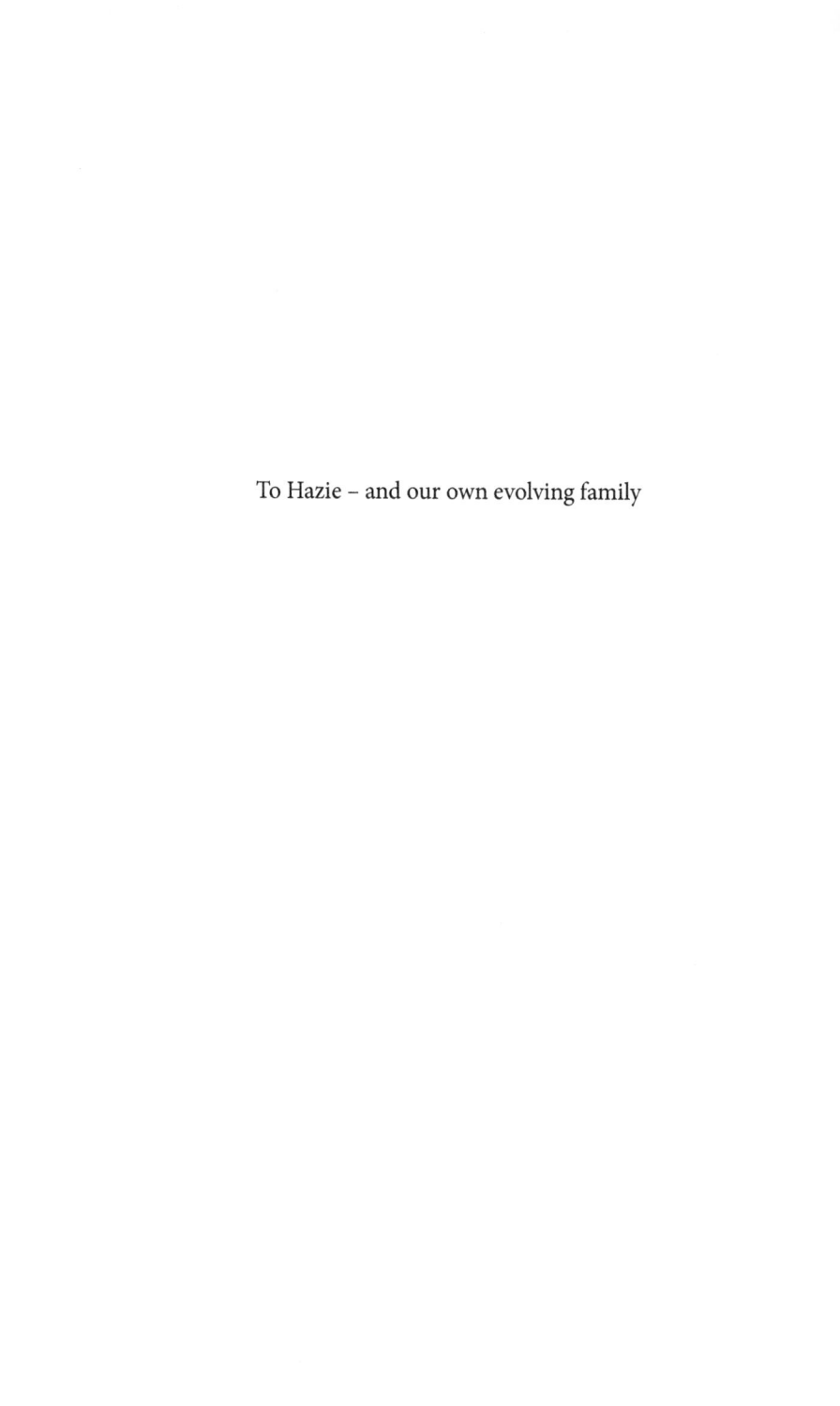

CONTENTS

INTRODUCTION		1
AUTHOR'S NOTE		3
A NOTE on PLACES, DATES and other REFERENCES		7

MAPS

1	NORTH-WEST EUROPE in the LAST ICE AGE – c. 20,000 years BCE	11
2	PEOPLES of SOUTHERN BRITAIN – c. 50 BCE to 150 CE	12
3	MAIN TOWNS, RIVERS and ESTUARIES – 1 to 800 CE	13
4	ANGLO-SAXON MIGRATIONS – 5th and 6th Centuries CE	14
5	THE MAIN KINGDOMS – 600 to 800 CE	15
6	ENGLAND – 910 to 939 CE	16

CHAPTERS

1	LAND and SEA – 10,000 to 4,000 BCE	17
2	BELIEFS and MONUMENTS – 4,000 to 1,200 BCE	35
3	METALS, CULTURES and CELTS – 1,200 to 55 BCE	48
4	ROMAN BRITAIN – 55 BCE to 290 CE	66
5	CRISIS and EXIT – 290 to 410	87
6	THE 'DARK AGES' – 410 to 600	105
7	MEANING, MIGRATION and MYTH	129
8	CHRISTIANITY and NORTHUMBRIA – 400 to 700	145
9	EAST ANGLIA and MERCIA – 600 to 825	167
10	LIFE in ANGLO-SAXON ENGLAND	183
11	ENTER the NORTHMEN – 790 to 900	194
12	WESSEX from DISASTER to TRIUMPH – 825 to 939	216

POSTSCRIPT – The EMERGENCE of ENGLAND	241
ADDENDUM	251

SELECTED READING and REFERENCES	253
INDEX	257
ACKNOWLEDGEMENTS	263

INTRODUCTION

Our history can be easy to overlook. From near where I now live on the Oxfordshire-Buckinghamshire borders, the Chiltern Hills frame the background as a pale blue-grey shadow. For years I walked the paths through the woods and fields of the complex Chiltern contours. Then one day I headed, for the first time, straight to the top of Pulpit Hill, a steady climb of about 400 feet to crest at around 800 feet above today's sea level. My objective was what turned out to be an easily bypassed Iron Age hill fort. Even if the great double ring of banks and ditches is now a shadow of its former self, the large central clearing can be clearly made out. I felt a sense here of a lost world which I might have missed.

In winter, the gaps between the bare tree branches offer views over the great plain ahead. Especially on misty mornings, or in soft evening light, it would be possible to imagine this as sea or a vast inland lake, as it was in aeons past. Around 12,000 years ago, it was uninhabitable tundra running up to the great icefields which ended more than a hundred miles to the north. Little could survive in these conditions, causing human life to retreat far to the south. Or perish.

This book is a story of what happened over the next 10,000 years, as Britain shed the ice and a new country, later to be called England, slowly and erratically emerged. As with dim morning or evening light, it can be hard to see clearly this far back, with shapes, colours and movement blurred by time. This is especially true of what is called *prehistory*, the period before written records were kept. Looking back, even with the many techniques of investigation now available to us, we are still left with an intricate, but incomplete, jigsaw, which needs constant reassessment.

This particular fort on Pulpit Hill is one of several studding the Chilterns, and seems to have been more a lookout point and occasional refuge than regular settlement. But to keep the trees back, early people would have had to make sharp axes from nearby flint and wood. For much else, including water, they would have gone down to the streams at the foot of the hills. Here too, a route known as the Icknield Way was gradually extended south-west to north-east, from the coast of Dorset to the land of the Iceni in Norfolk.

Along this track, to the left as we look over the plain, the small market town of Watlington for centuries hid a secret. There, in 2015, metal detectorist James Mather discovered a hoard of some 200 coins and cut silver which became known as the *Watlington Hoard*, later dated to the end of the 870s. The silver is of the kind used by Vikings as currency, and the coins throw a new light on the relationship between the two leading Anglo-Saxon kingdoms at that time, Mercia and Wessex. The hoard may even have been buried by remnants of the Viking army under Guthrum, on their way to a new Danelaw homeland in East Anglia in 879 after defeat by King Alfred. The year was a major turning point in this history, when a new level of cooperation between Wessex and Mercia laid the foundations for a partnership that, 60 years later, enabled Alfred's grandson, Athelstan, to become the first recognised king of the country that was England.

It was the Vikings themselves who were an original stimulus for this book. Over twenty years ago in a 'colombage' longhouse in Northern France, I gave a talk on the foundation of Normandy, whose Viking origins drew me into the bigger picture and complexities often bypassed in English histories. I wanted to know not just *what* happened, and *when,* but *who* really came, *why* – and *why then.* Gradually this took me back ever further, 10,000 years even before the Romans, to the point when an empty Britain lay locked onto the frozen north-western corner of Europe. Those who had lived there had fled south or died thousands of years before. Then, when the ice

INTRODUCTION

finally melted, the first intrepid explorers set out to cross the great land bridge into an unknown land.

Little about life was certain, especially at that time; and nature had played tricks before. When the thick ice had first started to melt, thousands of years of steady warming were followed by sudden intense cold, like the freezer door being slammed shut again. This period, called the *Younger Dryas*, is reckoned to have lasted over a thousand years.[1] After that, the warmth rose to the levels of more recent times – the *Holocene* period. This story therefore opens onto a mottled blue-white and grey canvas as great ice sheets shuddered across the northern landscape to melt into rivers and sea. We can make out newcomers entering a re-awakening landscape, following the food, be it big game or small fruits, seeking a way to survive in a new world. Never sure if the sun would rise again or that winter would turn into spring, they sought inspiration from the heavens and a closer community with the earth. Bold and cautious, fearful and intrepid, they moved with the seasons and the terrain. They survived if they had enough, and died if they did not, or when many of the other perils of existence struck them down.

This is the story of these people and those who followed in their footsteps. It is also a celebration of the land and countryside in which they settled, and the wonderful diversity it contains. We should not waste it.

AUTHOR'S NOTE

This book is an ambitious undertaking, not just to seek to summarise over 10,000 years of prehistory and history in twelve short chapters in an accessible way, but also to do so as a largely solo exercise. Like the early settlers, I've been able to move at my own speed, review the land ahead, choose my own path, pause as I wished, and learn as I moved on. This has limitations, but has also given me a degree of freedom not all historians have.

---

1   *About 10,800 to 9,600 BCE*

It was E H Carr, in his seminal work *'What is History'*, first published in 1961, who compared historical facts with 'fish swimming about in a vast and sometimes inaccessible ocean', suggesting that historians choose where to fish and what to try to catch. Following that principle, this book seeks to catch some of the bigger and better-known fish, some hiding in the shallows, and also something of the swells and currents of the historical oceans they inhabited. With so much to choose from, I've had to be highly selective, trying to understand the oceanic world better, rather than trawling up further shoals of facts. The reference section at the end covers just some of the many works I have consulted, including some less well-known. Like the fish in the sea, there is much more available in what is a very big ocean.

There have been challenges at every stage, not least in seeking to reconcile often conflicting expert views or to answer the big, unresolved questions that occurred in my 'investigation'. Overall, I've tried to present a balance. Where appropriate, I've also given a personal view on complex events that may, or may not, resonate elsewhere. No doubt there will be corrections, challenges and other views, which are to be welcomed. It's a joy to learn, and our history is, after all, *our* history.

To follow these immense periods of time I've been reliant on the many specialists who have taken pains to research, write and speak on the issues, without whom this book would not have got off the ground. My aim here is different; to construct a broader perspective, an overview from the hill as it were, of the ten thousand years of England's emergence. To try to understand who we are today I seek to follow who first came to the country, where from, and even why. I don't believe that there has been anything logical or predetermined about this. Indeed, one factor that becomes ever more striking when following history is not just that it is uncertain and often chaotic, but also that it can be incredibly *unfair*. These days, many of us try hard to address all kinds of unfairness; but the essence of life is that

INTRODUCTION

it is uncertain – and frequently unfair. We might (or might not) take comfort from the fact that we are products of evolution, where survival of the species, not fairness, is the biggest driver. Without that, we would probably not be here at all.

It's still important to seek accuracy and balance, but this is against an historical backdrop that keeps moving as new findings come to light or old ones are re-evaluated. Social and cultural attitudes also shift over time. New attitudes, heroines, heroes, and perspectives emerge, so that the icons of the past can suddenly become the fallen idols of the present. My approach therefore seeks the long view, focused on the area that would become England, but involving the neighbours who are an essential part of its past, and hopefully its future. Therefore, although this story focuses on England, its neighbours Wales, Scotland, Ireland, France, the Low Counties and Scandinavia are all vital players in the action.

There are many characters in this book, sometimes arriving and departing at speed, most of whom can be only lightly sketched. Other characters, however, include our natural surroundings, especially our rivers, seas and the countryside, all of whom have played a major role in the emergence of England. I make no apologies, therefore, for referring to some of the wonderful long-distance walking trails we enjoy in England, which have so enriched my own experience. Not all countries are so blessed. And my more recent involvement in environmental work has given me an extra perspective of a world changing all too fast in some respects, and all too slowly in others.

I now sense an England with an uncertain sense of its national identity. It may therefore be timely to look back at what helped 'make' England, and consider its relevance to what we face today. Given an empty land to start with, one recurrent theme, then and now, is migration. It's not a new issue, but one that pervades our intensely populated and unequal world. And it's not always an issue of immigration. At the onset of the last ice Age, those who did not emigrate far and fast enough soon perished. The ice came whether they liked it or not. And as the ice retreated, those who returned were all immigrants, each facing an uncertain future, but all with something to contribute to that future.

Charles Boundy – September 2024

A NOTE on PLACES, DATES and OTHER REFERENCES

Places

At the end of the last Ice Age the individual countries of Europe were far in the future and the United Kingdom undreamed of.[2] In this book, I've accordingly used the following, hopefully neutral, references:

* *Britain* is the island of Britain with its associated islands.
* *Ireland* is the island of Ireland with its associated islands.
* *Isles* covers Britain and Ireland together[3] with the Irish Sea between them.
* *The Channel* is the stretch of sea between France and Britain.
* *The Continent* and *Continental* refer to what is often called 'mainland' Europe.
* *France, Denmark, Sweden* etc. refer to the broad areas now covered by those countries.
* *Germanic* has a generic meaning, as explained in Chapter 1.

Britain

Why the name *Britain?* Early references are to *Albion*, possibly from the whiteness of its southern chalk cliffs (*alba* in Latin meaning white).[4] The Greeks used the term *Prettanike,* the painted ones, later

---

2 Great Britain is a later term for the whole island, including Scotland, Wales and England. The United Kingdom was created in 1801 and renamed in 1922 as the United Kingdom of Great Britain and Northern Ireland.

3 Following Norman Davies.

4 Also Albany, with Scotland later, for a time, called 'Alba'.

Romanised and 'anglicised', first as *Pretannia* and then *Britannia*, with its inhabitants switching from *Pretanni* to *Bretanni and then Britons*.

Dates

Compressing 10,000 years of history and prehistory into a short book means being highly selective about what to include, while providing enough detail with a sense of the flow and fluctuation of events. To help the reader with an overview, a short timeline is included in or at the end of many chapters. In terms of specific dates:

* Unless well agreed by experts, *dates are approximate*, based on my interpretation of sometimes conflicting sources. In some cases round numbers are used for economy.

* BCE (*Before Common Era*) has been used rather than BC (before Christ) and, later on, CE (*Common Era*) rather than AD (Anno Domini – 'in the year of our Lord'). After 43 CE (the start of the full-scale Roman invasion), dates are all CE unless stated otherwise.

* For older ('geological') eras, BP (before present) is used to accord with understood archaeological practice. For later periods reference to '*x thousand years BCE*' is generally preferred to '*x thousand years ago*' (or BP). The difference of 2,000 plus years is insignificant over millions of years but highly relevant closer to today.

* *Specific ages, such as the Iron and Bronze Ages*, are summarised in chapter 2, again with caveats, since British periods may differ from others.

DNA and other evidence

In prehistory we are reliant on disciplines such as archaeology, geology, radar, anthropology, radiocarbon-dating, ice-core findings, DNA analyses, strontium dating[5] and many more techniques. Each of these helps build up a picture, but that picture is never complete. DNA analyses, for example, are often lauded as 'breakthrough', whereas essentially they are really only additional clues. Over multiple generations, DNA gets mixed up and watered down. It seems that ancestral DNA can even become so diluted as to disappear from trace completely. This all means that DNA evidence has to be used with care; it may be more valuable in following larger groups and sweeps of migration than in seeking to pin down individual ancestries, but even then can raise its own issues.

Periods and people

Dividing history into 'periods', such as the (so-called) Anglo-Saxon or Viking periods, may help understanding, but can also confuse.[6] Saxons, for example, appear to have been present in Britain long before the Romans left and continued through and after the Viking inroads. Nor did the Anglo-Saxons and Vikings arrive en masse out of the blue. To appreciate who they were, and why they came when they did, means looking at a broader international picture and timeframe.

Italics

I've used italics to highlight something that is new, or from a different language or source, or to emphasise a section of text.

---

5   *Strontium in teeth is a valuable marker for diet and place of origin.*

6   *The overall period 410 to 1066 BCE is now often referred to simply as 'Early Medieval.'*

Man

Where applicable or unavoidable, '*man*' is used generically to include men and women (as it was in the past).

Addendum

With our understanding of history and especially prehistory changing faster than ever, a short Addendum is added at the end of the book to highlight some recent discoveries or changed interpretations, as marked # in the text.

* * *

Even with incalculable hours of reading, writing, research, review and re-editing, there comes a point to stop! It can be the hardest thing to let go. But a book, like a child, needs help and then to be left to find its own way. I've relished the journey – and hope you do too. And I've chosen to start with the mile-thick ice sheet as a sustained thaw finally took hold – and to 'go with the flow' from there.

MAP 1

NORTH-WEST EUROPE in the LAST ICE AGE
– c. 20,000 years BCE

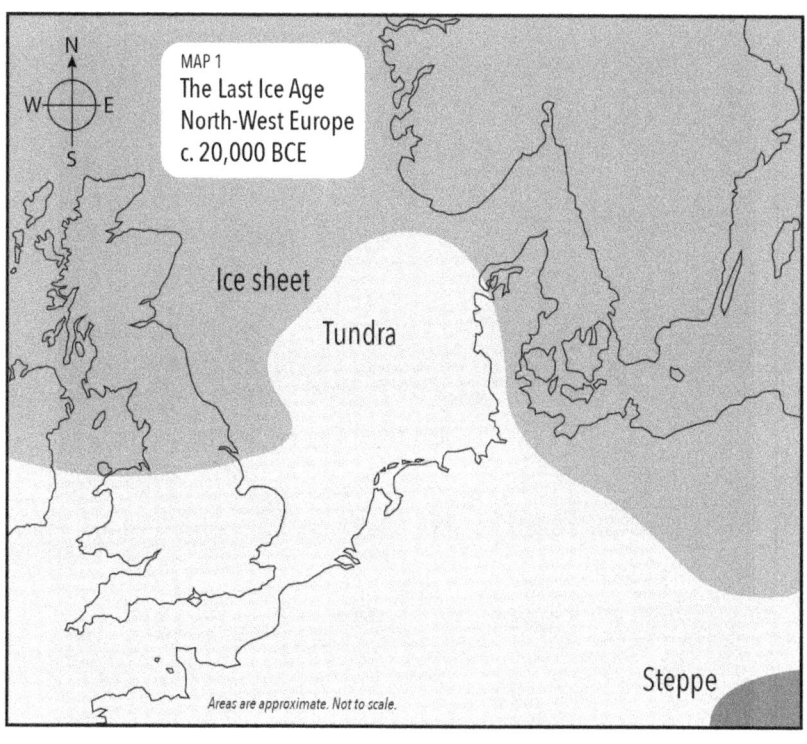

Note: All maps drawn by Paul Futcher and © Charles Boundy

MAP 2
PEOPLES of SOUTHERN BRITAIN – c. 50 BCE to 150 CE

MAP 3
MAIN TOWNS, RIVERS and ESTUARIES – 1 to 800 CE

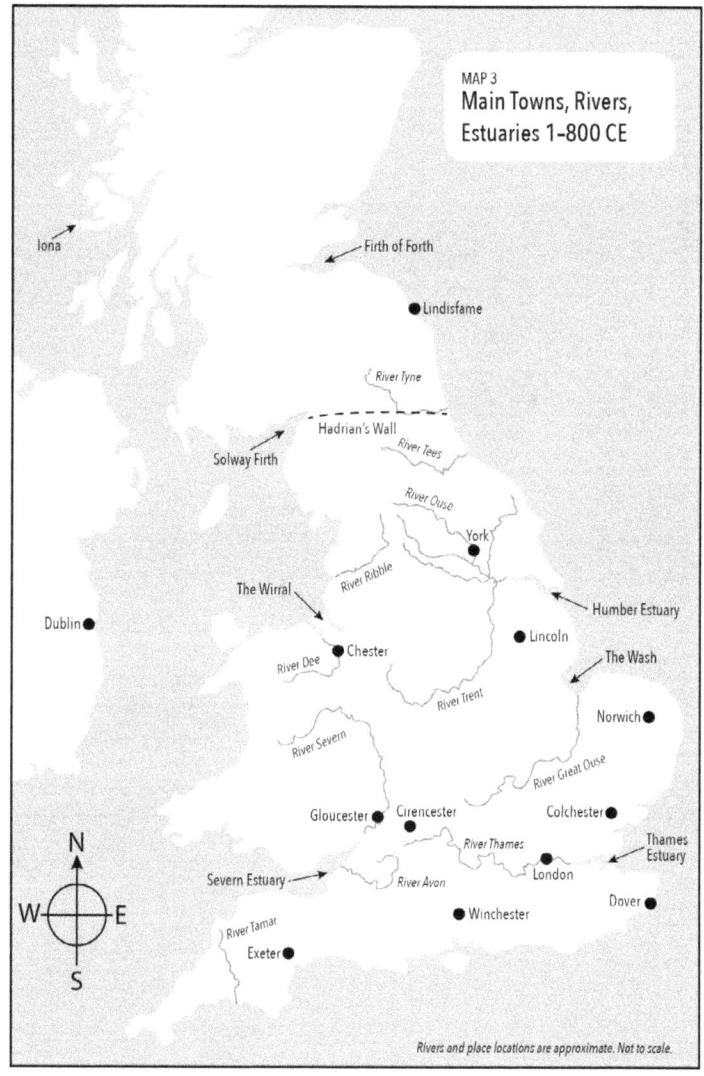

MAP 4
ANGLO-SAXON MIGRATIONS – 5th and 6th Centuries CE

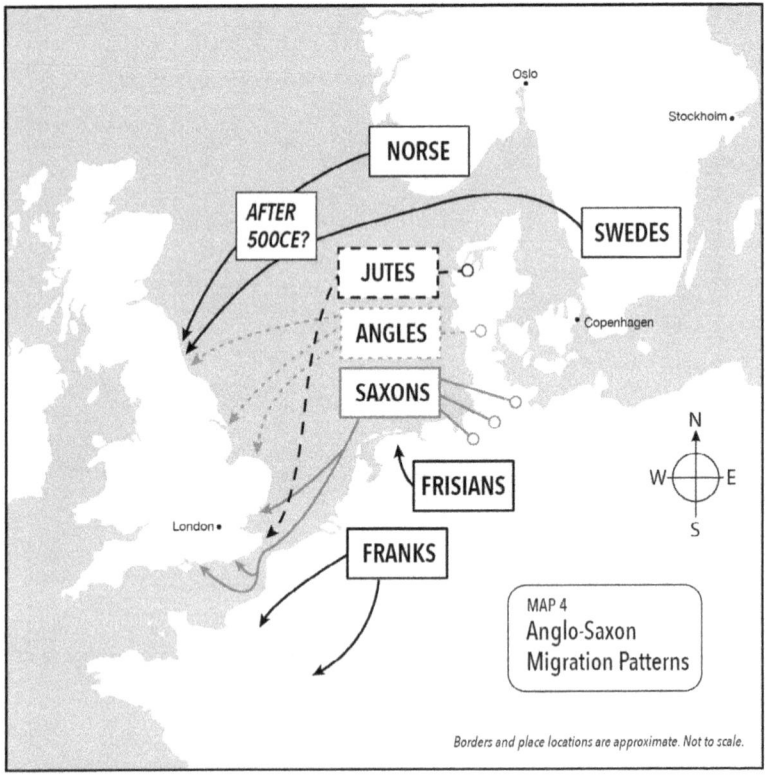

MAP 5
THE MAIN KINGDOMS – 600 to 800 CE

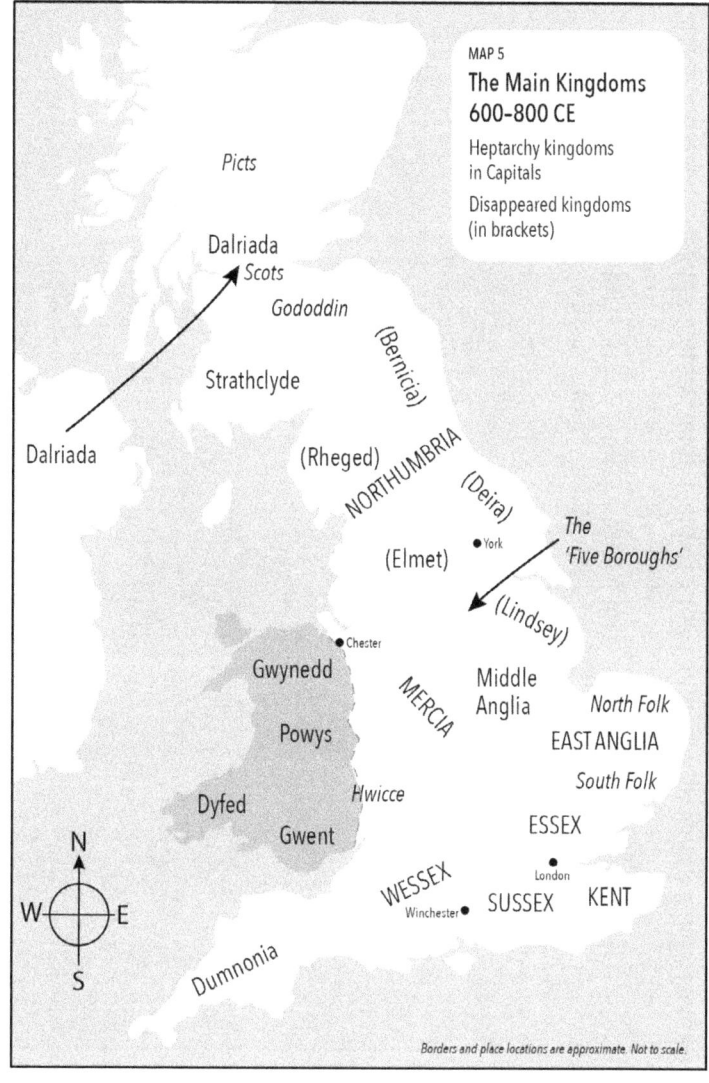

MAP 6
ENGLAND – 910 to 939 CE

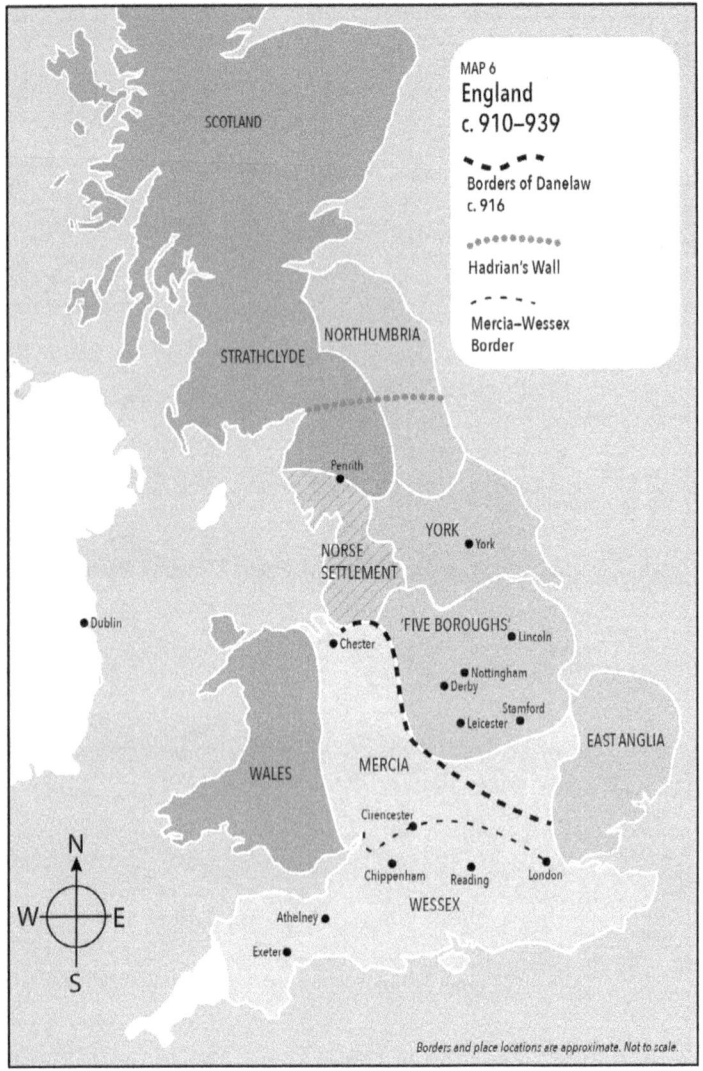

CHAPTER 1

LAND AND SEA

10,000 to 4,000 BCE

Millions of years ago Britain was part of a huge landmass basking in tropical waters in the southern hemisphere. But our earth is more changeable than it looks. Since then the land has moved, been raised up, battered down, and folded over in ways that are still hard to follow. As a result, the outlines of the land and sea today bear little relation to how they were in the distant past. Nor does change operate at a steady pace, but gradually and then in convulsions, often with dramatic results.

Tectonics

We now know that the earth's crust is overlayed with a series of large subterranean rafts, called tectonic plates. We are also now aware that these plates move very slowly, but inexorably, and not all in the same direction or at the same time. This means that the plates sometimes open up a gap between them and sometimes collide, literally with seismic effects. One visible example can be seen along the so-called Rock Route in north-west Scotland.[7] The rocks at Knockan Crag, north of Ullapool, believed to be a thousand million years old, once formed part of a far more extensive southern mountain range that fractured some 600 million years ago.

---

7   https://www.nwhgeopark.com/the-rock-route/

As the tectonic plates shifted, this great mountain range broke into four main sections as it moved north. Separate parts are now lodged in the Appalachian Mountains of USA; in north-west Scotland; in the rugged tops of Shetland; and in the snow-capped peaks of Norway. And when the 'Scottish section' of the mountain range crashed into the landmass that became Britain, the impact pushed some of the older rocks above their newer counterparts. This was the opposite of what Scottish geologists expected, until they worked out (what to them was) the astounding principle of plate tectonics. It may be an additional irony (or fatal attraction) that large parts of what is now Scotland, originally contiguous with the land that became England, took a very separate route north from the Antarctic, only to collide again close to their current location!

Before the last Ice Age

Life on earth depends on many things, including the right degree of *insolation*, the radiant energy from the sun that reaches the earth. But the way the earth orbits the sun, and thus the extent of insolation, fluctuates for many reasons, including alterations in the earth's tilt, or the shape of the earth's orbit, or the occasional terrestrial wobble on its axis. These variations affect ground and atmospheric conditions differently, which can in turn impact our climate. One result is that, although the current Holocene period has been substantially benign for modern humans, there has been nothing stable about our climate over the long term. At many times in the past there have been immense fluctuations of temperature with severe repercussions.

It was not always the cold. Around 250 million years ago the Permian-Triassic extinction event, probably caused by extreme heat, is believed to have killed some 90% of the world's then species. # One recent estimate suggested that the temperature increase causing this extinction was around 5%. It's a figure to be borne in mind when considering the level of current global temperature rises.

And change can be rapid. Some studies have indicated that, in the past, severe climate change may have swept away plant, animal and human life completely in Britain in as little as ten years.

Looking back at the period before the last Ice Age involves condensing past ages into a few paragraphs. We might start around 900,000 before the present (BP) for the origins of the earliest known hominid footprints found in Britain, in Happisburgh, Norfolk.[8] Later discoveries in East Anglia dating back to around 700,000 years BP suggest a balmy climate conducive to life, with the land sparsely occupied by a primitive species whose main tools were shaped stones. Although Britain was then largely an island, a broad land bridge connected the south-east to the Continent. Around 500,000 BP this link enabled so-called *'Heidelberg man'*,[9] possibly six feet tall (based on remains found in Boxgrove, Sussex), to cross over the land bridge, using hand-axes to hunt deer and rhinoceros.

From about 450,000 BP, however, the land cooled dramatically. This led to the Anglian, one in a succession of long-term ice ages, which drove out Heidelberg man. As the ice and tundra smothered the landscape from the north, life of all kinds would have had to flee south or perish. Some considerable time later, a huge glacial lake built up in the south-east. This eventually burst, causing a major flood that created much of the Channel, with the remaining narrow land bridge probably swept away in a second eruption.[10]

By around 125,000 BP Britain was therefore an island – and warm again. Modern man, *homo sapiens*, is believed to have reached Britain by about 45,000 to 40,000 BCE, and to have coexisted for

---

8   Pronounced 'Haysborough'. The term 'Hominid' broadly covers the family of great apes, including humans.

9   So named after remains first discovered near Heidelberg in Germany.

10 The Natural History Museum has some useful explanatory maps on its website, which will doubtless be updated as further research comes to light.

some time with resident Neanderthal Man. Recent skeletal and DNA tests even suggest some interbreeding between the two without sterility. One 'modern human' from this period was the so-called 'Red Lady' of Paviland, first discovered by the intrepid early 19th century geologist, William Buckland. Although later interpreted to be those of a man, the bones were later radio-carbon dated to around 32,000 BCE. Yet, having been a successful species for over 100,000 years, able to hunt, light fires and cook food, and for reasons still not clearly understood, Neanderthals seem to have disappeared by 30,000 BCE. #

Sometime after then, and possibly intermittently before, more fluctuations occurred, bringing periods of intense and lasting cold. This brought on what is called 'the Last Ice Age' ('last' in the past, if not necessarily in the future!) The cold was so pervasive that by around 20,000 BCE (known as the *Last Glacial Maximum* or *LGM*) an ice sheet covered nearly the whole of Scandinavia together with much of Britain and Ireland (see Map 1).[11] South of this, a great belt of north European mainland was largely lichen and moss-covered plain with frozen sub-soil, known as *tundra* – uninhabitable polar desert. In this period temperatures may have been around 20°C lower than those of today, with bitter winds and sharp variations between the seasons. In Britain the ice field shrouding the north may have been up to a mile deep, the locked-up water leaving sea levels about 250 feet lower than today.

With little able to survive these conditions, human life in Europe was pushed down to the temperate areas of what are now Spain and Italy to the south, and today's Balkans and Ukraine further east. Eventually, from about 20,000 BCE, Europe began to warm, slowly at first, and then erratically, with periods of alternate heating and cooling.

---

11   *Even if the last ice sheet may not have extended south of Lincolnshire, uninhabitable tundra covered the land far beyond that.*

By about 12,000 BCE life had returned and people were living in many areas across the south of Britain. But again it was not to last. In the Younger Dryas reversal (c. 10,800-9,600 BCE) temperatures plummeted once more. There is no clear evidence of anyone living in Britain in this period.

While a severe reversal, the Younger Dryas was (fortunately for us today) what is known as an 'interlude', and from around 9,600 BCE temperatures rose again, quite fiercely, to reach close to current levels. This was the start of the current Holocene period of greater stability, albeit with variations.[12] And as the climate warmed and the great ice sheet over northern Europe began to recede, much else began to change.

Flood – and early re-settlement

Ice and glaciers lock up huge volumes of water. As melting ice becomes freshwater this can have dramatic 'downstream' effects, especially flooding. Accordingly, as the glaciers receded, great rivers of meltwater formed and ran across the land. In the west, a developing Irish Sea re-opened an often turbulent seaway between the two Isles. In far north-east Europe, the Baltic became a freshwater lake and then a sea, with meltwater cascading into rivers flowing south through eastern Europe into the rising Black Sea.

To start with, sea levels remained much lower than today, leaving Britain still connected to the European landmass. Intrepid pioneers would have found a land scoured by ice, but trees and plants soon sprung up from wet, fertile terrain, and marched north as the ice receded. Behind the trees came the animals, and behind the animals

---

[12] *A noticeably warmer period from about 800 to 1300 CE enabled the British to grow grapes. Then in the 1400s temperatures dropped some 2°C in many areas, causing massive crop failures and widespread starvation in many places. This so called 'little ice age' is reckoned to have lasted about 500 years until the 1800s when Europe started to warm again.*

came the human hunters. This was all in the Paleolithic (old stone age), where access to a wooden shaft and a sharp piece of workable flint could make the difference between life and death for hunter-gatherers. They formed small communities, working together, and occasionally competing for scarce resources, venerating the animals they hunted. The Thames and the River Rhine emptied into the expanding North Sea, while the compressed Channel River cut a thin line between the chalk layers of southern Britain and northern France.

But ice melt has other consequences. When the ice first formed, its massive weight literally depressed the land; when it melted, the land sighed with relief and started to rise again (like a mattress released from weight). But the land rise was a slow process, known as isostatic or glacial rebound, compared with the faster rise in sea level (called eustatic) from the meltwater. This meant that the rise in sea level typically became apparent long before the land compensated. It also means that in some areas, long after sea levels increased from ice melt, the land continued to rise where the ice had been thickest. It's a process that still continues today.

As the ice receded and temperatures returned close to pre-glacial levels, Britain became warmer, greener and more fertile. Reindeer were replaced by elk, deer, boar, and massive oxen-like aurochs. And as forests grew, human foragers prospered. There were tubers and berries to be collected, and a wide range of animals to be trapped or hunted. The new settlers knew their plants for dyes and how to make rope from fibres and baskets from twine. They learned how to use all the parts of the deer, from antler to hide and guts, how to make clothes, how to prepare what they'd hunted, and how to make fire to cook. They also understood the benefits of working together. But not everything prospered; Britain's wild horses continued to be targets for hunters close to the point of extinction; millennia were to pass before new variants were imported.

Natural features inevitably influenced how and where people moved. The inhospitable high ridge of the Pennines separated cultures as well as communities. The mountains of Wales, the sharp valleys of the Lake and Peak Districts and the major rivers, though not impassable, all made their demarcations. People were used to walking long distances when required, but the rocks and soil conditions dictated where they could live, and how close they were to food, water and essential materials like wood and stone. Some locations seem to have held special appeal – *'landmarks-with-meaning'* – as Nicholas Crane calls them. Places such as the Mendips, a high ridge of hills in the mid-south-west, became revered. With limestone ridges riven by sharp gulleys and streams disappearing underground, caves in the gorges there acquired a spiritual quotient.

One of the earliest post ice-age sites discovered is Starr Carr in North Yorkshire, flourishing around 9,000 BCE. This was probably first accessed via *Doggerland,* a huge area of inlets, lagoons and rich hunting grounds in what is now the North Sea, but which then connected eastern Britain, the Low Countries and Denmark. Starr Carr is now an open moorland site, but discoveries buried in the peat deposits of what had been a great lake there yielded long-hidden secrets. These included tools and weapons, personal ornaments, and mounds of waste debris (known as *middens*) that revealed what people ate and threw away.

There were signs of past abundance; fish and wildfowl from the lake; seaweed, shellfish and seabirds from the nearby coast; berries, roots, tubers and prized hazelnuts from the ground and trees; and deer, boar, elk and auroch from the land. The finds indicated that the area may have been a summer camp for processing food, animal skins and tools, as well as providing storage ahead of winter. Starr Carr's treasures also highlight symbols and ceremony, notably red deer antlers with barbed points cut into them, and stag skull headdresses with the facial bones cut away, suggesting very early, and probably inherited, ritual practices.

Meanwhile, sea levels were steadily rising. It was perhaps around 7,000 BCE before the main glacial melt had largely run its course, by which time much of the original coastline (and evidence of early occupation there) had been submerged, overwhelming some islands and creating others. Doggerland was being steadily eroded. But the climate remained variable, and from around 6,700 BCE there was another intensely cold period that lasted several centuries.

Island

There were new floods to come, this time with the power of the sea unleashed by dramatic movements of the land. This is what happened in the North Sea sometime around 6,200 BCE, when Doggerland still connected Britain and the Continent. North of this, three massive underwater sections[13] of the Norwegian continental shelf, close to the outer rim of today's Arctic Circle, collapsed into the sea. Now known as the *Storegga Slides*, the collapse caused a huge tsunami, possibly some 30 to 40 feet high, growing to 50 or 60 feet by the time it struck the Shetland Islands north of Scotland. Doggerland, right in the wave's path, was largely obliterated, together with its inhabitants.

Massive volumes of water ran down the east coast of Britain, funnelling where the Rhine, Thames and Channel River fed into the North Sea. Combined with subsequent turbulence, by 6,000 BCE rising sea levels had submerged most of the rest of Doggerland, leaving a broad North Sea between Britain and Norway and a wide new Channel between Britain and the Continent. Britain was once again an island – with all that entailed.

Back on land, trees that best tolerated cold, like birch, willow and juniper, had grown first, with elm, lime, oak, alder and other broad-

---

13   *Reckoned together to be some 180 miles in length.*

leaved specimens developing as the climate warmed. The animals took full advantage, as did the hunter-gatherers, who were attuned to the seasons and natural resources. Theirs was a life of moving on with the conditions and the seasons, the animals, and the fruits of nature.

Over time, communities cut clearings or set fires to provide open grazing land and easier hunting. But clearances, together with reduced plant transpiration, weakened the topsoil and encouraged the silting of streams, leaving some areas to become bog or marsh. Much of this clearance was down to the stone axe, a multi-purpose instrument to fell and shape trees, provide frameworks for dwellings, handles for tools, and much else. There were spearheads too, with plentiful supplies of fish and birds to be speared, snared or netted, plus a range of delicacies along the sea shore, many rich in fish oils for good health and iodine to aid fertility.

Even so, the elements were unpredictable. Rising seas could carry away tracts of land and even villages overnight. And in the course of the one and a half millennia after 5,500 BCE, the climate was hit by succession of dramatic changes. These included years of harsh winter rain, cooler summers and a shortened growing season following a huge volcanic eruption in Sumatra. There were also more (if smaller) tsunamis, a deep solar minimum and then extreme cold.

Despite these adversities, social and trading relationships grew up between those on either side of the new divides, especially along the western coasts of the Continent and the new Irish Sea. The new Channel sea route and improved seafaring techniques made it generally much faster to move goods and people by water than land, encouraging exploration and exchange. With different natural resources available in different lands, there were 'imbalances productive of change'[14] which proved a perfect recipe for trade.

---

14   Braudel (1987)

A short timeline up to 4,000 BCE

The Paleolithic (2.5 million years ago to 10,000 BCE – all dates approximate)		
900.000	Early human footprints in Britain	*Happisburgh ('Haysborough'), Norfolk*
700,000	Fertile, balmy climate in Britain	*Early hunter-gatherers Stone tools found at Pakefield, Suffolk*
500,000	Heidelberg man in Britain	*Boxgrove Man, Sussex*
450,000	Anglian Ice Age	
120,000	Modern man (homo sapiens) leaves Africa	*Second 'wave' c 60,000 BCE*
75-50,000	Toba Volcano (Sumatra)	*Devastating widespread effects*
45-30,000	Homo sapiens spread in Europe Neanderthals decline	*'Red Lady' of Paviland*
37,000	The Isles separated	
30,000	Last Main Ice Age develops	*Land bridge*
20,000	Last Glacial Maximum (peak ice) (LGM)	*Humans driven to margins Sea level c. 330 ft below now*
16,000	Slow warming; deglaciation starts	
12,000	North Sea starts to emerge	*Doggerland fertile*
11,000-9,500	Last Main Ice Age ends (Holocene)	*Little Dryas freeze c 10,800 – 9,600*

The Mesolithic (10,000 to 4,000 BCE)		
9,300	Temperature improves	*Back to pre-glacial high*
9,000	Starr Carr, Yorkshire	*Site occupied c 300 years*
8,200	Cold weather returns	*c 100 to 200 years*
8,100	East coast of Britain emerges	*Sea level rise slows*
6,700-6,000	End of glacial melting? Sea level c.100 m higher than LGM	*Reduced growing seasons. Temperature drops by c 5C, heavy flooding + tree loss*
6,200-6,000	North Sea tsunami and flooding of Channel River	*Doggerland largely washed away – Britain an island*
5,000-4,550	Wetter winters and cooler summers	*Growth and food affected Spread of peat in lowland areas*
4,350-4,300	Two lesser tsunamis + deep solar minimum depress temperatures	*Adds to food etc. problems*

The Neolithic (4,000 to 2,400 BCE)

Ther pace picks up after 4,000 BCE as the Mesolithic moves into the Neolithic (from the Middle to the New Stone Age). Even these millennia cover timescales that are hard for our minds to grasp.

Fernard Braudel called them the *'longue durée'* – lengthy periods that give a clearer perspective on human history than can be distinguished by those actually living through them. But the dates given to those periods depend on the location being considered, with Britain, in the north of Europe, a relatively slow starter. This means that the British Neolithic, Iron Age and Bronze Age periods occur later than their southern cousins.[15] For current purposes the dates are as shown in the charts and section headings.

An overview of the immediate post Ice Age period in Britain might identify four main stages:

* *Ice to Neolithic: 10,000 BCE (end of the last Ice Age) to around 4,000 BCE.*
* *Neolithic: 4,000 BCE onwards – intensive farming, monuments and early cultures.*
* *Iron Age – Tribal era from 800 BCE through to 43 CE.*
* *Roman Britain – From 43 to 410 CE.*

The Landscape – Chalk and Flint

One distinctive feature of English downland is chalk, the white, crumbly residue of an infinite number of tiny marine creatures whose shells were deposited on the seabed, ground to microscopic powder or turned into sedimentary rocks, some 90 million years ago. Today, chalk gives many of England's uplands its thin soil, soft grasses, distinctive flowers and scooped slopes. It can shine brightly under a clear sky, gleam when the turf above it is cut, or be grey and slippery when wet. Chalk is also permeable, enabling rainwater to seep through until it finds a waterproof layer, such as clay. The water will then collect along this layer, sometimes escaping at a bubbling hillside spring. Many chalk valleys accordingly have no rivers, but

---

15   *The dates of the different ages, even in Britain, also seem to vary between different authorities!*

possible seasonal *bournes* linked to water levels beneath, whose intermittent flow can struggle to support settlement.

We can see chalk in the Ridgeway and its extensions, the Lincolnshire and Yorkshire Wolds and along the North Downs, to culminate in the white cliffs at Dover, or the South Downs at the distinctive Seven Sisters outside Eastbourne. And the line continues in many places across the Channel, such as the cliffs of the Pays de Caux (*chalk* in French) and along the great sinuous banks of the Seine, where impressionist painters used the pale backdrop to frame their vibrant foreground colours. Where chalk combines with soils such as clay and greensand, rain can filter down and freeze between layers of rock. When this occurs near cliff edges, such as at the 'Jurassic' coast in Dorset, sudden landslips can expose fossils long locked into the earth.

A walk over chalk downland is likely to show scatterings of pale and dark grey stone, often bone-like in shape. Much of this is flint, embedded within the chalk as an insoluble hard silica or chert, a crystalline structure giving it sharp edges when fractured. Pick up and break a piece of flint and be reminded why, in the words of one distinguished geologist, 'flint has exercised more influence on early human history than almost any other rock in Europe.'[16] For aeons of time the sharp edges and points of broken flint acted as the tools and weapons that could make the difference between human life and death.

As can be seen in the thin black line across some chalk cliff faces, quality flint for tool-making is often embedded in seams deep in the earth. This was a realisation that encouraged early flint-mining in Britain. With vertical pits leading down as much as thirty feet and branching off into side tunnels, flint-mining was backbreaking and dangerous. The vast quantities of earth and stone removed to make even a scattering of axe-heads could leave the land scarred, as

---

16   *AE Trueman in Geology and Scenery in England and Wales (1949) – Penguin Books*

at Grimes Graves in Norfolk. Here, some 400 access pits were dug after about 2,500 BCE, leaving a pock-marked, lunar-like landscape.

High quality flint also became a valued trading commodity, notably that from the Langdale Pikes in Cumbria's Lake District. This was especially prized for ceremonial purposes, as if its original closeness to the heavens made it more precious. And as the need for better tools and weapons grew, so did the arduous work and skill involved in chiselling or 'knapping' it into the fine blades or spear points that an increasingly competitive world demanded. This was rarely a quick job. As a good axe became a valued tool, a weapon of deadly efficiency, or a venerated possession of beauty, the sound of flint knapping became a dominant backdrop in many settlements.

Farming and family

The greatest change in the early British Neolithic came from the intensification of farming. From developments in the Fertile Crescent (today's Iraq, Iran, Israel, Syria and eastern Turkey) around 9,000 BCE, new farming techniques spread like an incoming tide across the Continent, reaching the northern shores of France by about 5,000 BCE. After an apparent pause,[17] new farming practices spread rapidly in Britain, with crops including wheat, barley and peas, plus livestock of cattle, sheep, pigs and goats. Three different strands might be distinguished:

* *horticulture – the intensive growing of food plants,*
* *arable – ploughing and planting the land surface, and*
* *pastoral – leaving herds or flocks to graze on natural vegetation.*

It's also arguable that basic farming started much earlier, as long ago as 40,000 BCE, when humans began consciously to manipulate

---

17 *The idea of a 1,000 year gap before farming really took off in Britain (from 4,000 BCE) remains debated.*

their environment.[18] After meltwater from the last Ice Age pushed sea levels higher, causing intensive flooding, proto-farmers sought improved yields from crops that were amenable to more intense cultivation. The change to hours of back-breaking work might have made farming an unappealing occupation for many but, as populations surged and there were ever more mouths to feed, there may have been little alternative. The family diet would also have undergone fundamental change.[19]

The effects of farming

More intensified farming reduced the land and scope available for hunter-gatherers, forcing many to adapt or perish. And with farming leading to higher population growth, it would not have taken many generations for any slower-reproducing hunter-gatherers to fall behind in percentage terms. Farming also involved new ways of thinking and planning, which, with luck and some skill, could lead to abundance. But abundance can lead to a higher birth and survival rate, with more mouths to feed, requiring more investment. Farming also freed up some people for other work, enabling more specialist trades and time for weaving, spinning and pottery, which encouraged new styles and markets.

Marriage was another factor. Healthy offspring meant moving outside a close circle of several families, with a wider 'tribe' of 900 or more estimated as being a large enough network for the viability of future generations.

This was, however, no bucolic paradise. More lives meant more deaths, requiring new burial plots outside main living areas.

---

18 See Colin Tudge: *Neanderthals, Bandits and Farmers – How Agriculture Really Began* (1998) Weidenfeld & Nicholson)

19 See Yuval Noah Harari: *Sapiens – A Brief History of Humankind* (2011/4) Harvill Secker

Crops needed proper grain storage, and corralled animals needed winter food and shelter. Farming encouraged disease through soil degradation and close human proximity to animals, and denser populations could stimulate virus transmission. Over time, most people developed immunity to many of these ills, but when those people moved or traded elsewhere, they could carry germs or viruses that might prove fatal to others.[20] Human attitudes to animals also changed as more farmers regarded their stock as something to be eaten, traded, used for valuable by-products, or even sacrificed. Dairy milk became more widely available, aiding nutrition but at the risk of lactose complications until, over time, higher levels of tolerance were achieved.

Farming also required investment. As land was cleared for other uses, its value could increase, a concept that remains dominant to the present day. Crops and livestock needed protection from human and animal scavengers. For all these reasons land needed defining and protecting, leading to fences, ditches, walls, hedges and even ramparts, like a proliferation of 'Keep Out' signs springing up across the land. Meanwhile, the wildwood was coppiced and pushed back, oaks felled for houses, ash for fences, and hazel for wattle. The added effect of sheep, cattle and goats enjoying tree bark and leaves plus rootling by pigs led to extended clearings. Great swathes of land became treeless, with poor soils being further damaged by acidity and erosion. Wild animal populations crashed in consequence, and by about 1,350 BCE that great beast of the open country, the auroch, was extinct.

Pests did not help either. Even the great elm trees suffered from an infection brought in by insects, killing up to half of Europe's elms in the 4th century BCE, and opening further gaps in the woodland and forest floor. Even more significantly for the future, as land use, farming and trade intensified and became more competitive,

---

20 *Cambridge-led research into ancient HSV-1 genomes indicated a sudden rise in infections around 3,000 BCE. This might be linked to increased migration, possibly accelerated by the (supposedly) new social phenomenon of kissing!*

more disputes could be expected between neighbouring groups. Neighbours might combine by consent or through force, actual or feared, sometimes driven by ambitious leaders, with the main groups becoming larger and more tribal.

It remains unclear how much violence was induced, and whether skeletal remains found with embedded arrowheads were really grave goods or evidence of human aggression. The number of skull and limb disfigurements discovered across disparate burial sites certainly suggests increased violence at some times and in some areas. In the 4th millennium BCE at Crickley Hill, for example, on the Cotswold scarp in Gloucestershire with a superb view over the plain below, the ditch around the site was reinforced by a timber palisade with defensive gates across the causeway to the interior. This may, however, have proved inadequate, judging by the remnants of burnt-out houses, timbers and gateways, and the presence of over 400 flint arrowheads, nearly all pointing to the entrances to the settlement.

Migration

We still don't really know how much of the population increase came from new arrivals. Archaeologist Francis Pryor believes that farming spread through Britain steadily rather than rapidly, with around 20% of the population of Neolithic Britain being newcomers arriving with farming over lengthy periods.[21] There are, however, conflicting opinions about how far incomers progressively replaced the native population at this time, as well as later, and ongoing research will doubtless continue to challenge previous understandings.[22]

In the longer term, however, if one goes back far enough, many of the prehistoric migrations into Britain seem to have had their

---

21 *Francis Pryor: BBC Article – 'Overview: From Neolithic to Bronze Age' from 2011. #*

22 *Newer evidence includes samples of mitochondrial DNA (DNA passed down the female line) as well as aDNA (DNA from ancient bones).*

distant origins in substantially the same area, the great grasslands of the Eurasian steppe. At the risk of over-simplifying matters, we might see their routes to Britain as largely following three main trajectories – north-west towards Saxony and the Baltic (summarised in this book as 'Eastern'), west along the Mediterranean coast to Iberia and up the Atlantic coast ('Western' or 'Iberian'), plus a mix of middle routes through central west Europe ('Central').

These migrations – like the 'Cultures' considered in Chapter 3 – would have been in waves moving at different times and speeds, often breaking into smaller surges or cross-currents. Some became ethnic groups, some tribes and some cultures, while others were subsumed or merged into more dominant communities over the course of time and events.

What ultimately mattered more for the future England was what the newcomers brought with them, how peacefully they settled, how they were accepted, and how far they adapted and contributed to the future. In the meantime we might prefer the thought that, however and whenever our ancestors got here, we all go back a long way in time and ultimately come from much the same place!

CHAPTER 2

BELIEFS and MONUMENTS

4,000 to 1,200 BCE

Human development is not just about farming and survival. From early days we have sought to understand our position on earth and make sense of our environment. This chapter therefore focuses on how the neolithic landscape became marked with a mix of features and monuments that can be hard to understand today. It's even been said of southern Britain in this time that 'as much effort went into cultivating the gods as went on cultivating the land!'[23] Prehistory left us no instruction manual, but tantalising clues, which we try to interpret through archaeology, dendrochronology (tree-ring dating), ice core and soil samples, ground penetrating radar, DNA and the like. Each new piece of evidence fills in detail, but also raises further questions.

Tracks and traces

As settlements and trading grew, so did the routes that connected them, many of which became well established before the Romans overlaid them. Not all survived, however. The *Post Track* and the *Sweet Track* (named after Ray Sweet, its discoverer) have been dated to around 3,800 BCE. These were pathways of long oak planks, laid end to end and supported by posts driven into the

---
23   Miles p73.

ground. But they lasted just ten years before being overwhelmed by the Somerset Levels. *Flag Fen* is another small area of wetland, in East Anglia, originally linked to the great bay of the Wash. It was rich in fish, wildfowl, trees and reeds for thatch, but early settlers faced a constant battle with rising and falling waters. Francis Pryor's excavation there indicated a half-mile long causeway built from successive layers of timber, secured by wooden pegs and overlaid with brushwood and wooden planks scrubbed with sand and gravel for grip.

On higher ground, by contrast, as the ice retreated and the valleys and plains became heavy swamp or thick forest, the southern Ridgeway provided a clear, high-level route for the four-footed beasts moving slowly across the ground in search of new vegetation. Not far behind came man, the two-footed hunter. But, as tools and techniques improved, many animals were driven to the margins, hunted to extinction, or tamed. Valleys were drained, woods reduced to make way for pasture, and the uplands fenced for grazing. The Ridgeway's terrain shows ancient signs of having been flooded, folded and compressed. Long escarpments furrowed with ditches, studded with burial mounds, or marked by sculptures chiselled into chalk on prominent hillsides, are linked by ancient trackways and drovers' roads. Starting near Avebury in Wiltshire, the Ridgeway runs for about 40 miles before it dips down to the River Thames as it flows through the Goring Gap on its way to the London basin. Following the Ridgeway can still feel like walking through history under the great immensity of the heavens.

For early farmers, however, the more they invested in the land, the more they had to lose. Yet even the basics seemed uncertain. What brought the clouds and rain, and what drove them away, leading to aridity, withered crops and dead animals? Why did the seasons change, and how could people better assure a bountiful spring and a healthy harvest? Where did disease come from, and when people died, where did their spirit go? Were they even really dead?

How could neolithic man begin to understand this except as the operation of some higher being?

Seeking meaning and structure to improve their lives and chances, some societies spent vast efforts in building monuments on the land. Communal effort and shared space were highly valued, the experience heightened by large groups feasting and singing together, helping forge stories, language and community. As such events still do. Coming together in a special, social space with believed spiritual qualities, whether to mourn the dead, praise the rising sun, or to celebrate the death of winter and the victory of spring, seems to have given communities literally the faith to move mountains.

People looked to the sky for possible answers, developing great skills in alignment and measurement of sun and stars, planning for equinoxes with accuracy and noting the changes in visible heavens. But there was still the impenetrable question of *why*, and *how* to ensure the best outcomes for their crops, their livestock and themselves. Their stories might have harked back to a rumoured past, perhaps to a land of fire and ice (still envisaged by modern writers), evoking a sense of elemental, other-worldly, forces.

Might they have tapped into ancestral tales from long-gone generations, just as awareness of a great flood seared itself across the collective consciousness of many regions?

Even the cave art from these times brings its own questions. Creswell Crags, a limestone gorge full of caves on the border of Derbyshire and Nottinghamshire, for example, bears the marks of astonishing art, some dating back to paleolithic times, before the Last Ice Age. Within that complex, Church Hole is notable for engravings on the walls of a narrow chamber which could only have been accessed by contorted crawling in and out. These were not images intended for casual visitors; was the artist going into the depths to communicate at higher levels?

Water itself was often associated with spiritual qualities, and perhaps access to the underworld. Rivers, deep ponds, or pools with believed supernatural powers could attract sacrificial deposits of weapons and precious items. Elsewhere, small hillocks crowned with ancient trees and washed by a nearby stream were often seen as spiritual, and many early English churches were later built over 'pagan' shrines in such locations.

One irony of prehistory is that most of what we can learn about the *life* of people comes from how they were treated in *death*. Even so, early signs can be ambiguous. The so-called *Red Lady of Paviland*, who turned out *not* to be either red or female, serves as a warning against over-hasty judgment. And when freshly unearthed stone age remains from Gough's Cave in Cheddar Gorge, Somerset, showed evidence of possible cannibalism, opinions rapidly polarised. *Cheddar Man*, as he was quickly called, was first thought to have died around 13,000 BCE, before the re-freezing of the Younger Dryas. But newly discovered bones found later (in 1986) *underneath* 'Cheddar Man', caused something of a 'feeding frenzy' when analysis suggested that they had been expertly picked over *after* death. Was this cannibalism or part of a funeral rite?

Painstaking analysis finally indicated that the Gough's Cave bones had been gnawed clean by human teeth and the available marrow sucked from them, probably soon after death. Even more dramatically, some of the skulls appeared to have been de-fleshed and cut to make drinking vessels. Not just that. Cheddar Man himself turned out to have lived and died much *later* than previously thought, around 7,000 BCE, perhaps 5,000 or so years after the cannibalised bodies buried beneath his own grave. The even greater surprise was that DNA reconstruction indicated that Cheddar man had blue eyes and a dark skin, causing challenges to many old beliefs, and its own sensation when publicised in 2018.

With living and dead meant to have their own, separate places, some locations associated with the dead became liminal, with boundary markers to keep the 'unauthorised' out. Death was part of life, but had to be respected, and to cross the wrong lines or fail to honour the ancestors could bring calamity on all.

As Alice Roberts has suggested,[24] our ancestors may even have differentiated between the recent, still decomposing, dead, whom they feared, and the bare bones of those who had moved on long ago, which were revered. This approach might explain why, in the days of multiple burials, some human remains were either left to decompose (natural *excarnation*) or de-fleshed and 'dis-articulated' – broken up and even mixed with the bones of others when interred. As if to ensure that the dead should truly stay dead.

Stonehenge and other monuments

As to the land itself, one dramatic marker could be *menhirs*, large upright stones placed singly or in combination, typically in lines or circles. We can't tell what drove the effort involved or how the stones were celebrated, but we can see that such monuments spread far and wide. Other stones were installed in rings, as witness the 1,300 or so pre-Stonehenge stone circles from windswept Orkney to emerald Ireland to Carnac in Brittany to Stonehenge. These indicate that people travelled, traded and shared their experiences over great distances. Here the dead could be almost as present as the living, with the stones acting as a possible intermediary between this world and beyond. Very often these circles were enhanced by a deep circular ditch with the spoil heaped outside it as a steep bank. This is the classic *henge*.

At first sight there is little about one site in central southern England that marks it out from the great rolling Wiltshire plain of which it forms part. Yet the land clearly had a quality that attracted people as early as 8,000 BCE, when Britain was still linked to the Continent. This was some 5,000 years before the creation of what

---

24   *See Selected Reading list at end.*

we now know as *Stonehenge*, the major celebrity of Neolithic times. At its peak the site's reputation seems to have drawn people from far away, coming together to absorb its spiritual qualities and to bask in the glow of a common experience (as they still do). Why does it have this appeal? Partly because it is graphically striking in its own right – like the stark outline of an ancient world; partly because of its ongoing association with the solstice; and partly because it retains its mysteries.

Its attraction includes the primaeval nature of the great stone slabs and their cross lintels, dark-edged against the sky, gateways for the equinoctial day. Even if we now better understand where the great stones came from and how they were transported, *why* that happened and *how* the site was used may long remain a mystery. In seeking answers, we get more questions, and new discoveries. To follow what happened it may be best to break down the apparent stages.[25]

* From early times the Stonehenge area had spectacular long barrows and causewayed enclosures, suitable for large gatherings. It maybe also had a cursus, a set of wooden poles or parallel banks thrown up from a ditch, sometimes hundreds of yards long. Some of these earthworks or structures were aligned with the solstices, literally the times when the sun 'stands still' at the longest and shortest days of the year. Finds at causewayed enclosures suggest these were places for large periodic meetings, where many came from far and wide to join in – perhaps for stock-trading, ceremonial tribal occasions, family gatherings, and even as an informal marriage marketplace.

* Stonehenge, as we know it today, seems to have started with an enclosure, over 100 yards across. This was bounded by a circular ditch and bank with at least two entry and exit points. Then,

---

25 *The English Heritage website gives a useful summary. For more detail see Garrow and Wilkin (2022).*

around 3,000 BCE, some 56 pits or post-holes (known as 'Aubrey holes') were dug just inside this circular bank, possibly to take bluestones (weighing two to five tons each) which were later removed.[26] The holes were then used for cremation burials.[27]

* Stonehenge is best known now for the great inner horseshoe of immense sarsen stones with capping lintels (trilithons – literally three stones) which were erected, over the course of a century or so, around 2,500 BCE. Around 16 feet tall, weighing 25 tons on average, and of a wholly different dimension from most other megalithic rings (stone circles) elsewhere, these sarsens are believed to have been hauled across from West Woods, some 20 miles away.

* Between the sarsen inner horseshoe and outer circle, arcs of the smaller bluestones were raised. These were probably the bluestones removed from the Aubrey holes; stones which, it's now believed, were originally transported from the Preseli Hills in distant Wales.[28] They probably came via a nearby production site where the stones were prepared, dressed (laboriously worked into shape by flint and antler tools) and moved into place before being hauled upright. They were later relocated several times in different configurations. #

* The large trilithon sarsens and many other remaining stones incorporate mortice and tenon stonework joints (still used in modern woodworking) to help secure them.

* Around 1600 BCE, new holes were dug at Stonehenge, possibly

---

26 *Called bluestones as they tend to look blue when worked or wet.*

27 *Mostly of local people of all ages but some of possible Welsh origin.*

28 *Of the possible 80 Preseli bluestones, transported 140 miles (bird's eye) or 250 miles by boat, over 40 have so far been identified. They may even have formed their own circle in Wales before being transported.*

to accommodate bluestones. But they were never filled, with the site left close to what we see today.

During pitch black nights crowded with mysterious stars and an unsettling moon, the midwinter solstice might represent the death of winter and the birth of new life, with the great trilithons acting as entrances to another world. Stonehenge then could be seen as a link to the unknowable qualities of life and death, the vicissitudes of climate within a pattern of sunrise and sunset, summer and winter, and a homage to the omnipotent forces holding sway over humankind. The many carvings, especially of axes, found etched into the sarsen stones, might have been offerings to a supernatural power, suggesting Stonehenge as a portal to another world.

Some other locations

Amesbury – From Stonehenge, an avenue with a bank and ditch on each side follows the solstice line northwards and then south-east down to the nearby River Avon at West Amesbury, some two miles away. This may be where the Welsh bluestones arrived by boat before being hauled up to the Stonehenge plain.

Durrington – This lies nearby, with its own mysteries and deposits indicating its possible use as an interim construction and accommodation site. And Durrington Walls stirred the world of archaeology in 2020 with the discovery of a massive ring (up to 1.2 miles in diameter) encircling a series of huge pits measuring about ten yards across by five yards deep. Optically stimulated luminescence (OSL)[29] tests date the soil in the pits to around 2,400 BCE, largely contemporaneous with the main activity at Stonehenge. The pits seem to have been used much later, before silting up, leaving another, so-far unsolved, mystery.

---

29 *Among other uses, OSL is able to measure the date when the sediment was last exposed to daylight.*

Avebury and Windmill Hill – Around 20 miles north of Stonehenge, Avebury in Wiltshire remains intriguing, where a massive henge, some 350 yards across, encloses much of the village. This site too was reworked several times before the current stones were erected – with one weighing up to 100 tons. Nearby is the south-western end of the Ridgeway and the great marker of Windmill Hill with its large hilltop causewayed enclosures, in this case concentric earthworks cut by several access points. This open gathering space is thought to have been constructed around 3,700 BCE, to have taken some 62,000 worker hours to construct, and to have been used for just over a thousand years before being abandoned.

Silbury Hill – Close to Avebury is Silbury Hill, a giant sandcastle-shaped mound up to 100 feet high that might have taken four million hours of human labour to create. But why? Rather than the hill containing treasure, bodies or other archaeological secrets, thorough investigations have revealed nothing inside except stones and earth. We can only surmise why people spent such concerted effort to produce these monuments. Were they simply creating a manifestation of communal belief that would be strikingly visible across the landscape?

Long barrows – Not far away lie two long barrows and a plethora of smaller round barrows. These include *West Kennet Long Barrow*, over 300 feet long and 10 feet high, and the mystical *Wayland's Smithy*, redolent of folklore and ancient beliefs. Long barrows were increasingly visible in open country after 4,000 BCE, often as long, vaulted chambers, later overlaid with stones and turf to protect against decay or fire. With average life expectancy in those times not exceeding twenty years, the dead could have been seen to require more lasting protection than the living. But we still don't know who was consigned to the barrows, or why, although their prominent position might point to some having been territorial markers, adding a spiritual quality to a boundary.

Stone chambers might also have given astonishing acoustics, with motifs and patterns carved on the walls sometimes accentuated by dramatic painted colours. Lines, circles, spirals, swirls, zigzags and chevrons, especially in a dark tunnel-like space with pinpoints of brilliant light and the overweening presence of the long dead, could have accentuated disorientation with potentially hallucinogenic effects. Was this another case of a ritual space or a tantalising glimpse of an effort to communicate with another world?

With all these monuments we are left with the great mystery of how the enormous human effort in finding, transporting and erecting these monuments was coordinated – and why. Was this really down to ancestral power or the product of high-level, visionary and forceful leadership?[30] Or could many early sites have evolved by near-spontaneous communal drive, belief, and adaptation as new ideas came forward? If so, the great henges and monolithic presentations of antiquity might also be monuments to the immense potential of collective human spirit and collaboration.

'Seahenge' in Norfolk – Some way distant, around 2,000 BCE, a circle made out of 55 tall oak sections was erected in the saltmarsh near the sea, with the entrance on a solar midsummer alignment. The centrepiece was the upturned base of an oak, its roots reaching out to the sky as if linking the underworld to the heavens. The imprints of 51 different iron axes identified on the wood of the henge indicate both the number of people and the intense level of activity involved. Seahenge is an example of a liminal presence on the edge of two worlds, the land and the sea, and the separation of the living from the dead.

---

30 *For example, Ackroyd (2011) sees 'evidence of a controlling power that could organise vast numbers of people in a shared project', suggesting that by the time of Stonehenge, there was an aristocratic, rather than a tribal, society.*

Changing practices – 3,000 to 1,500 BCE

From around 3,000 BCE (or earlier), and on into the later Iron Age, there were waves or trends of new styles, art and attitudes introduced into Britain, mainly from the Continent. These are what we now call *cultures*, whose relevance and complexity are explored further in the next chapter. One example is the *Beaker (or Bell Beaker) Culture*, which took its name from pottery moulded into the form of an inverted bell, a shape then used for funerary rites and other distinctive artistic and social styles. Some cultural shifts took advantage of new ways to fuse tin with copper to make bronze, enabling more durable and much finer items to be made with distinctive new designs.

By about 2,000 BCE, an extensive network in Beaker items developed and spread widely, valued as gifts and treated with reverence as grave goods. Metal produced in thin sheets could now be worked with fine patterns and inlays, with images of the crescent moon especially popular, known as *lunalae* or little moons, along with the sun or stars associated with the farming year.[31] Slowly, perhaps over a thousand years, the crescent moon became a heavily embossed and intricately worked (often gold) collar called a *gorget*, from the French for throat, worn as an explicit symbol of wealth and power.

One notable discovery relating to this period was the so-called Amesbury Archer, who died around 2,300 BCE. He was buried in his own grave a few miles from Stonehenge in a distinctive way, complete with a wrist protector and a wide array of grave goods (some hundred objects in all), seemingly donated by mourners from many different areas. Isotopic dental analysis surprised many by indications that the archer had lived much of his 40-odd years on the Continent, possibly near the Alps, bringing with him early examples of metalworking

---

31 *The famous Nebra Sky Disk found in Saxony, Germany, featured the seven stars of the Pleiades.*

hardly known in Britain at that time. These reflected, or could have given him, the special status apparent from his burial. The archer indicates both the range of artefacts then in circulation and the huge distances often involved.

Sometime around 1,500 BCE there was a material change, with a move away from great communal monuments and henges. With life increasingly centred around the farm, demarcated by fields and animal enclosures, the ritual landscape appears to have become less relevant. There was also a change in grave goods and a shift from communal tombs to individual burials. Burial practices in Britain still varied regionally, and even within localities. In southern Britain there are signs that many people were cremated, or left exposed to wildlife and the elements before being buried. When interment switched to cremation around this time, ashes were sometimes buried in pots or other small urns,[32] in line with the *Urnfield Culture* on the Continent. Changes in fashion were essential elements of social evolution.

A short timeline for Chapter 2

4,000 to 2,400 BCE – NEOLITHIC (New Stone Age) in BRITAIN[33] – *all dates BCE and outline*		
4,000	Climate improves – farming intensifies in Britain.	*Newcomers have farming equipment and skills + new beliefs. Different groups gather to feast together. Rise in woodwork + pottery. Long barrows start to appear.*

---

32 *Apparently very tedious to excavate!*
33 *The Mesolithic, Neolithic and Bronze Ages quoted here are based on British Museum dates, which may vary from other authorities and different parts of the world.*

BELIEFS and MONUMENTS

3,800	Early causeways and causewayed enclosures	*Post Track, Sweet Track, Somerset* *Windmill Hill near the Ridgeway*
3,700 to 2,600	Neolithic sarsen stone and henge building	*Multiple burial grounds – often with local variations*
3,400	Waun Mawn	*340 feet diameter stone circle in Presili Hills in Wales*
3,300 to 3,000	Ness of Brodgar and Skara Brae, Orkney	*Vibrant civilisation around Orkney*
3,000 to 1,500	Active Stonehenge Period	*Active flint mining*
2,600	Avebury bank and ditch	
2,500 on	Grimes Graves in Norfolk	*Intensive flint-mining*
2,400-2,300	Beaker Culture appears	*Death of Amesbury Archer*

CHAPTER 3

METALS, CULTURES AND CELTS

1,200 to 55 BCE

Several interrelated themes dominate the next period. In the background, intensive farming continued to affect the landscape and environment, directly and indirectly. Wood clearance, soil erosion, river silting, and the growth of peat bog all contributed to the degradation of much of the agricultural land in central southern Britain by around 1,000 BCE. The continuing development of bronze and then iron encouraged more mechanisation, better tools, and more powerful weapons. Then, as production and trade progressed, powerful elites started to emerge. Interwoven with these factors were the changes brought in with new cultures, along with the challenge of distinguishing incoming fashions from major inroads of new people.

The period also takes us towards the domination of Greek and Roman 'civilisation', with a surge in written records as we move from prehistory into recorded history. This gives us more information, but also more opinions from the commentators of the time, often with questionable perspectives (as we'll see.)

Late bronze – 1200 to 800 BCE

With bronze now the wonder material of the age, sourcing its raw

METALS, CULTURES AND CELTS

ingredients, copper (90%) and tin (10%), took on a new urgency. Hard to find tin was available in Cornwall in the far south-west. Copper could be extracted from mines such as Alderley Edge in Cheshire and several sites in Wales. These locations meant that new sources of supply and trade routes were often required, with resultant economic implications.

After 1500 BCE there was a step-change in productivity and population, driven by new materials and techniques and also by newly harnessed forms of land transport. Horses originating from the eastern Steppe started to become regular features of life in Britain. Either for a sole rider or a basic transport to be harnessed to a cart, horses helped revolutionise both short-haul traffic and warfare.[34]

Bigger herds encouraged more droveways, compounds and stockyards. The need for better access, travel and transport led to causeways, fords and jetties, with the resultant increase in river traffic served by more moorings, boatyards and coastal luggers. All this boosted trade and competition – and more activity.

Curiously, one by-product was an apparent growth in *votive offerings*, in graves or in mass deposits in rivers or deep bogs.[35] Such items were often jettisoned beyond hope of recovery, with swords or dagger points deliberately (and carefully) bent, preserving the item while removing its threat. This early 'throw-away' society suggests a wealthy elite able to afford such displays, as evidenced by the rash of bronze jewellery, necklaces, bracelets, finger rings, pins, clasps and torcs of many kinds that marked wealth in life and status in death. But recycling was also active, evidenced by salvage from the sea floor

---

34 *The earliest chariots so far discovered date from the 5th to 4th centuries BCE (in the Iron Age). And one significant recent discovery was that not all prehistoric warriors were male, with reliable accounts also of women driving chariots in pre-Roman times.*

35 *Votive offerings are deposits of valued possessions in perceived sacred places to appease the gods or spirits.*

which suggested that materials were being imported for melting down and recasting in Britain.

Archaeologists rightly remind us that 'absence of evidence is not evidence of absence'. In other words, that something hasn't been discovered yet does not mean that it did not exist or happen. That's especially true near the coasts. After the early floods from deglaciation, a great deal of our prehistory is now literally underwater. But with sea-bed exploration now uncovering some of what was formerly out of reach, we can expect fresh challenges to old understandings. In addition, improved metal detecting, together with compulsory surveys of sites of potential archaeological significance before re-development, mean that excavations for new airports, inter-city railways, housing estates and even house extensions are changing our understanding of these early periods faster than ever before.[36]

Some discoveries indicate social trends, such as the flesh hooks for roasting huge joints of meat and massive cauldrons found at Battersea on the Thames, dating from around 800 BCE. Nearby vast middens of animal bone and other waste, built up over centuries, suggest continued large-scale farming and feasting at that time. And at just one Wiltshire site,[37] based on animal bone remains, 600 cattle and 3,800 sheep appear to have been consumed *annually* for 100 years.

Outside hillforts and major centres, settlements might range from small farmsteads supporting one or more extended families to communities of two or three hundred people. At this stage houses typically remained circular, with hazel sticks and wattle woven walls between upright posts, or sometimes stone walls.

---

36 For example, survey work on the A6 Manchester Airport Relief Road at Bramhall near Stockport exposed features containing pottery of Bronze Age appearance and cremated human remains, radiocarbon-dated to the Middle Bronze Age. A technical paper on the discoveries is available at <Bronze age in Bramhall (semmms.info)>

37 *East Chisenbury* – Crane (2016) p 155.

Angled roof supports were held together in the centre, topped by reeds, straw, or turf, according to locally available materials. Such roundhouses were generally not divided into rooms but had separate spaces for cooking, sleeping and indoor activities. Doorways often faced east or south-east to secure the first rays of the rising sun, and the hearth would be in the middle, with no need for a structural central post. Avoiding a central roof opening, liable to draw sparks up into the thatch (with potentially disastrous results), the smoke would normally rise into the roof space and dissipate through the thatch.

Fire was certainly a constant threat, as evidenced by one noted discovery at *Must Farm* in Cambridgeshire, near the Flag Fen archaeological site. Must Farm was a Late Bronze Age settlement of a small group of houses, built on a platform supported by wooden piles sunk into wetland. Early in the first millennium BCE, fire broke out which resulted in the collapse of the houses into what was then a slow-moving river. The preservative effect of the river sediments has left many of the structural features and house contents largely intact, even if charred.[38]

Iron – and its implications – from 800 BCE

While flint continued to be widely used, the transition from bronze to iron from about 800 BCE took place gradually. And although iron became available across the country and was a superior substance for tools and weapons, it required a great deal of work to create, often involving whole families. The ore had to be dug out from a pit, washed, dried, and then heated over charcoal in a furnace to around 800° C. The resultant lump of iron was then heated again and beaten to extract the remaining 'slag' – the unwanted minerals – from the original ore. It was only then that the iron was re-heated and forged into shape. All this took great reserves of effort plus massive supplies of wood to heat charcoal to the temperatures required.

---

38 *Now on display at Peterborough Museum.*

As more mineral resources brought new trade routes and settlements, rising sea levels re-shaped Britain's coastline, producing new islands, such as in Tamit (Thanet) in Kent. One coastal beneficiary was *Hengistbury Head* at the entrance to the protected waters of Christchurch Harbour, close to modern Bournemouth. This became a significant protected settlement, enhanced by nearby iron-ore deposits, and a growing smelting business, later with its own coin mint. These benefits helped it become, for a time, a major centre for export. Silver, lead, tin and copper from the west and south-west, as well as iron, salt and shale, were exchanged for wine, figs, pottery, coloured glass and new handicraft production techniques.

The eastern Mediterranean had now recovered from an earlier drought, leading to new levels of prosperity there. But not so in Britain. As Athens approached its peak with the Parthenon around 430 BCE, Britons huddled together for warmth and security where they could. Cold and rain caused flooding, with reduced useable land and a short growing season heightening pressure. In the midlands and south, many communities coalesced in larger and more protected settlements. Old field systems were overridden by huge new ditch and bank demarcations, sometimes backed by palisades, marching boldly over the contours and cutting across old boundaries. The broch, a tall, double-skinned, near impregnable brick tower, became a feature in the far north and Scottish islands.

The switch to iron brought other implications – changing fashions, new sources of supply, new customers and merchants, which created new opportunities, and new rivalries. But with up to one and a half million people in Britain by the end of the Iron Age, life for many remained short and painful. Violence was never far away, and iron added to the power of weapons. All this seems to have encouraged the growth of powerful elites from around 500 BCE, while improved techniques in archery, able to bring silent death from some distance away, caused a rethinking of defence.[39] Defensive hillforts and enclosures grew larger and harder to penetrate, with higher-protective banks.

By about 100 BCE these warrior elites controlled ever larger areas, becoming confident enough to display their wealth openly. One huge hoard found at Snettisham in Norfolk included 150 *torcs* and torc fragments, necklaces of Celtic-style twisted gold or silver, suggesting major riches and powerful symbols of authority.[40] There was also a move towards a monetary economy, as coinage increasingly became an accepted means of exchange or tribute, possibly spurred by the use of Gallo-Belgic *stater* coins by southern Belgic tribes expanding their remit in Britain. But producing reliable coinage needs close supervision by a powerful authority, encouraging some southern tribal leaders to establish their own legal mints and *oppida*, fortified production and trading settlements.

Some other locations

River Witham, Lincoln – The River Witham at Lincoln, far inland today, was once a thriving port, the word *lind*, meaning pool or lake, perhaps giving its name to the settlement of what was Lindcolm. Below today's mighty Lincoln cathedral, on the northern bluff of a cleft widened by ancient glacial action, the Brayford Pool formed a large lake. The area provided a good living for early hunter-gatherers, later settlers and subsequently a base for the local Corieltauvi, meaning the 'host of the land of many rivers.' Prestigious ritual deposits found here include the *Witham Shield*, dated to 400 – 300 BCE, now in the British Museum.

---

[39] Even so, the bow and arrow seems to have had limited use at this time, with some groups preferring the (highly skilled) use of the sling (a leather strap) to hurl stones with bullet-like force.

[40] Dated to around 70 BCE, these may have belonged to an early leader of the Iceni tribe.

Dorney Reach, near Maidenhead – Some wetlands retained an attraction for votive offerings, with hoards, swords, helmets and shields deposited in bogs, lakes and rivers often showing the developed skills of smiths.[41] Excavations to create the boating lake at Dorney Reach, near Windsor and Eton, revealed part of a former course of the River Thames, studded with islands linked by connecting bridges to the mainland. These appear to have become favoured places from which to make offerings to the river gods, including broad slashing swords of the type used by warlike horsemen around or after 1,000 BCE. The finds support the idea of an evolving warlike elite, the sword design enhancing both artistic merit and military prowess. Such swords must have been highly treasured, making their ritual deposit seem all the more significant.

Dorchester-on Thames – Major gravel extractions near Dorchester on Thames have unearthed a huge volume of iron age coins, and signs of raised ancient earthwork embankments as evidence of a substantial pre-Roman settlement. Dorchester and nearby Abingdon would have been impressive settlements, equidistant from the estuaries of the Severn and the Solent as well as being on the banks of the Thames itself, giving a direct river route to the north and west.

Danebury – This fort, near Stockbridge in Hampshire, now extensively excavated, is an example of the change in this period. It was designed around 750 BCE, apparently as an area to store livestock and crops for surrounding communities. Then, sometime after 500 BCE, Danebury was substantially remodelled as a fortified settlement. Rings of earthworks and a once-hidden entrance protected dwellings for some 300-500 people, valuable grain stores, and workshops for ironsmiths and potters. Even today, while much has subsided or eroded, the depth and sheer sides of some of the outer ramparts feel dramatic.

---

41 *Sometimes the equipment had been used, like the magnificent Pocklington shield found in the Yorkshire Wolds, and at other times it was pristine, like the Battersea shield found by the Thames.*

White Horse – Adjacent to the Ridgeway, the White Horse of Uffington, a 350 foot long, stunningly graceful, chalk inlay rears out from a hillside in West Oxfordshire. The crumpled downs here are visually arresting, leaving the hillfort castle and the horse prominent, but almost spectral. The horse is elusive, best seen from above. But by whom? Was the horse a reminder of a controlling presence above – or below? And the shape of the design, graceful and fragmented, seems to echo a design from old Macedonian coins from the time of Alexander the Great. If so, it goes to show how far great design, as well as valuable coinage, can last – and travel! Non-invasive *Optical Stimulated Luminescence (OSL)* has helped date the deposits to around 800 BCE, another marker for a time of major transition in southern Britain.[42]

Huckhoe Settlement and Shaftoe Crags, Northumberland – At Huckhoe, there is evidence of a triple layer of oak palisades enclosing an early defended settlement for stone or timber roundhouses and perhaps some livestock. The oak has been radio-carbon dated to about 580 BCE, with similar palisaded hilltop enclosures found locally, indicating the likely extent of woodland there at the time. Shaftoe Crags are an even more dramatic feature in the open Northumbrian landscape, with commanding views all around. Within the natural defences of the crags and a defended settlement from Roman times, it appears that there was an Iron Age settlement here, protected by a rampart.

Cultures and Celts

The last chapter mentioned two specific cultures, *Bell Beaker* and *Urnfield*. These so-called *cultures* highlighted new styles, decoration and use of pottery introduced into southern Britain in the late Neolithic and early Bronze period. As the Bronze Age was succeeded by the Iron Age, the flow of new ideas and technology

---

42 See Miles (2005)

increased, confirming the readiness of people to absorb and adapt.

Cultural change could be seen in different ways with different groups, not just in distinctive styles of dress, art, pottery and religious practice, but also by increasing signs of social and demographic change in values, beliefs and sense of heritage.

It is less clear (then and now) how such changes come to be adopted. Does it require a few trailblazers to inspire others or a considerable body of like-minded incomers bringing material change with them? And what degree of evidence is needed to support the idea of a new culture? For an archaeologist this may be shards of new style pottery appearing widely over an area. A historian may require more written records, and a geneticist may be more focused on identifiable traces of common DNA. Culture is therefore a useful, but essentially elusive, concept. And with Britain still thinly populated at this time, a few 'early adopters' might easily have stimulated what could appear to be widespread cultural change.

An example is the so-called *Arras Culture*, which seems to have taken hold in the mid-Iron Age (c. 400 to 200 BCE) in certain parts of the Yorkshire Wolds. The culture is evidenced by burial mounds (barrows) containing the remains of carts, chariots, grave goods, and, in some cases, human and horse bones. These burial practices are common to, and suggest links between, the Yorkshire Parisi and the similarly named Parisii tribe of northern Gaul.

This introduces a further complexity – the *Celtic* influence. Here we really have to start by accepting that there was no single race or people called 'the Celts.'[43] Instead, *Celtic* is probably best seen as a description of similar cultural aspects across widely-spread peoples. Some Celtic influences in Britain might even be traced back to the early intensive farmers from 4,000 BCE onwards, but with

---

43 *A similar issue arises with 'the Anglo-Saxons' and 'the Vikings' – see later chapters.*

reservations. It would be easy, therefore, to highlight some features as typically Celtic, even if the wave that brought them to the fore had no other Celtic connections at that time.

Another major difficulty is the limited use of the names *Celts* and *Celtic* at the time. We don't know whether those identified by others as Celtic thought of themselves as such, but might suspect not. One name origin is ascribed to the Greeks who, with typical cultural bias, used the word *'keltoi'* to refer to *strangers*. By this they meant tribes beyond the Greek borders who were supposedly uncivilised, dangerous, and implicitly inferior, outsiders. The Romans followed suit, calling such people *Celtae*, or, more commonly for outsiders, Barbarians.[44] Once victorious over Celtic groups, however, the Greeks raised their own glory by re-inventing their defeated enemies as noble savages, with a stoic quality to their suffering. Similarity, the Romans first dismissed the Celtae as primitive, ill-disciplined, aggressive, alcoholic, superstitious, prone to human sacrifice, and generally unreliable! Nevertheless, they noted with appreciation the Celtic bardic traditions and abilities together with their honourable hospitality, nobility and defence of honour.

Closer to today, the term *Celtic* has become associated with a distinctive style of art, poetry and music, often with a strong Irish, Scottish, West Country or Breton emphasis. This has been accompanied by a belief that Celtic people were the major constituents of pre-Roman Britain, continuing a traditional and peaceful way of life before being driven out, or to the margins, by the aggressive Anglo-Saxons. As so often, these stereotypes now appear misplaced. So far as there were commonalities, the impression we now have is that the groups who might be called *Celtic* were ready to pursue farming and fighting with equal vigour. They settled large areas with intensive agriculture, and were highly aware (and superstitious) of nature. In regarding war as a way of life, they tended to privilege personal glory and honour, leaving

---

44 *Dismissing their language as just 'bar-bar-bar'.*

them liable to attack with bravado rather than discipline and strategy.

In broad terms, therefore, we might think of Celtic groups as having common origins with other early people movements, moving through western Europe, and typically settling in areas conducive to trade and farming, or (in the west) a coastal and maritime life. Later we can see some such groups settled in Gaul, especially north-eastern areas, integrating with the Gauls and the Belgae (Belgic people), groups of whom later moved to central southern Britain. At times Julius Caesar, despite his famed division of Gaul into three parts, seems to have seen Gauls and Celts as almost interchangeable. Either way, the Celtic elements in Gaul were unprepared to accept the Roman yoke, with the result that they were systemically driven out, enslaved in great numbers, or massacred by Caesar's troops.

One feature regarded as distinctive to Celtic groups were the Druids, who appear to have been a highly learned and respected group within mainstream Celtic society. A twenty-year apprenticeship in such subjects as law, history and medicine was mixed with an intensive study of magic, divination and astronomy, giving them a learning and mystical authority that few could challenge. It was the Druids' authority over people, partly through Celtic belief systems and a reverence for ancestors, that gave the Romans cause to fear and then hate them.

Another distinctive feature of Celtic people is that they originally shared a common language (or linguistic) base. Then, as they dispersed and settled across wide areas, their language continued to change. In the Isles a *Brittonic* (or p-Celtic) strain led to Welsh, Cornish and, with a Gallic strain, Breton. Elsewhere, Manx, Irish and Scottish Gaelic derived from the *Goidelic* (or q-Celtic) strain, with other variants developing as identifiable Celtic languages[45]. In Gaul, apart from Brittany, local Latin dialects changed into the

---

45 E.g. the 'Celtiberians' in modern Spain and Portugal.

modern Romance language of French. In Britain, on the other hand, even if it kept to the margins, Celtic survived under Roman rule (adopting a few Latin terms), but was still to face the impact of later Germanic languages. These areas apart, the Celtic language appears largely to have evaporated in mainland Europe by around 400 CE.

The original split between Celtic and Germanic languages has been estimated at around 4,000 BCE.[46] If so, this would coincide with the advent of serious farming in Britain. In any case, as was to happen with Old English, a common language does not require a common lineage. People copy others, intentionally or otherwise, and absorb languages like ideas. Similarly with art. While Celtic art was primarily Iron Age art, not all Iron Age art was necessarily Celtic, any more than modernist art comes from a single artist.

Celtic art, with its intricate, interlaced, and energetic patterns and whirling designs, might even be seen to echo early Mesolithic carvings on passage-grave walls. But with new materials from a new age, artists we might think of as Celtic developed a mastery of method and movement that still dazzles the eye and mind. They also loved adornment. Museum exhibits display stunning, intricately wrought and decorated, 'Celtic' objects, mostly in bronze, but also in materials such as gold, silver and pottery. Chief among these in collections are the plaited necklaces, the torcs, which became a hallmark of Celtic culture before being copied and developed for other areas, times, and wearers.

Here again, Celtic originality coupled with fine workmanship and technology was not confined to art. It was also put to harsh practical use; Celtic people are credited, among other things, with the invention of chain mail and several ship-building techniques that the Romans later felt free to appropriate.

In the last three centuries BCE Celtic groups made stunning advances in art and technique, but because they were not a single people and

---

46   *E.g. Oppenheimer p 111 fn 4.*

cooperated only as a necessary and expedient, they became vulnerable to the regrouped and now intensely coordinated Romans.

The Hallstatt and La Tène groups and their aftermath

Within this overall mix two distinctive Celtic 'civilisations' can be traced as coming to prominence in central Europe from around 1,000 BCE onwards. The first were the *Hallstatt (or Halstadt) Celts*, settling north of the Alps over hundreds of years. An aristocratic and militaristic society with wealth built from long-distance trading in tin, copper, salt, and other luxuries and essentials, they left their mark in strategic hillforts, earth barrows and valuable grave goods.[47] From 600 BCE, their links with Greek Marsalia (Marseilles) left them well placed as merchants in trading furs, salt, tin, gold, amber and slaves. Then, by c450 BCE, the Hallstatt culture seems to have disappeared, to be replaced by La Tène, who seem to have been even more warlike than their predecessors. Their self-contained settlements and powerful elites led to more population surges and eruptions beyond their borders with knock-on effects. Although these events seem far away from Britain, two points are especially worth noting here.

The first is that the demise of the Hallstatt culture seems to have been driven more by trade than war. When the Etruscans moved into northern Italy (around Lake Como), they opened up a new, and more direct, eastern route to the fur and amber markets of the Baltic and north-east. This enabled the La Tène groups to benefit, but meant that Marsalia and the lower French rivers were bypassed, with severe economic consequences for the Hallstatt and other groups relying on the old routes.

The second point relates to the sense of peace-loving Celtic groups in Britain later becoming innocent victims of the more

---

47   *Including distinctive wheeled vehicles, horse harnesses and long swords indicating a warlike society.*

aggressive Romans and Anglo-Saxons. The La Tène Celts belie that image. When one group crossed the Alpine passes into northern Italy, they defeated the Etruscans and founded a settlement near modern Milan. Spreading out across and southwards in Italy they soon defeated a large Roman army and entered Rome itself in 390 BCE. After they had sacked parts of the city they were bought off by the Roman authorities, collecting a vast amount of booty as the price of their departure. The indignity was something the Romans were unlikely to forget!

In retrospect, the Celtic decision to take the money and abandon Rome in 390 BCE might seem one of the great mistakes of history. In other ways, however, it highlights the issue of cultures and civilisations. It seems unlikely that the Celtic forces could or would have wanted to adapt to Roman cities and lifestyles, any more than the Anglo-Saxons in Britain some 500 years later. And the Celts were not to know that the enemy they defeated in 390 BCE was to become the mighty, and for a long time invincible, Roman Empire. But after the Romans commissioned a navy, established military discipline, defeated Carthage, and controlled the sea, there was little to stop their inexorable advance.

By 275 BCE, the tide had turned as Celtic societies successively fell to Roman trade, Roman arms or the lure of Roman lifestyles. Then, between 58 and 50 BCE, Julius Caesar, claiming that Roman interests were threatened, pursued his Gallic wars against the Celtic tribes with chilling efficiency, killing, enslaving or driving out an estimated one third of the entire Gallic population at the time. No wonder many sought to escape to Britain. With Celtic traces almost expunged in northern Gaul, the implications would not have escaped the Britons across the narrow Channel. Yet, for all their unruliness, many Celtic institutions were smoothly incorporated into the conquering Roman system, after which it was an easy step for the remaining Celts themselves to be absorbed. For the elite able to adapt, this became the good life as they attuned and adapted to Roman ways.

Reprise

The following is put forward as a very tentative, broad-brush summary of the Bronze and early Iron Age migrations affecting Britain.

* *Three main streams* – In Chapter 1 three main streams of settlement into Britain were suggested following the last Ice Age. The Eastern stream had early land access into eastern Britain across Doggerland, evidenced by discoveries at Starr Carr in Yorkshire and elsewhere, until the North Sea flooding closed that as a land route. The Western stream, meanwhile, was persistent and powerful in bringing people, trade, and ideas up the Atlantic west coast of Spain and France, and across to Ireland and south-west Britain. The Central stream, if it really existed, appears to have been much more widespread, with diffuse groups settling in different areas, often assimilating with resident groups there.

* *Language* – Some sections of the Central stream appear to have developed and shared with the Western stream a distinctive root language which we think of as Celtic, with its speakers sharing other cultural similarities.

* *Celtic groups* – Various cultural changes, including the so-called Urnfield culture mentioned earlier, are linked with movements that might be thought of as Celtic. Much later, the Hallstatt and La Tène groups appear to have been more distinct, with a more cohesive social and mercantile structure with its own characteristics. After that, while the Western (Iberian) stream continued to flourish, we next really become aware of Celtic peoples in northern Gaul before their Gallic language and many of the Gauls themselves were obliterated by Caesar.

METALS, CULTURES AND CELTS

* *Tribes to kingdoms* – This was also a time of rapid change in southern Britain, including Bronze Age arrivals from the Central and Eastern areas. New ideas and approaches spread quickly. As populations increased and families developed into tribes, land became more congested and contested. And as weapons became more sophisticated, tribes coalesced for trade and mutual support. This was probably encouraged by elites, who increasingly dictated the culture of the tribe. Some of these tribes consolidated into kingdoms, looking over their shoulders for defence, consolidation, or expansion. Origins may rapidly have become less important than loyalty.

* *Belgae in Britain* – Latterly, the Belgae became prominent. These were similar but semi-independent Belgic tribes, seemingly with a material Celtic ingredient, from the broad area between the Rhine delta and the Seine valley. In the late 2nd or early 1st century BCE, sections of Belgae crossed to Britain and established a base close to what later became Winchester. The Atrebates were another Belgic-linked group, centred around Calleva (south of Reading), as (probably) were the Catuvellauni to their north-east. All these groups were soon to play a critical role in the next phase, and Rome was already casting its shadow over Britain.

* *Immigration or replacement?* – It seems hard to estimate the extent of Celtic influence in Britain before the Romans came. In his major work, published in 2006, Stephen Oppenheimer writes: 'There was no Celtic replacement, any more than there was an Anglo-Saxon replacement.'[48] Although more recent DNA research challenges this, we might fairly conclude that, from the 5th century BCE until the Romans came, there were many waves of immigration into southern Britain that might be thought of as Celtic.

---

48   *Oppenheimer (2006)*

* *Celtiberian* – These waves especially included a strong Western/ Iberian connection along the Atlantic seaboard of Europe (thus 'Celtiberian'), with ancestral connections between indigenous Britons and the Basque areas going back thousands of years. Barry Cunliffe, a noted expert on this period, suggests that we might 'think of the Atlantic coast as a continuous corridor from Morocco to the Shetland Islands', a vast span of contrasting regions. Within this corridor people considered Celtic were constantly moving up and down the sea routes exchanging goods, information and ideas. Sharing many beliefs and cultures in the process, they were aided by similar linguistic roots and common experiences of the maritime coast. There was an especially strong connection between Brittany and Cornwall, who were near neighbours when Britain was physically linked to the European landmass, with strong social and trading bonds. Even after Britain became an island around 6,000 BCE these joint Atlantic coastal connections put Cornwall a world apart from the people of eastern and north-eastern Britain who had initially arrived via the Eastern Stream.

Perhaps it suffices to end this section with the words of Barry Cunliffe. 'The concept of the Celts is an ancient one that has changed with time. The Celts are always being reinvented, sometimes by outside observers, sometimes by the people themselves.' That was in 2003, and the process is ongoing. This analysis suggests that 'the Celts' were not all driven to the margins of Britain in the 5th and 6th centuries by the Anglo-Saxons. Many were already there by choice and long settlement.

A short timeline for chapter 3
All dates BCE and approximate

1,159	*Icelandic volcano eruption – Northern Britain in darkness*
1,200-600	*Old Field Systems Overridden – New major ditch and bank boundaries*
1,000+ 800	*Solar minima in Britain – Earthquakes in Mediterranean*
800	*More hillforts created – Uffington White Horse*
700	*(or earlier) Hallstatt Celts in Europe*
550	*Danebury hillfort lived in*
500- 100	*Emerging elites in Britain*
450	*La Tène Celts (to c. 50 BCE)*
430	*Parthenon built in Athens*
425	*Solar minimum – Bad weather possibly lasts until c 200 BCE*
390	*Celtic groups attack Rome*
275	*Romans drive back Celts*
200	*Climate stabilises*
100	*Hill forts abandoned – People move into valleys. Population c 1 to 1.5 million*
70	*First British coins? – Major expansion of trade*
60	*Growth of oppida – At least 12 oppida in SE Britain*
58	*Caesar starts Gallic Wars – Mass exterminations in Gaul*
55 + 54	*Caesar in Britain*

CHAPTER 4

ROMAN BRITAIN

55 BCE to 290 CE

This history now moves into a new phase. As Julius Caesar butchered his way through Gaul, his influence would have been felt in Britain long before his ships were launched. He came, he saw, but he did not conquer, and when the real invasion finally came under Claudius, it was fortunately not as destructive as Caesar had been in Gaul. In many ways the Romans conserved and moulded Britain, before retreating centuries later. The heaviest level of control, and thus the main part of Roman Britain, was the area we now call England, with Hadrian's Wall marking the main northern boundary for over 250 years. But to grasp how and why Roman involvement in Britain played out as it did, we need to see the wider picture.

Caesar in Britain

Rome is regarded as having been founded around 753 BCE. It was led by kings for some 250 years before they were ejected and the Roman Republic was established in 509 BCE. Although far from a democracy, the constitution was designed to prevent future domination by a single individual. Despite various upheavals and the occasional dictatorship in times of crisis, the succeeding nearly 500 years saw the Republic's power grow with the widespread, often violent, imposition of Roman rule across vast areas. But Julius Caesar's action in leading his army to Rome in 49 BCE violated the constitution, leading to a five-year civil war (with Pompey). Caesar emerged from this with effective supreme power, culminating in his assassination in March 44 BCE. This plunged Rome into further vicious conflicts, from which Caesar's great-nephew and godson, Octavian, ultimately emerged as victor. Despite dressing it up as a renewal of the old Republic, claiming to be 'first among equals', Octavian became effective dictator as Augustus, the first Roman Emperor.

Meanwhile in the last century BCE, Britain's trade was flourishing. Valued cross-Channel exports included tin, cattle, corn, animal hides, hunting dogs, gold, silver and slaves, with imports featuring wine and other luxuries. Trade suffered from around 60 BCE, however, as Caesar ferociously prosecuted his Gallic Wars, with the Roman victory in 52 BCE proving fatally decisive for the Gauls. After their Celtic leader, Vercingetorix, was hauled to Rome, kept in chains for six years and then executed, the Celtic Gauls largely perished as a mainstream force.

As a typical bully, Caesar resented apparent British sanctuary for his enemies. But, quite apart from the uncertainties of the Channel, Britannia remained a land of mystery and unknown hazard for Roman troops, accentuated by an intense Roman fear of the druids and the alleged practice of burning people alive in so-called Wicker-Man wooden cages.

Finally across, Caesar's first landing in 55 BCE was inconclusive, with the harassed Romans barely maintaining a foothold on British soil. Caesar spun the story of triumph over adversity well enough to gain the thanks of the Senate in Rome. He also sent emissaries to Britain to seek allies for the Roman cause. Undeterred, he returned in July 54 BCE with a substantial army. This time the landing was on open ground unopposed by the Britons, partly because they elected for guerrilla war, and partly because they were at odds with one another as to how to respond.

At that time in Britain two major southern groups had been in conflict for some time: the *Catuvellauni,* who controlled a wide area north of the River Thames, and the *Trinovantes*, their neighbours to the east in Essex and Suffolk. (See Map 2.) As Roman influence grew, the Trinovantes – tired of being pushed around by the Catuvellauni – aided the invading Romans by showing them the otherwise hidden route across the Thames at Brentford where the Catuvellauni were massed. Once across, with Roman military discipline seen to prevail, many tribal leaders came forward to make their peace with Caesar. But not Cassivellaunus, leader of the Catuvellauni.

Despite having got this far, Caesar turned back to pursue bigger ambitions than ruling Britannia. Securing pledges of allegiance from many southern British tribes he took himself, his army and some hostages back to Gaul, leaving trusted placemen in Britain to ensure that treaty terms were observed. Some of the hostages were treated well and Romanised, then encouraged to return home and extol the advantages of Roman ways. The intention was for Rome to control Britain without taking the trouble to defeat and occupy it.

The *Atrebates*, to the west of the Catuvellauni, benefitted greatly from Roman sponsorship. At modern Silchester in Hampshire they built what was effectively a new city to a grid pattern in a fusion of Roman and local styles. This was given a latinised Celtic name, Calleva Atrebatum, the first known example of British town planning, long before the Romans came back in 43 CE. In Calleva, Roman ways, household goods, food (such as oysters), wine and other luxuries would have been on display, such that visiting Calleva might have been like walking from Iron Age subsistence into Roman decadence. Some of this might have been down to a man called Commius, installed to rule the Atrebates in Britain to showcase and foster support for the Roman cause in return for many privileges, including freedom from taxes. This wide-ranging power was passed on to a successor called Verica, who ruled from about 15 BCE until shortly before the Claudian invasion in CE 43.

He may not have conquered, but Caesar had left his mark, and his placemen, in Britain. It only needed a trigger, plus a successor keen enough to take the risk.

Augustus thought about it, but had other priorities. His successor, Tiberius, had the military qualities, but was preoccupied on Capri. Next was Caligula, who planned an invasion with some care, before becoming distracted and then murdered. This left Claudius, dragged out from behind the curtains and thrust into the imperial purple. With many physical disabilities, and in the midst of a murderous family, Claudius was not the fool he appeared to be. Lack of charisma and military background hid a calculating brain, and he seized on 'unconquered' Britain as a means to make his mark with the Roman people. There were unruly tribes to be 'pacified' and valued British exports to be protected, but the real driver must have been Claudius's wish for glory and a formal triumph back in Rome.

Tribes

In-fighting between the southern British tribes provided the pretext. Some 15 or so *main* tribes or peoples have been identified south of the River Tweed and east of the Welsh border (See Map 2.) Starting in the north (with reference to modern locations for ease of reference) these were:

* the *Votadini* who occupied the east between Northumbria and the Firth of Forth,
* the *Brigantes*, probably a combination of smaller groups, dominating the large area around and south of the future Hadrian's Wall,

- the *Parisi* around the Yorkshire Wolds, noted for their links to Gaul and distinctive burial practices,
- the *Corieltauvi*, covering much of the East Midlands, centred on Leicester and Lincoln; and
- the *Cornovii* occupying land to the west of the south Pennines, today's Lancashire and Cheshire.

South of these and north of the Thames Valley, between the Severn Estuary and the North Sea, there were the:

- *Iceni* in Norfolk and eastern Cambridgeshire,
- *Trinovantes* in Essex and Suffolk,
- *Catuvellauni* in Oxfordshire, Buckinghamshire and Hertfordshire; and
- *Dobunni* across the Cotswolds (centred on Cirencester) to the southern Welsh border.

South again, along and inland from the south coast, ranging from east to west (with their broad modern county equivalents) were the:

- *Cantiaci* (or *Cantii*) in Kent, with a capital at Canterbury,
- *Regni* in Sussex, with a capital at Chichester,
- *Belgae* in Hampshire, with a capital at Winchester,
- *Atrebates* along the Thames Valley (Berkshire/ upper Hampshire), with a capital at Silchester,
- *Durotriges* in Wiltshire and Dorset, with major bases at Hengistbury Head and Dorchester; and
- *Dumnonii* (or *Damnonii*) to the far south-west, centred on Exeter.

As seen in the last chapter, many of the south-eastern tribes by then had close links with nearby Continental areas and groups. Most notably these were the Belgae in much of (modern) Flanders, Belgium and Holland, the Regni, and the Atrebates, meaning 'settlers', who (as seen earlier) became clients of Rome early on. The Iceni in Norfolk, the Dobunni in the Severn Valley, the Durotriges in the mid-south-west, and especially the Dumnonii in the far-south-west, were more self-contained.

Things were more contested north of the Thames Valley, where the expansionist Catuvellauni seemed so dominant that the Roman historian Suetonius even referred to their leader as 'king of Britain.' This was *Cunobelinus*, also known to us as Cymbeline.[49] As he moved east against the Trinovantes' capital at Camulodunum (Colchester), one of his brothers drove west into the land of the Atrebates, capturing their capital, Calleva, by about 25 CE.

Cunobelinus also had three ambitious sons, more than ready to mount their own attacks. One was *Caratacus* (also Caractacus), of whom we'll see more later. But when another son, Adminius (alias Amminius), attacked Kent he was (according to Suetonius) banished by his father in 40 CE. With lucrative cross-Channel trade and supplies now at risk, and spurred on by neighbouring tribes and a disaffected son, Emperor Claudius dusted off Caligula's invasion plans and put them into action.

The Channel deserves special recognition here as a key character in English drama. Even after the fear of druids, painted ones and mysterious beasts had diluted, there was the Channel itself, a sea which might suddenly turn from calm to maelstrom.

Caesar's first sight of Britain in 55 BCE was of high white cliffs bristling with British spears. Even when the Romans had finally secured a foothold on land, their ships were battered by a fierce storm. And when, the following year, Caesar came back with more ships, men and supplies, the wind was against him and penned his ships back in Gaul for about 25 days. Although the sight of this fleet lining the horizon caused the Britons to withdraw from the

---

49 Shakespeare's play of that name, however, has little relevance to the real history of the title character!

beachhead, the Channel was still to have its say. After the landing, a violent storm destroyed 40 of the 800 moored Roman vessels, requiring the Roman commander to build new ships in Britain to get his men (plus captives) back to Gaul. The cause may have been a storm surge, accentuated by the full moon and wind direction. The effect might have raised the sea level by as much as ten feet, tossing and beaching many ships over the shoreline.[50] On this occasion, crossing the Channel did not stop Caesar (little did – until the Ides of March), but it seriously mauled his plans.

The Claudian Conquest and aftermath
(Dates now CE unless stated otherwise.)

Claudius's 43 invasion was led by Aulus Plautius, supported by seasoned commanders. Having driven back the native fighters under Caratacus in mid-Kent, Plautius advanced to the Thames. He also sent for Claudius to join him, since politically the next stage needed to be the triumph of the emperor, not that of his general. For his part, Claudius resolved to make the conquest in style, accompanied by a large troop of elephants! Massing his troops, he stormed the effective British capital at Camulodunum, modern Colchester, and received the surrender of some eleven British kings. Job supposedly done, after just 16 days in Britain, Claudius returned to Rome to enjoy his imperial glory. In fact, the conquest took some 40 more years to complete.

A later supply port seems to have been established near modern Chichester in West Sussex. At the time the sea would have lapped the shores close to where the remains of Fishbourne Palace now stand, a magnificent former Roman villa with some of its stunning mosaic floors largely intact. The area may have been useful as a base for subsequent campaigns in the west, but the opulence of Fishbourne remains something of a mystery. Shortly after the invasion, a man

---

50   *Gerald Grainge – The Roman Invasions of Britain; Tempus (2005)*

called Cogidubnus (or Togidubnus),[51] possibly descended from Verica, son of Commius, seems to have emerged as a major ruler in the area, acknowledging the overlordship of Rome. If Fishbourne was indeed his, it suggests material thanks from a grateful Rome.

After Claudius's departure, the Roman army fanned out in three main directions – west, north-west and north – pacifying the tribes they met, but ready to administer Roman deterrence when persuasion failed. As they went, they left garrisons to maintain order in new forts or castra, later anglicised with the suffix chester that remains with us today.

Leading one army to the west was Vespasian, the future emperor, who is reported to have fought some thirty-three battles as he forced his way west and south-west. In many places he met little resistance but, even when retreating behind the defensive lines of massive hillforts, the natives were no match for the seasoned Roman troops. Not everyone received the conquerors peacefully. There were skirmishes, ambushes, and the occasional open battle before the Britons realised the folly of standing in the open, or even in their hill forts, against the ruthless Roman fighting machine.

One noted site is Maiden Castle in Dorset, which had begun life as a Neolithic causewayed enclosure before being adapted as a self-contained Iron Age hillfort for several hundred people. When skeletons with signs of trauma were unearthed by the noted archaeologist Sir Mortimer Wheeler, alarm bells rang out. But the idea that this was the site of a massacre has since been heavily doubted; there were certainly deaths from combat, but little evidence of mass slaughter at Maiden Castle – or elsewhere at that time.

Undeterred, Caratacus continued to harry the Romans wherever he could, working with local leaders and operating successful guerrilla tactics from the mountains of the Welsh marches. Then, for some reason, he chose to engage the Romans in open battle near the River

---

51   *Not to be confused with Togodumnus, brother of Caratacus!*

Severn in 50. The end result was probably inevitable, yet while his family were captured by the Romans, Caratacus again escaped. This time he sought sanctuary with Queen Cartimandua of the northern Brigantes, unwisely as it turned out. The queen, a Roman ally, promptly clapped him in chains and handed him over to his enemies. Even then Caratacus was unbowed. Paraded in Rome by Emperor Claudius, he passionately defended liberty, successfully persuading the emperor that he had more to gain by sparing his prisoner's life than ending it. Caratacus survived, but stayed in Rome.

The biggest rebellion, however, was yet to come. Having early on made peace with the invaders, Prasutagus, king of the Iceni tribe, continued to rule as a Roman affiliate. When he died in 60, the king's will appointed his two daughters as his co-heirs jointly with the Roman emperor. That, however, was not how things worked with Rome. And even if Prasutagus was being naïve, the Romans acted abusively when they took over complete control, a situation not helped when Seneca, Emperor Nero's then right-hand man, called in his extensive loans to the locals. The Iceni and their neighbours were already seething with discontent from Roman confiscations, huge Roman buildings and monuments being imposed on their land, and especially the enforced surrender of their beloved weapons. But what now lit the fuse was the treatment of the late king's widow. When she protested at Roman actions, she was flogged and her daughters raped in her presence. When she called for support in a revolt against her oppressors events rapidly spiralled out of control.

We now know the queen as Boudicca, whose treatment ignited many other tribal grievances and whose exploits seared a passage through history. Combining with the Trinovantes, the Iceni took out their fury first on the new, and bitterly resented, imperial capital at Colchester, massacring locals and Romans indiscriminately, then on Verulamium and London, burning large areas of the three cities to the ground. The Roman historian Tacitus reckoned that some 70,000 people died in this orgy of killing and destruction.

Early in the revolt, part of the Ninth Legion had been destroyed by the rebels. This was while Governor Suetonius Paulinus was on campaign against the druids, who had withdrawn to the apparent sanctuary of the Isle of Anglesey, off the north Wales coast. After a wait, Paulinus managed to lead his men across the turbulent straits to a fierce reception on Anglesey, with the druid leaders prominent among the massed ranks of Britons. Once again Roman military prowess, weapons and discipline prevailed, and the wholesale massacre that followed ensured that druids were never again a serious threat to Rome.

Annihilation complete, Paulinus turned round to march south-east, picking his spot to meet Boudicca's rebels somewhere in the Midlands. His army's flanks were well protected, forcing the massed Britons to tackle the Romans head-on. The undisciplined British charge, including whole families shouting howls of outrage, collapsed before the spears, shield-wall and short stabbing swords of the Romans. At the end of the day, with their escape route blocked by their own baggage wagons, some 80,000 British men, women and children lay dead on the battlefield, including Boudicca by her own hand.

Although Boudicca is sometimes taken as a symbol of early female emancipation, this might be viewed in the context of the mass slaughter that followed. Her actions certainly alarmed the Romans, who still saw compliancy in marriage, household management and bashful piety as the chief womanly virtues. To them, Boudicca was not just 'foreign' but also 'unnatural', and even if fascinated by her, Romans recoiled from such behaviour in a woman. That said, and after setting up a huge central military encampment against future trouble and a probably too efficient 'clean-up' operation in many areas, the Romans may have learned not to push the Britons too far. There were some gross purges to come, with ongoing outbreaks of unrest continuing, but no more major rebellions for centuries. It may have been bloody, but perhaps Boudicca had made her point.

The Iceni, however, racked by retribution and famine, were never the same again.

The Northern Boundary

It's possible today to walk across northern England from sea to sea by following the bracing and beautiful 192-mile Coast to Coast route over the Lake District, the Pennines, the Vale of York and the North York Moors. By contrast, the Hadrian's Wall Long Distance Path is further north, more remote, with a very different terrain and, at 73 miles, about a third the length. But this route compensates with ever-changing estuaries, wall remains, ruined mile castles and old forts. Geologically mixed, the Hadrian's Wall highlight is the dramatic Crag Lough section near Haltwhistle, where the Roman Wall seems briefly to compete with wilder sections of the Great Wall of China. Here is the Whin Sill, whose scarp slope is moulded from igneous rock, molten material injected upwards into softer areas and twisted into folds and faults. The result is the drama of sharp crags above, and windswept tarns in ice-scooped hollows below the bluff.

Renovated structures like Housesteads and Vindolanda now house tantalising exhibitions and artefacts, such as the renowned Roman writing tablets, written in ink on thin sheets of folded wood. These give glimpses into the daily life, concerns and gossip of the Roman soldiers, wives and families based there over 1,500 years ago, many having originated from distant lands where their broader families remained. When not fighting, on patrol, or occupied with construction projects, they seemed to have been as involved as anyone else with medical concerns, food and drink, parties, or requests for supplies from relatives or friends elsewhere.

With no obvious border to overcome, but supported by ruthless discipline, direct roads and supply lines, Roman policy was often just to keep going. So when Agricola campaigned in the far north in 78-83, he carried on up to the 'Highland Line', the deep fissure of the Great Glen, running diagonally across Scotland from modern Inverness to Fort William. On the way he managed to lure the northern Caledonians into the open at an unknown location known as Mons Graupius, possibly the modern Grampians. Here the natives suffered massive losses and the Romans supposedly few.

But Agricola's success was watched with jealous eyes by Emperor Domitian who, granting him a triumph at Rome, recalled him from active service. After Mons Graupius, the Romans effectively abandoned Scotland until Emperor Trajan chose to reinforce a more southerly border across the Solway-Tyne divide. His successor, Hadrian, generally more of a consolidator who lived life on the move from one border to another, commissioned the building of his eponymous stone wall in 122 as part of his strategy to secure all the imperial borders. Only twenty years later, however, with attacks continuing, Hadrian's successor, Antoninus Pius, established a revised, shorter, 40-mile-long 'Antonine Wall', built of turf, between the Clyde and the Forth,[52] south of Agricola's Highland Line but north of Hadrian's.

This 'Antonine Wall' also proved unsustainable, so that twenty years later the Romans fell back to Hadrian's line. Even so, Hadrian's Wall was overwhelmed between 180 and 184, and also in 205/6. In 208/9, therefore, Emperor Septimius Severus, something of a military dictator, took his forces far north against the Caledonians and Maeatae.[53] They, perhaps learning from the disaster at Mons Graupius, avoided a frontal engagement, and relied on demoralizing guerrilla attacks to erode Roman ranks. Short of a comprehensive victory, Severus opted for a diplomatic solution that masqueraded as success. He then withdrew to York, where in 211 – as his successor Constantius Chlorus was to do nearly a hundred years later – he died.

---

52   Broadly where Glasgow and Edinburgh are now located.
53   Later to merge and become known to the Romans as the Picts.

The northern groups had held out, this being the last time they were to be seriously threatened by Rome. For the next few centuries it was the Caledonians and their successors who would be the aggressors. Though far from impregnable, the border was now set in Hadrian's stone for some time, even in the imperial anarchy period from 235 to 284.

The Votadini were then the dominant tribe north of the wall up to their northern stronghold at Din Eidyn, Edinburgh-to-be. And even if they were aided by Roman 'investment', they may well have helped maintain relative peace for some time. In any case, the wall was not just a defensive structure; it was also a customs post and a clear statement that to the south was Roman territory. Anyone who sought to cross the line must have good reason to do so – and pay a customs tariff. And just south of the wall, a wide and open ditch called the vallum, with twenty feet high banks on either side, reinforced the message.

Romano-British Society

Having imposed peace on Britain, the Romans turned their attention to its government. Key to their approach was to give the local Britons scope to manage their own affairs within Roman constraints. They used old tribal boundaries to fix new, largely self-governing, regions (*civitates*), with capitals either in old centres or on newer open ground. Local elites in growing towns were encouraged to donate to major construction works and handle routine administration, channelling their competitive instincts into public works rather than opposing Rome. These Romano-Britons were thus compelled and seduced by turns to become 'Romanised', with togas, hot baths, personal hygiene, theatres, amphitheatres and private dinner parties, which gave them a taste of the good life that proved too powerful for most to resist.

In these early years, security and prosperity owed much to the governorship of Agricola (77–85) who respected local laws where these did not challenge Roman principles. Roman ways, proficiency in Latin, and education generally were encouraged, with the occasional possibility of a taste of *la dolce vita* in Rome. The Roman historian Tacitus questioned why the British elite adapted so readily, commenting that they did not realise this was a new style of 'servitude.' But Tacitus, concerned about Roman degeneracy at home, was also implicitly mocking the Romans' own slavery, evidenced by their increasingly decadent way of life.

The Romans now sought to extract the maximum revenue from Britain at the minimum cost without provoking a violent backlash. But maintaining four legions ready for action with all necessary support was hugely expensive. By the 2nd century this cost may have absorbed up to around 10% of the entire imperial army strength in order to guard under 5% of its total population.

The army, however, helped keep the peace and maintain stable roads, which facilitated trade which brought greater wealth, all improving the net Roman return on investment. Meanwhile, the well-honed Roman legal system made some inroads into ancient British practices, such as the traditional blood feud. At the same time, rights for the wealthy contrasted with the often arbitrary and brutal punishments for the underclass and slaves. More generally, and despite great Roman constructions in and between towns, rural Britain may not have changed greatly following the conquest. Modern aerial photographs and laser scans indicate that much of the extensive agriculture of pre-Roman times was left to continue, helping to feed the empire's insatiable appetite for grain. And in the fenlands of East Anglia many more marshes were drained for production or to become imperial estates.

But where things did change, normal benefits for well-off Romans would have been stunning novelties for Britons. Straight, stone-built house walls, running water and plumbing, glass in the windows, and underfloor heating, would have been extraordinary luxuries. In the well-to-do kitchens new dishes, fruits, exotic spices and fine wines encouraged experimental palates. In town streets new merchandise became available, plus markets for local produce. And, following the old Roman policy of 'bread and circuses', entertainment was available through gladiatorial contests in amphitheatres and some chariot-racing tracks (*circuses*) with up to 15,000 seated spectators.

Valuable mineral resources were another matter, leading to substantial quarrying, which dramatically changed some landscapes. Tin had long been a main attraction, iron production was extended in the foundries of the Weald and Forest of Dean, gold extracted in parts of Wales, and lead processing developed in full swing in Derbyshire and the Mendips. Indeed, the iron from the Weald of Kent was so valuable that distribution was controlled by the Channel fleet, while the lead industry was carried on through accredited middlemen called *conductores*. Higher production needed more transport and roads, encouraging facilities and markets to grow up around the main routes and junctions. Greater wealth increased demand for products such as household furniture, quality clothes, objets d'art, wine, olive oil and fish sauce, plus Roman-style services such as baths, barbers and hairdressers.

Tacitus wrote that his father-in-law, Governor Agricola, 'had to deal with people living in isolation and ignorance, and therefore prone to fight; and his object was to accustom them to a life of peace and quiet and the provision of amenities.' When Tacitus wrote of the 'unsuspecting Britons' being lured and lulled by 'arcades, baths and banquets' as 'civilisation', he was really speaking for an elite few. But how else might the Britons have behaved? With possession of a military weapon now a criminal offence, was there only a stark choice between Stoic acceptance and Epicurean self-indulgence?

Tacitus was describing a tiny minority. While a few people developed artistic skills in pottery or jewellery design and production, most remained tied to their scrap of land for animal husbandry, basic farming or worse. Working conditions in many areas would also have condemned many to a life of gruelling poverty in the fields or mines. Many skeletal remains show bodies worn down by labour, decay and injury, and some of the environmental destruction is with us still.

Many of the towns developed then are familiar to us today (see Map 3). From west to east on or near the south coast were Exeter, Dorchester (Dorset) and Canterbury (near Dover) in Kent. Cirencester, Winchester and Silchester lay a little further inland. Further north came Gloucester, St Albans (Verulamium – on Watling Street) and Colchester. Towards the Midlands were Wroxeter, Leicester and Castor-by-Norwich in the east, with Chester and Lincoln beyond them. In the north, York became increasingly dominant. These were the main towns where the new establishment and entrepreneurial class used Latin for social, political and business dealings, causing a spike in education and Latin literacy, while those on the land retained their old language and most of their traditions.

There would have been steady integration with Roman legionaries from various overseas countries. Signed on for 25 years at the army's command, the roughly half who survived battle and disease received handsome pensions and permission to marry. Long required to read and write, those who stayed on and married local women became a backbone of a new British middle class, with Roman citizenship being extended to wives and families.

Many previous fortified *oppida* became towns under new management, with a forum and administrative buildings, and some with extra defences. Local markets continued to flourish, building up natural contacts around them. So long as they remained peaceful, provided food, and paid their taxes, they may have enjoyed reasonable lack of constraint. London apart, most towns at this time were small. Even those such as Winchester or Leicester may have had populations of only around 2,000 to 4,000. Most production remained in the countryside, with goods and produce being carted into urban areas, leaving towns as centres of consumption and transport rather than the centres of industrial production that were to spur urban growth in later periods.

The wealth of the few became apparent in the villas that appeared in the countryside, outside but often close to towns, as the new elites sought more space, refinement and privacy than towns afforded. Many had mosaic floors, glazed windows, central heating and dedicated rooms for bathing. Some stood alone whereas others became centres for substantial estates, a material contribution to local economies. Local potteries prospered along with mosaic workshops, while estate hunting brought employment and opportunity for many. Overall, and even with great disparities in society, the Roman period saw a peak in the British population which was not regained for a long time.

Some locations

Wroxeter – One key Roman camp in the north-west Midlands lay close to Watling Street where the River Severn turns south from its source in the Welsh hills. This was Wroxeter, close to modern Shrewsbury, little known today but the site of well-preserved remains as a reminder that, at its peak, it was the fourth largest town in Roman Britain. When the local garrison was relocated to Chester, Wroxeter was reconstructed as a civilian town and administrative centre for the region. The town grew and prospered, adding baths and heated stone houses for the well-off, plus defences in the more turbulent late second century before steadily declining thereafter.

Bath – Bath is still known for its water, for the warm springs that bubble up from the depths, and their health-giving properties. And it did not take long for the Romans to discover and adopt these benefits. Recognising the similarities between the local goddess, Sulis, and their own Minerva, the Romans pragmatically combined the two into a joint goddess, Sulis-Minerva, and named the settlement Aquae Sulis – the waters of Sulis. They could be diplomatic when it suited them.

Buxton – The caves and dry valleys of the Derbyshire Peak District in the centre of England are typical features of porous limestone terrain. The Romans were drawn to Buxton, on the western reaches, for its water, especially at St Ann's Well – a natural spring in the town centre (with strong myths attached) where water flows out at a steady 27 degrees Celsius (80 degrees Fahrenheit). The percolation process is so slow that the water we can sip there today is reckoned to have originated from rain that fell in the later Stone Age, some 5,000 years ago![54]

York

As the Celtic Brigantes tribe (or tribes) north of the Humber had accepted the status of a Roman client kingdom, the Romans initially paused at the Humber Estuary. The neighbouring Parisi ruled the Wolds and further north-east, so that peace reigned until the leadership of the Brigantes changed in unusual circumstances. Cartimandua was the queen of the Brigantes, possibly (unlike Boudicca) queen in her own right before the Claudian invasion in 43. As a Roman ally, she was left relatively untroubled, and well rewarded when she handed Caractacus over to the Romans.

When her Roman allegiance was not shared by her husband, Venutius, Queen Cartimandua divorced him and replaced him with his former armour-bearer. Unsurprisingly this went down badly with Venutius, who, with some outside support, wrested control of the kingdom back from his ex-wife. While Cartimandua then seems to have disappeared from history, Venutius, by removing a Roman client ruler, provoked the Romans to send the Ninth Legion north under Cerialis to evict him.[55]

---

54 For more see *The Goddess of the Grove* by Sue Mortin (2013), published locally – ISBN 9781301156245.

55 *This is the same 9th Legion that worked with Vespasian, whose infantry were partly wiped out by Boudicca, and whose later adventures inspired the historical fiction by Rosemary Sutcliff: 'The Eagle of the Ninth.'*

In 71, having marched up from their base at Lincoln to crush the latest revolt, the Romans created a major fortification and garrison at York, calling it *Eboracum*.[56] Their camp was on a raised plateau close to the junction of two rivers, the Fosse and the Ouse which, wider than today, gave a fully navigable route to the Humber and North Sea. To the west loomed the great dark ridge of the Pennines, to the north-east the sweeping heathland of the North York Moors, and to the south-east the steep, dry valleys of the Yorkshire Wolds. The new camp rapidly attracted people keen to serve the soldiers, growing into a fully-fledged military and trading town. This became the effective northern Roman gateway, base and refuge for those fighting in the north. Archaeological finds suggest that the town developed a good standard of living for the soldiers and the well-to-do. Around 200 York became the capital of so-called Britannia Inferior (perversely meaning Upper Britain), with London the centre of its counterpart, Britannia Superior (Lower Britain).

London

As yet there is little evidence of London being anything more than scattered settlements in prehistoric times. This may have been because it was on the border between the Catuvellauni and Trinovantes to the north, the Atrebates to the west, and the Cantii to the south. A muddy tidal area in the middle of a major river between competing tribes might not have seemed an ideal town base at that time! London itself lies in a great basin of (largely) chalk overlaid with clay, earth and gravel, cut through by the serpentine Thames on its way to the wide mouth of the estuary. To north and south the land rises steadily, and on the nearby north bank of the river two small hills, with a plateau between them, stood out above the marshy ground. These are what we now call Cornhill and Ludgate Hill, with the Walbrook then running between them and the Fleet river just to the west below Ludgate Hill.

---

56 *A romanisation of an original Celtic name which appears to refer to a yew tree.*

On reaching the south bank, the Roman advance guard had found Southwark as a promontory of firmer ground to construct a pontoon bridge for their troops to cross over. The significance of the location would not have been lost on them; a crossing point well placed for ships sailing down the Thames, both for essential supplies and for trade and commerce.

Accordingly, after they had established their grip on the area, the Romans returned to London to start a major building programme in the period 48 to 52. The first London Bridge across the river from Southwark then provided a hub from which many of the main roads across the country radiated, some of them already settled trackways from previous centuries.

* *Watling Street* ran to London from the south-east, near Dover, continuing north-west through Verulamium, Letocetum (Lichfield) to Deva (Chester), gateway to north-west Britain and north Wales.

* *The Portway* led west to Calleva and then split, south to Venta Belgarum (Winchester), south-west to Durnovaria (Dorchester), west to Aquae Sulis (Bath) or north-west to Cirencester and Gloucester.

* *Ermine Street* ran north via Lindum (Lincoln) to Eboracum (York).

* Spur roads ran east to Colchester and southwest (*Stane Street*) to Chichester and the south coast.

* Other lateral routes included the *Fosse Way*, which crossed from Exeter through the Midlands to Lincoln.

A logical centre for trade, London soon attracted tradespeople, dealers and brokers of all kinds. After being looted and burned by Boudicca's wild army in 60, rebuilding started soon afterwards, including fort, forum, basilica[57], baths, shops and stalls. An amphitheatre instigated by Vespasian in 74 emphasised Roman power, and by the end of the 1st century CE the city had become the political, administrative and trading heart of Roman Britain, with a population of perhaps 30,000. There do appear to have been setbacks. Archaeology has revealed a series of skull remains and a dark, seemingly burned, layer dated to 125, but not what caused it. An apparent serious decline in pottery, construction and population in the decade from 160 also suggests a major crisis.

Another crisis struck in the second century, when the then governor of Britain, Clodius Albinus, made a bid to be Roman emperor, marching troops out of Britain to support his challenge against his main, and ultimately successful, competitor Septimius Severus. After the defeat and death of Albinus in 197, Severus visited Britain, and when not campaigning in the north he ordered major rebuilding, including the first real London wall. It was a sign of the times, and an indication that all was not well. The wall was up to twenty feet high, with a three-mile-long boundary. Starting with five gates it later added another two.

Further turmoil followed in the period around the middle of the 3rd century, but again the cause is uncertain. The town wharves were cut back and imports seem to have dried up – even wine for the troops, a serious issue! One possible reason is the advent, or feared advent, of the Plague of Ciprian, which ravaged Rome and much of the Empire from 251. An alternative, or possibly additional, cause may have been rampant piracy, either Saxon or Frankish or both. For a city to destroy its own wharves seems an extreme act, but perhaps unrestrained piracy or plague might be seen as justification, seeking to stop *any* ships landing there. Once again, however, the city revived and prospered, and by 313 had its own bishop.

---

57   *The basilica was a multi-function administrative building for many of the affairs of state.*

CHAPTER 5

CRISIS AND EXIT

290 to 410

Many British histories leap straight from Roman Britain to the Anglo-Saxons. We learn that a series of would-be usurpers from the late 4th to early 5th century left Britain to seek imperial glory, that Britain continued to be assailed by Picts, Scots and Saxons, and that in 410 the Emperor Honorius declined to come to Britain's aid. From a British perspective there is a sense that the Romans, having milked the land dry, had decided to walk away and leave them to their fate.

It is of course rather more complex than that and, as ever, our individual perspectives will vary. Do we sympathise with the Romans or the beleaguered Britons? Do we associate with the Britons or the Anglo-Saxon drive for a new life? Either way, to ignore the cataclysms in mainland Europe that preceded and accompanied the Anglo-Saxon arrivals is to miss a vital part of the bigger picture. But the dramatic 500-year history of the Roman Empire and the decline and fall of its western half covers a huge canvas. A few scenes have therefore been selected to throw some light on why what happened to the empire mattered to Britain and the future England. And it's worth starting with an improbable sailor-emperor, who might have been more at home in later times as an Elizabethan pirate-admiral.

Carausius – and a short-lived Brexit

The second half of the 3rd century was a troubled time in Roman Europe, and a climate dip in Britain, with high rainfall and persistent flooding, added to a sombre mood. Many of the Empire's borders were under pressure, its resources stretched to near breaking point, and its emperors having a decidedly short life expectancy. In the fifty years leading up to 284 some twenty-five emperors died trying to hold things together, many of them murdered by their Praetorian Guard. It was *Diocletian* who rescued the Empire from anarchy in 284, going on to establish the Tetrarchy, the 'rule of four', with a co-emperor in east and west, each supported by a caesar (effectively a sub-emperor).

Meanwhile, pirate groups continued to plague the coasts of Britain and northern Gaul. With Roman mercantile interests threatened, an experienced captain called *Carausius* was chosen to command the Roman Channel fleet and remove the raiders. His apparent success attracted a different kind of attention when rumours circulated that it was attributable to Carausius conniving with the pirates. Maximian, then joint western emperor, ordered Carausius to return to Rome, a command which the admiral saw as a likely death warrant. He also saw that his fleet was his best protection. 'Going for broke' in 286, Carausius proclaimed himself Emperor of Britain and Northern Gaul, but his wish to rule jointly with Diocletian and Maximian was not reciprocated.

Roman Emperors were a diverse bunch. Even so, Carausius was unusual, his coins of around 290 showing a double-chinned, bull-necked man rather than the imperious brow of the stylised military hero. Initially a down-to-earth type, Carausius seems to have enjoyed loyalty among his men, and possibly among his enemies too. Issuing new coinage to stabilise the economy, and with the fleet controlling the Channel, he managed to hold sway for seven years before being overcome by his growing hubris and assassinated by his own chancellor, *Allectus*.

For the next three years Allectus managed the realm, with the Caledonians still rampant to the north and the sea protecting the south. But by late 296 time and imperial patience ran out when a Roman fleet left the Seine Estuary under cover of a thick Channel fog to take the 'home' fleet by surprise. Landing a large military contingent on the south coast, the Roman forces finally brought the rebels to battle near Calleva, the old capital of the Atrebates. Allectus perished in the conflict, and the rebellion largely died with him. Meanwhile London was 'liberated' by a Roman fleet commanded by the recently-appointed western caesar, *Constantius Chlorus* ('the pale'). Thus ended the Carausius experiment, highlighting a structural fault and a dangerous precedent.

Constantine

Today, York Minster dominates an area inside the restored Roman walls around the narrow city streets. Just outside the minster a verdigris-coloured statue may puzzle the casual visitor. A young, regal figure, seated on a throne with left hand extended over the hilt of a sword, gazes impassively into the distance. The plinth below the statue carries the engraving: *'Constantine the Great, 274-337 – Near this place, Constantine was proclaimed Roman Emperor in 306.'*

In fact, Constantine was not *proclaimed* emperor by Rome; he was actually (and illegally) *acclaimed* by his father's troops then stationed in York and had to fight all the way to achieve his later eminence. Yet 306 was pivotal for his impact on both the Roman Empire and the island of Britain. When, in 305, Diocletian unexpectedly chose to retire as emperor, Constantius Chlorus, the man who had liberated London from Allectus in 296, was elevated to western emperor. Returning to Britain in 305 he attacked and drove back the far northern tribes before retiring for the winter to the Roman base at York, where he became ill. With his son at his side, Constantius died in July 306. The son was *Constantine*, already a popular and seasoned campaigner in his mid-30s, whom the northern legions now acclaimed in his father's place.

But it was not that simple. Noting the past disasters of unsuitable sons following their fathers, Diocletian had insisted that new emperors and caesars were formally appointed, with no automatic succession. Constantine's action was therefore potentially treasonable. As with Carausius and his fleet, Constantine's best protection lay with his army. He therefore left Britain with his men to secure his father's base at Trier (now in north-west Germany) before cautiously moving south towards Rome. Finally, in October 312, after much manoeuvring, Constantine faced his western rival, Maxentius, at the Battle of the Milvian Bridge on the edge of Rome. The result was an overwhelming victory for Constantine and the death of Maxentius in the Tiber, leaving Constantine in effective control of the western empire.

Just before the battle Constantine claimed to have experienced divine inspiration in the sky. Even if this might today be seen as a sun halo, it suited Constantine to interpret it as a Chi-Ro, the first two letters of the word Christ in Greek, and a sign of divine support. The next year the Edict of Milan adopted Christianity as an official religion of the Roman Empire. And it never looked back.

The religion already had established roots in Britain, with its own martyrs. Yet as it grew, doctrinal and other differences became more apparent, to which the Roman Church responded by seeking greater adherence to its adopted beliefs and processes. Many Romans, used to living with a pantheon of gods, struggled to accept the concept of a single omnipotent being (other than the emperor), but Constantine soon saw the benefits of combining heavenly approval and state power in his own person. Also recognising that Rome was now well away from the centre of the Empire, he set his sights on Byzantium, gateway between the Black Sea and the Mediterranean, and between Europe and Asia.

Here was a worthy site for an imperial city, sitting astride the trade and affairs of two continents. But Constantine (inconveniently) had a co-emperor there, Licinius, and it was to be 327, fourteen years on, after much more manoeuvring and some brutal battles, before Constantine triumphed in the east. Three years later, in 330, he moved the imperial capital from Rome to Byzantium as a Christian city, modestly renaming it Constantinople after himself, and later bringing to it the full trappings of its own senate and magistracy. Here, he thought, was a suitable location and memorial for his omnipotence.

The Constantine Inheritance

Despite being hailed as 'the Great' after his death in 337, Constantine left a mixed reputation, partly due to the contradictions of his character. His contribution to Christianity assured him eternal acknowledgement from the Catholic Church, but the communion cup was also a potential poisoned chalice in terms of doctrinal disputes.[58] Doubts also remain as to exactly what he believed in, even if he knew it himself, as he seems to have hedged his bets with the sun god, Sol Invictus. He also left a disastrous legacy with family complications of near-labyrinthine proportions. While his mother Helena was later hailed as a saint, one of his sisters-in-law also became his step-mother when she married Constantine's father. On Constantine's own death, this left an extended family with three sons and three daughters plus four grandsons on the male side. Constantine himself is held responsible for putting to death both his first wife, Fausta, and his son by her, Crispus, for unexplained reasons.

Perhaps noting the risks, the emperor's sons seem to have learned to look after themselves before others did. The result was that, within

---

58 *Especially as to the Trinity, and whether God the Father, God the Son and God the Holy Spirit were of the same substance or (the Arian view) only a similar substance.*

months of Constantine's death, most of his father's second family had been murdered, leaving only two young grandsons. Constantine's three sons then turned against one another, leaving the second son in age, Constantius II, as the last man standing. But there were other contenders for the top job, including successful generals, many of Germanic descent with similar names.[59] Nor was Britain immune, with many of its troops drawn into ill-fated campaigns, depleting Britain's reserves.

When, in 353, the mean-spirited Constantius II, suspecting the country to have supported his rivals, sent a man called *Paulus* to Britain to bring to justice those responsible, the implications were severe. Paulus was vicious, treating evidence of guilt on the part of those 'investigated' as an unnecessary luxury to dispensing justice. His violent campaign and cull of the army plus higher ranks of civilians earned him the name of Paulus Catena ('chains') for his excesses in dragging his chained victims through the streets. The ensuing bloodbath left the people of Britain demoralised and in little position to defend themselves. Paulus was later to suffer in turn, being burned alive under the next emperor, but the scars of his butchery left a lasting impression on the collective British memory.

Constantius II was left with two young cousins, but the leopard had not changed his spots. Once the elder, Gallus, had finished helping Constantius defeat another rival, he was intercepted and killed. This left, *Julian*, the only other adult male in Constantine's family, to be pressed into service as caesar in 355. Having pushed back the Franks along the Rhine, Julian's troops declared him emperor, but this time it was Constantius who fell ill and died, leaving Julian sole emperor in 361.

Julian, however, proved to be equally brutal and unreliable, being prepared to make and break truces as he chose. He also harboured

---

59 *By the fourth century an estimated 25% of the Roman army in the west was of Germanic background, with many reaching high command.*

a secret; although feigning adherence to Christianity, he 'came out' as a pagan, growing his goatee into a ragged philosopher's beard. Having restored the pagan temples and the sacrificial practices that were such an anathema to the Catholic church, Julian, now the 'Apostate', became caught up in the old imperial obsession, Persia. After a good start, the Roman campaign became bogged down. When Julian, perhaps believing he had supernatural powers, rushed out into the fray without his breastplate, he was fatally speared. He was the last of the House of Constantine, and although this was far from the end of paganism as such, henceforth the rulers of Rome would all be Christian.

The Saxon Shore

In the late 3rd century, around the time of Carausius, accounts start to refer to the *Forts of the Saxon Shore*, later supervised by the 'Count of the Saxon Shore'. Nine such forts have been identified over a broad shoreline from Norfolk through Essex, Kent and Sussex to Hampshire. Some remains are still evident, with Porchester near Portsmouth a fine example. A similar line of forts had also been built across the coastal areas of northern France, suggesting a composite approach to what must have become a major piracy problem along the Channel.

But why the reference to 'Saxon' shore? The Romans could be very generic with the names they used for other people, often using 'Saxons' as a catch-all term for pirates or raiders based elsewhere. Rome also employed former outsiders from Saxony as auxiliaries, so that the name might not refer to pirates but to the 'Saxons' already in place in Britain to protect British and Roman trade, ships and supply lines. Then there is the renegade admiral Carausius himself. To defend himself against the Roman fleet, might he have built, or rebuilt, the forts to keep the *Romans themselves* out?

Even if the forts later became customs outposts, a visit to the still massive walls at Richborough in Kent, erected in the late 3rd century, does reinforce the view that, while also used as storehouses, at least some of these sites *for some periods of time* were real forts, especially when protecting vital sailing channels and townships within their walls.

The significance is that a large number of 'Saxons' seem to have been present in Roman Britain at least two centuries before the full Anglo-Saxon surge occurred. This would have had material implications for what was to come.

The decline of the Empire – 350 to 410

Despite some turbulence, the first half of the 4th century seems to have been something of a golden age for Roman Britain, at least at the upper levels. Trade still nourished wealth and status for some, while providing a valuable revenue stream for the Empire. Roman administration developed with the beginning of a civil service; the governor of Britain, based in Trier, had reporting to him a *vicarius*, deputy governor, who had four provincial governors, probably operating from London, Cirencester (mid-southwest), Lincoln (midlands) and York (north), each with his own support team.

But while Britain remained in need of defence on all sides, so did the rest of the Empire. The constant drain on the island's resources was leaving Roman Britain increasingly vulnerable. And that weakness was sensed by its neighbours.

The groups north of Hadrian's Wall were meanwhile growing in strength. Yet even here the picture is complex, nor helped by continuing confusion over the groups involved. By using the term *Picts* and *Scots (Scotti)* as a generic term for aggressive raiders from untamed far northern Britain, the Romans conflated two, originally separate, groups. The Scotti originated in the northern areas of Ireland before expanding across the sea into Argyll and western Scotland, creating the kingdom of Dalriada (or Dal Riada) in the process. The Picts (the 'painted ones' from their prominent warlike tattooed designs), were from northern Scotland, coming to Roman attention from around 300, seemingly as a collection of recently-merged far northern tribes (perhaps including some Caledonians). As so often, each group might join with others, sometimes fight against them, and at other times act independently.

To try to reduce the confusion, this book uses *Scotti* for the 'Irish' while Ireland remained their main base, adopting the name *Scots* once they moved across the sea to settle in what became south-west Scotland. In good times there would be relative peace, and Hadrian's Wall acted as a controlled gateway for people and trade, with a buffer zone up to the Forth-Clyde isthmus.[60] But breakouts across the border, and sometimes full-scale and devastating invasions, were to remain a persistent problem for centuries to come. By about half-way through the 4th century, the northern groups felt strong enough to go on the offensive. And they were not alone.

In 353, 360, 363/4 and again, most extensively, in 367, southern Britain came under ferocious onslaught from all sides. The last of these was so widespread, so contemporaneous, and so strategic in its locations, that the Romans, taken unawares, believed it was a conspiracy. This was the so-called 'Barbarian Conspiracy' between Picts, Scots and Saxons, perhaps assisted by aggressive Franks from Gaul.

As Roman Britain reeled from these offensives, back on the Continent the next stage of Rome's military decline explains why Rome was ultimately unable to help. Large groups of *Goths*, driven by Huns attacking from the east, had reached the north bank of the Danube, the major imperial frontier. Having finally received imperial permission to cross they were viciously exploited and attacked by the Roman military. When the Goths retaliated, the then Emperor, Valens, returned from Persia in 377 to face the Goths

---

60 Possibly later in cooperation with the more compliant local kings or tribes such as the Votadini.

at Adrianople, deploying his tired troops across the face of the Goths' lines. The Goths then lit bush fires, with the prevailing wind fanning heat, smoke and confusion across the Roman lines. For once, Roman discipline broke, and the Goths' follow-up is estimated to have ensured that some two-thirds of the imperial Roman army perished, including 35 tribunes and the emperor, whose body was never found.

Adrianople showed that the Romans were beatable. But the Goths' success in battle left them no nearer their dream of a homeland in which to settle, or even the money to buy the food they needed. The Roman refusal to deal fairly with them, even with many Goths later becoming valued Roman mercenaries, did not ultimately benefit the Romans either. The imperial vacancy was filled by a 32-year-old proven army leader, *Theodosius I*, whose reign was marked by continual fighting on and near the borders. He also has the distinction of being the last emperor of the combined east-west Roman Empire. But Theodosius was also volatile and, after recovering from a near-death illness, he went on the religious offensive with his Edict of Thessalonica making Nicene (as opposed to Arian) Christianity the official religion of the Roman Empire.[61] In January 395, a few months after his last great battle near the River Frigidus, close to Aquileia, Theodosius was struck down with illness and died. His sons and successors were just 16 and 10 years old, *Arcadius* in the east and *Honorius* in the west. As it turned out, the split Roman Empire would not come together again, partly as the sons were young, inexperienced, and pliable. Although hemmed in between Christian powerhouses on one side and an expansive Muslim homeland on the other, it was the eastern 'Byzantine' Empire that lasted a thousand years longer than the western, before falling to the Turks in 1453. None of this would have looked likely in 395.

---

61 *Those who believed otherwise, he decreed, were 'suitable to be smitten first by divine vengeance and secondly by the retribution of our hostility.'*

Nor might it have seemed likely at the time that the leadership of Rome would pass to the Catholic Church. When in 390 Theodosius viciously responded to a rebellion at Thessalonica by massacring thousands of its inhabitants, Bishop (later Saint) Ambrose refused him communion until he had done public penance, proving an early precedent for future confrontations between church and state. And the Goths? In one sense the Gothic advance across the Danube had lit a slow fuse that was, decades later, to burn through to the centre of Rome itself. A gathering Gothic force moved into Italy, with Honorius, western emperor, hiding in his new, largely impregnable, palace at Ravenna, issuing threats and unwilling to negotiate. Finally, the Goths under Alaric, as much out of frustration as anything, sacked Rome in 410. Note the date, and the name of the emperor – Honorius the unsuitable younger son of Theodosius and titular ruler of the Western Empire.

We can now see why Emperor Honorius would not wish, and was in no position, to come to the aid of a now largely redundant Britain. There may well have been many others who knew it too, and had started to make their moves.

Meanwhile back in Britain, by about 375 there seems to have been increasing Romano-British discontent about Rome's ability to protect its citizens, who were also paying heavy taxes. This may have spurred the then military governor of Britain to make his own bid for glory. Sporting the hyperbolic name of *Magnus Maximus*, in 383 he crossed to Gaul and held sway there for some five years. Although finally falling to Theodosius in 388, the fame of Maximus grew into legend, notably in Wales where he was called Maxen Wledig, and later credited with being the ancestor of the kings of Dyfed.[62]

When, around 405, the High King of Ireland, Niall of the

---

62 *Not the (fictitious) Maximus of 180 CE portrayed by Russell Crowe in the Ridley Scott 2000 film 'Gladiator'.*

Nine Hostages, attacked the British south coast, the Britons were in a quandary. Organising their own defence might be seen as insurrection, but to do nothing would leave them at the mercy of the attackers. The Irish king was eventually beaten back but there followed an extraordinary period from 406 when a succession of British-based usurpers lay claim to the imperial title. After the early death of the first two aspirants, the third took the title *Constantine III* in 407 and set off with a Romano-British army to save Gaul from a huge army of Vandals and others. Having defeated one renegade force, he reached Spain before returning to Arles in southern France, which put him in striking distance of the Roman heartlands. Honorius played for time, as was his custom. Constantine III's support started to ebb away, and he was finally defeated and executed in 411.

With repeated troop depletions, foes massing at the edges, and law and order fracturing, even before a devastating Saxon attack in 408, many in Britain were in revolt against Roman masters who were unable to protect them. Despite this, others saw their country as still an integral part of the Roman Empire, possibly also wanting to distance themselves from the rebellion led by Constantine III. It may be this last group, whoever they were, who decided to write to Emperor Honorius asking for help.

The young, self-indulgent, western emperor, Honorius appears to have remained uninterested in the fate of the far-away and troublesome province of Britain. When it came, his response to the British request for aid, possibly in 409 though often attributed to 410, was to confirm that the Britons must provide their own defence. But although Roman records of the time say that in his reign Britain was lost 'for ever' to Rome, Honorius's refusal to help was not expressed as a permanent abandonment. Many expected the Romans to return. But the reality was that the old Roman Britain, the England of the future, was really now on its own.

Britain and its civilian population may have been spared the massive rolling battles that spread across central Europe around this time, but they suffered in other ways. While its coasts acted as a sufficient barrier to deflect the huge swirling migrations that beset the Continent, Britain had lost most of the troops needed for its own defence. The great adventure of Constantine III would have been especially galling, withdrawing ever more support from Britain, paid for by taxes on those who only became more vulnerable as a result. They were spared the vengeance of another Paulus, but that may have been small comfort. By 409 day-to-day life in Britain was suffering and its citizens would have become increasingly aware of Rome's inability to protect it.

Roman Britain reviewed

In his afterword to his book *Britain BC*, Francis Pryor mildly berates the lack of appreciation of the qualities of the native British and the over-glamorisation of the benefits of Roman 'civilisation'. He quotes the observation of Tacitus that the Britons became lured into pleasure without realising that it was a form of slavery. Pryor suggests that the Romans found in Britain a 'network of complex and constantly changing relationships', which they were unable – and probably never wanted – to unravel and understand. The Romans relied on first rate military intelligence, understood military strength and weakness, and knew how to exploit division or discord among their enemies. But in the event, the early Britons resisted so forcefully that it took vast numbers of legionaries, plus auxiliary and support personnel, to contain them. This was a commitment which, over time, Rome proved unable to maintain. One sustaining factor, in Pryor's view, was the Britons' belief in individual freedom, which even if they have sometimes fallen short of their own ideals, has continued as an ongoing feature of the British races. Perhaps we have not changed so much after all.

So, what long-term effect *did* the 360 odd years of imperial occupation have on the social fabric and future prospects of the people of Roman Britain?

* *Continuity?* – Perhaps the overriding impression is of effective continuity in many occupied areas during much of the Roman period. After Boudicca, Caratacus and the challenges of policing the Welsh and Scottish borders, despite raids, piracy, border skirmishes and inroads from imperial aspirants, Britain largely escaped the worst of the many civil and other major wars that assailed the Continent in that period. Not just that; Roman garrisons brought work, trade, prosperity and a large degree of order to a country that had previously been riven by tribal rivalries and differences. Three hundred years of relative peace was a remarkable achievement in highly turbulent times when the Continent itself was convulsed by massive migrations that accelerated the demise of the once-mighty Western Empire. It was not until 367 and the 'Great Barbarian Conspiracy' onwards that serious inroads into the social fabric of Romano-British life threatened centuries of relative peace and stability. In fact, many archaeologists and historians now take the view that, although the Romans occupied Britain for centuries, they did not materially change its social structure or essential culture.[63] In that sense (as Barry Cunliffe observed), the Roman occupation of nearly 400 years could be called an 'interlude.'

* *Respect* – Even if grudgingly, the Romans had learned to respect the spirit of independence in Britain. As time went on, the distinction between native Britons and Romano-British could have blurred to the extent that the Roman occupation might have seemed more a joint venture than a takeover.

---

63 *It might be argued that the Romans introduced Christianity to Britain, but that was only after Constantine in the early 4th century, and after 300 years of seeking to suppress the religion!*

Compared with the initial aggressive Roman attitude or the wholesale dispossession and top-down hierarchy imposed by the Normans after 1066, later Roman control of Britain seems to have become almost consensual. Over time, for example, the army appears to be as much a protector as an oppressor of the people, all aided by the trades that grew up around the main military camps and by soldiers retiring and marrying locally. But with Roman policy not to use local troops in their own areas, Britain would have progressively been drained of many who might otherwise have been able to defend it.

* *Language* – Another factor is the existence or otherwise of a common language. Before and after the Roman invasion most Britons are believed to have spoken a form of Celtic-derived Brittonic (or Brythonic) language, whereas the occupying forces at that time spoke Latin, as did some of the would-be new elite. In Gaul, by contrast, Latin remained a living language after the western Roman Empire fell apart, while spawning a new Romance (i.e. Latin-based) language as the Frankish influence grew. Latin also became the language of the Christian church, by then well established in Gallic society, though not in Britain. As a result, Latin largely disappeared from everyday speech in Britain in the early 400s, leaving space for what became Anglo-Saxon Old English. Thus, where the Franks/French retained Mars (Mardi), Mercury (Mercredi), Jupiter (Jeudi) and Venus (Vendredi) for the days of the week, the Anglo-Saxons adopted (and the English have retained) the Germanic gods, Tiw, Woden, Thunor and Frig for Tuesday, Wednesday, Thursday and Friday.[64]

* *Slavery authorised* – The better-off or more socially mobile may have prospered during the years of Roman control, but life

---

64 *Sunday and Monday are the days of the sun and moon respectively; Saturday reverts to the Roman Saturn.*

for most of the low-born, servants and slaves remained tough. There were cases of slaves spending valued lives and even being freed, but the power of life and death over the unfree that Romans took for granted and exercised with impunity would have condemned untold numbers to misery and some to agonising ends. And when change did come, they were unlikely to be the ones to benefit. Although we see things very differently now, we should also recognise that slavery was not a Roman prerogative; it had been practised, and would continue to exist, in varied forms and across many societies from time immemorial for thousands of years to come.

* *Civil society* – The big change for Britons would have been what Romans regarded as the essence of civilisation – towns, streets, imposing structures and an ordered society. Much of this was wholly new to Britain, but in other respects the Britons learned to work for and obey new masters. And when the time did come for change in the 5th century, it was the towns, streets, and structures that were to suffer most as the key tenets and tenements of Roman civilisation crumbled away.

* *Towards the end* – In the late 4th century many well-off Britons started to suffer as social and financial structures came under strain. As agriculture collapsed, countryside patterns changed. Drainage ditches silted up, leading to many areas of formerly productive land being lost to flooding and marsh. Ploughing continued, but in a more restricted way. Pottery imports fell away, and it took time before local British production filled the gap, much of it on a near industrial scale at a few specific sites. Similarly, iron production became more concentrated, creating major employment in some areas, but leaving great quantities of iron-slag in its wake and reduced occupations elsewhere. The signs suggest that many industrial activities were now in the hands of a new style of industrial baron or oligarch.

When Rome could no longer pay its soldiers, the last bulwark protecting Romano-British society collapsed and the financial system started to seize up. As coinage dried up, it became debased, sometimes with sections clipped off existing coins to make new ones. Potteries and brickworks closed, leaving most urbanites having to find new ways to survive. For a while farming may have been able to continue as it had been, with the burden of heavy Roman taxation lifted. But with the export market largely closed, demand and employment were reduced, pushing farm prices down with consequent effects.

Perhaps worst of all, a dangerous power vacuum had been created.

A short timeline for Roman Britain

27 BCE – 14 CE *Augustus as Roman Emperor*
43 *Claudius' invasion*
50 *Foundation of London*
51 *Defeat and capture of Caratacus*
60/61 *Boudicca's revolt*
69 – 79 *Vespasian as Roman Emperor*
71 – 84 *Conquest extended to North, Wales and Scotland*
100 *Northern border back to Tyne-Solway line*
122 *Hadrian's Wall started*
143 – 160 *Antonine Wall started and then given up*
208 – 211 *Severus campaigns in Scotland*
235 – 284 *The Anarchy – ended by Diocletian*
286 – 296 *Carausius and Allectus – Britain regained by Constantius Chlorus*
306 *Constantine 'the Great' acclaimed in York*
312 *Constantine defeats Maximian at Milvian Bridge and enters Rome*
313 *Christianity recognised in Rome*
330 *Constantine establishes Constantinople*
337 *Death of Constantine I – sons as joint emperors*

340 – 69	*Turbulent period with attacks on Roman Britain*
353	*Purge in Britain by Paulus 'the Chain'*
367 – 9	*'Barbarian Conspiracy' attacks*
378	*Goths defeat and kill Emperor Valens at Battle of Adrianople*
379	*Accession of Theodosius*
383	*Magnus Maximus acclaimed in Britain*
395	*Theodosius dies; Honorius becomes western emperor*
406/7	*Two usurpers and troops leave Britain plus Constantine III (died 411)*
409/10	*End of Roman rule in Britain*
410	*Goths sack Rome*

CHAPTER 6

THE 'DARK AGES'

410 to 600

We can now see that the Romans did not all line up and take ship back to the Continent in 410. They had been leaving for years, including those who had probably become more Britons than Romans by then, but bound to follow military orders. Despite this, some remnants of administration did appear to continue in Britain, with no reason for the country immediately to fall into anarchy. Nor did the Anglo-Saxons arrive en masse, like the earlier Romans or later Normans. When they came, Anglo-Saxon inroads were ongoing, intermittent, often localised and sometimes haphazard, in a process best viewed over a long period.

This takes us into the obscure period still sometimes called 'the Dark Ages'. The term is used with caution today, but can still be apposite. It reflects how little we know for sure because of the near absence of contemporaneous written records. It evokes the spiritual darkness felt by the Catholic Church with Britain being overrun, as they saw it, by pagans, and also the more literal darkness after 530, when the country was assailed by a debilitating volcanic ash cloud, followed by the plague.

Terms used

To help navigate the complexity of the period and try to limit misunderstanding, here's a summary of the ways certain terms are used in these chapters. Inevitably some of these beg further questions, which are explored later.

Briton, British and Brittonic – refer to the bulk of those 'settled' in Britain by the end of the Roman occupation.

Germanic – This refers, not to a nation or ethnicity, but to the groups of people who lived on or near the North Sea coasts of the Continent, including Saxons, Angles, Frisians, Jutes, the original Rhineland Franks, and some from Scandinavia.

Saxon – includes the *foederati* (auxiliary soldiers) and other 'Saxon Shore' groups described earlier plus those incomers who predominantly originated from Continental Saxony (see Map 4).

Anglo-Saxon – The term seems to have come into use from about the 7th century to distinguish the Saxons settled in Britain from those still living in Continental Saxony. It then became a useful description of the Angle, Saxon and other mainly Germanic people then settled in Britain. The Anglo-Saxons are not a distinct racial group, and the term does not carry any ethnic overtones.

English – Although there was no England at that time, *English* is progressively used after about 600 to refer to the people of Mercia and Wessex, extended later to others who saw themselves as English, rather than (for example) Scots, Welsh, Danish, Norse or Swedish.

Dates – The precise timing of the various arrivals, of many of the key battles for control, and the succession and inter-relationship of leaders, are all highly complex. These chapters come with the usual caveat that this account is a suggested outline summary of complex issues, based on current understanding. It does not attempt to be a complete history, and the issues raised will leave fertile ground for new discoveries and renewed debate for years to come.

Chronicle – The Anglo-Saxon Chronicle was begun in the late 9th century under the aegis of King Alfred. Copies were distributed to monasteries across the country, where many were updated independently. The result is the 'Common Stock' version of Alfred's time plus many other regional versions as extended over time, some of which may reference earlier sources since lost to us.

The longue durée view (as described in chapter 2) – To try to give a preliminary overview of the next two centuries, perhaps about ten generations, events are now broken down into four half-century periods.

400 to 600 – An overview

400 to 450 *(Adjustment)* – Starting ten years before the 'you're on your own' message from Emperor Honorius, this initial period now appears to have been one of steady civil and social decline, marked by attacks from the Picts, Scots and others. As time went by, the supply of coinage dried up, buildings and services fell into disrepair, with little money or skills to repair them, and lawlessness increased. The evidence suggest that life went on, but at a more basic level than before.

450 to 500 (*Inroads*) – It was probably around 450 (or slightly earlier) that serious insurrection occurred in Kent, possibly orchestrated by Jutes rather than Saxons. After being penned back, they broke out and attacked Kent, gradually taking over and installing a king there by 500. They were followed by Saxon groups arriving in Sussex and further west. Meanwhile, over on the north-east bank of the

Thames Estuary, the East Saxons founded Essex and inroads of Angles settled in East Anglia and along the north-east coast. As ever, much depended on time and place, and while most evidence to date indicates a relatively peaceful process of integration, there do seem to have been places and times of slaughter and enslavement. Near the end of the period, however, there was a significant British fight-back.

500 to 550 *(Dark Years)* – As a culmination of the fight-back, around 500 there was a major battle at a place called Mount Badon, whose location and context remain the subject of much conjecture (see below and chapter 7). The battle appears to have resulted in a major victory for the Britons against the Saxon forces, halting the main Saxon offensives for several decades. The relative peace that followed was broken by years of darkness and plague.

550 to 600 *(Takeover)* – Renewed waves of immigration into Britain resumed, including substantial numbers from Scandinavia. The Anglo-Saxon forces renewed their advances, to the extent that, by around 600, they controlled much of the southern, central and north-eastern territory of the future England.

Evidence – how do we know what (we think) we know?

Before investigating further, we need to recognise the very limited contemporaneous sources available. In effect there is only one, *The Ruin of Britain*,[65] written by a monk called Gildas sometime between 490 and 530. As such, Gildas needs to be taken seriously. Unfortunately, his highly vivid account lacks coordinates in time and place, and also suffers from a surfeit of spiritual angst.

In essence, Gildas wrote as a Briton who saw the Saxon inroads as a disaster for his people, which he could only ascribe to God's desire

---

65 *De Excidio et Conquestu Britanniae.*

to punish the Britons for their lack of faith and religious discipline. His message of hell fire and damnation, and his anguish in fleeing to Brittany for the rest of his days, may also have led him to dramatise and generalise events.

A little more information is given by a cleric based in southern France called Constantius, who wrote his *Life of St Germanus of Auxerre* about 480. Germanus, apparently confident of moving around the country unmolested as late as 429, seems to have regarded Britain as a still wealthy island at that time. After Constantius, we move briskly forward in time to the Venerable Bede's much-lauded *The Ecclesiastical History of the English People*, probably completed in about 731/2. This was a far more detailed and meticulous approach, focused around the growth of the Christian Church in Britain.

Unlike Gildas, Bede was a staunch Anglo-Saxon, writing in a period of relative peace in Northumbria when it was the foremost kingdom in the land. Yet while Bede was more balanced in his approach, his work displays a clear Anglo-Saxon bias, written to extol the praises of those he called 'his' '*gens Anglorum*'. The normal translation of this as 'English people', however, really anticipates 'the English' of the future. And, while toning down the language and improving the balance of Gildas, Bede relied substantially on him for earlier periods.

A century and a half later, when the country was plagued by Vikings, *King Alfred* (called 'the Great' very much later), ruling a very different area of the country from Bede's Northumbria, actively promoted the concept of the '*Englisc*' and the early English language. But Alfred too had his own bias in glorifying his kingdom of Wessex, using his strong Christian faith to generate a powerful vision of 'the English' as a galvanising force able to free 'his' country from the Vikings. The Chronicle (see above), which he sponsored, is in parts unashamedly pro-Anglo-Saxon (especially pro-Wessex), giving the native Britons short shrift, at times almost seeming to relish their suffering.

To add to this is a 9th century *History of Britain*[66] compiled (or 'heaped together' as the writer himself put it) by a man called Nennius. Although causing no small amount of confusion for later scholars on many issues, Nennius gives some substantial insights into the history of northern Britain in the 6th and 7th centuries. Mention should also be made of *the Annals of Wales,* seemingly collected in the 10th century. Beyond those sources, together with some poems, songs and anecdotes that have survived, we are largely left with non-written sources, especially archaeology, which continues to inform and, sometimes, surprise.

Gildas was especially vague on dates. So when he refers to 'anarchy, devastation and famine' occurring 'after the legions departed' we don't know when or which legions he means. As most of the legions had long gone by 410, Gildas's legions might well have been the troops who left with Magnus Maximus back in the 380s.

Adjustment (410 to 450)

There may have been some apparent stability, but, as suggested in the last chapter, below the surface things were fracturing. From about 407 no *new* coins went into circulation in Britain, with barter replacing such coinage as was left by 430. The 'manufacturing base' of the country had also suffered. The huge production of pottery from the previous century was replaced by a limited supply of high-value handmade goods for those who could afford them, with many basic wares again being made from wood and leather. Lawlessness increased, causing some to move back within town walls for greater security. Metal recycling grew, as did looting. Villas were vacated, deteriorating as they were misused, damaged, recycled, or sometimes deliberately wrecked.

After Constantine, the Catholic Church had steadily assumed leadership of the western ecclesiastical world. But there was

---

66 *Historia Brittonum*

nothing like a heresy to stimulate action, especially a fundamental difference of belief in the nature of man's responsibility for his own soul! Augustine, known as *Augustine of Hippo* and later St Augustine (354 – 430),[67] was a leading voice in the early Christian Church. A philosopher familiar with the works of the Greeks, he had nonetheless a dogmatic disposition, with a fixed belief in 'original sin' which became a fundamental tenet of the Catholic faith. This held that that man was essentially frail, and that his salvation was entirely dependent on God's grace, which (in practice) it was up to the Church to interpret.

Such views were contrary to those of Augustine's contemporary, *Pelagius*, probably Celtic British, highly educated and originally well-respected in Rome for his erudition and personal austerity. Pelagius rejected original sin, teaching that man had free will and was able to control his own destiny by his actions on earth. His beliefs were at first tolerated, until Augustine pressed the Roman Church to treat Pelagius's teachings as anathema. With the approval of Emperor Honorius, Pelagius was excommunicated in 418.

Pelagianism, however, appealed to the Celtic mind and rapidly became popular in Britain, gaining such a hold by the 420s as to cause the resident Catholic bishops to seek help from Rome. In 429, carrying both spiritual and military credentials, the remarkable 'fighting Bishop', *Germanus* (later St Germanus) of Auxerre, arrived in Britain and soon drew large crowds to hear him. An experienced lawyer as well as a former Roman general, Germanus impressed many by his message and his military style when he put on physical armour to help secure a British victory (reportedly against Pictish and Saxon insurgents).

Having converted many by oratory and baptism, Germanus led newly inspired soldiers into battle with a chorus of vigorous 'Alleluias' that

---

67 Not to be confused with the Augustine sent by Gregory to convert the Anglo-Saxons in 597 (see chapter 8), who later became the first Archbishop of Canterbury and effective founder of the English Church.

reportedly terrified the opposition and won the day. This was muscular Christianity at its most fervent.

After 410 we might imagine that some factions wanted the Romans back, and others did not.[68] The vacuum seems to have given the opportunity for a group of powerful local chieftains to emerge. Gildas calls them 'tyrants', generally interpreted as rulers with considerable authority, not necessarily as acting tyrannically. Chief among these was a man who appears to have held sway from about 425-430 to around 450. Reports suggest that he was known as *Vortigern*, but not where he came from, how he got there, or whether *Vortigern* was really a title rather than a specific person. Whoever he was, it seems that he progressively extended his realm east from near the Welsh border to achieve substantial influence over southern Britain, possibly with the help of mercenaries owing him personal allegiance.

About this time we also hear of the brothers *Hengest* and *Horsa* (literally *gelding* and *horse*), commonly regarded as Jutes. Such alliterative names were, however, a common device in Anglo-Saxon creation myths (see next chapter). Bede and others attribute their arrival to 449, but they might have arrived earlier and lain low until they saw real opportunities. After helping Vortigern repel other invaders, the brothers claimed that he had reneged on a deal he did with them, although it must be just as likely that the Jutes increased their demands, bolstered by new North Sea recruits. There are also reports of a classic ploy by Hengest, using his daughter to seduce a drink-affected Vortigern into offering her half his kingdom as a marriage gift. Whatever the truth of the matter, the claim was enough for Hengest to demand the whole of Kent, compromised for a while by the Jutes being permitted to settle on the Isle of Thanet on the south-east tip of Britain. The lid had been put on the Jutish-Saxon cooking pot, but the pressure mounted, and did not take long to blow. Meanwhile, inroads were being made elsewhere.

---

68   *Perhaps an early polarisation of opinion like the 21st century Brexit division.*

Inroads (450 to 500)

We should probably think in terms of a series of migrations from the mid- to late-5th century, followed in the later 6th century by others, including many from Sweden. All would, at some point, have had to undertake a tricky sea crossing. Many may have first moved down the Continental North Sea coast to seek the shortest, safest crossing to Britain, but by the 6th century they may have come from Norway and Sweden, either direct or via Denmark, to East Anglia.

Bede's breakdown of the incoming groups has been much followed (see Map 4):

* *Saxons* from a large area south of Jutland (mainland Denmark) – named after the seax,[69] their distinctive and powerful short sword,

* *Angles* from central Jutland (where there is still a town called Angeln); and

* *Jutes, Frisians and Franks* – a more complex group. The Jutes' probable homeland is north Jutland, but they also had links with the Frisians, prime traders further south-west along the North Sea coast. The Franks were originally a Germanic group from the Rhine area, who were now emerging as a powerful proto-nation expanding into (and giving their name to) the emerging Frankia or France.

Northern Scandinavia deserves special mention. Much of the land dividing the future Norway and Sweden from one another was thickly forested. Near impenetrable woodland also cut off the central part of Sweden around Lake Mälaren (near modern Stockholm)

---

69   *Probably pronounced 'sax' – as in 'Saxon.'*

from the Skåne or Scania southern area more closely associated with adjacent Denmark. And in Norway the immensely long, habitable part of the west lies narrowly between the heavily indented coastline, with its deep-cut fjords and a dazzling multitude of islands, and the lengthy physical barrier of the Keel Mountains. To the south the Norwegian coastline curves into the Oslo Fiord and round southeast to the Swedish border. As might be imagined, these geophysical separations in both countries were for a long time a regular cause of contention between the rulers of the separate areas.

In comparison, Denmark is tiny and fragmented. The major part of Jutland (or *Jylland*, formerly the *Cimbrian* peninsular), runs largely north-south, dividing the North Sea to its west from the Skagerrak accessing the Baltic to the east. This location, with a few large islands and innumerable small islands, all low lying, made Denmark a key location in east-west maritime trading routes. Sweden's main outlets, by contrast, were onto the Baltic or via the treacherous Kattegat above the tip of Jutland. Norway was further away, but with several exits to the North Sea and the northern isles.

Note also the distances involved. A straight line between Southern Jutland and the north point of Norway (well inside the Arctic Circle) is some 1,200 miles, which is further than a straight line running from southern Jutland to Rome.[70] With this enormous range, Scandinavian climactic conditions varied hugely, the gentle farmland of central Denmark being a world apart from the rugged tundra of the Arctic Circle, where the midnight sun of high summer is repaid by winter months without sunlight. People there had to be exceptionally tough, resourceful and patient just to survive.

When it finally came, the Scandinavian Bronze Age brought huge improvements in metal work and extended trade. Scandinavia had furs, ivory and highly valued amber (sap hardened into stone) to export, in return for ornate Roman pottery styles and motifs copied on cooking and storage pots, together with luxuries such as jewellery and plate. Trade with the Romans and others (including supplies to

---

70   David M Wilson – *The Vikings and their origins* (Thames and Hudson 1989)

the Roman Rhine armies) enabled some Scandinavians to sport a proliferation of pendants, arm rings, and other jewellery. All this wealth fuelled the growing warrior elites in their own competition for wealth and power.

A pattern thus emerged of wealthy but militaristic and highly competitive groups with prime loyalty to their chief or king. Over time, with not enough to sustain the growing population or individual ambitions, the lure of a brighter future elsewhere might have sufficed to generate major social change.

Given geography and trade, many Anglo-Saxons would have lived close to, and worked with, the sea, estuaries and tidal rivers. With the intense interior of Sweden and Norway making progress on land slow, laborious and dangerous, water became the faster and preferred method of transport. This had encouraged the Scandinavian, as well as the Germanic, groups to become adept shipbuilders and sailors, with knowledge of shifting tides, currents, sudden enveloping mists, and varied shorelines.

One example of improved ship technology, although dating from the 4th century (c 320), was the *Nydam*. Remains excavated in Jutland indicated a sleek ship around 75 feet long with a beam of ten feet. With a freeboard of just three feet, it would have been fast, capacious (able to carry up to 45 people) and highly manoeuvrable.[71] While not at the level of later Viking longships, such vessels would have been capable of hugging the North Sea coasts and, later, of more extended sea crossings. Limits to the number of people and goods each ship could safely carry might have restrained the speed of migration, but seemingly not its persistence over many years. Such voyages would not have been especially comfortable but, as we are reminded today, if people are desperate or determined enough to cross the sea, they will find a way to come. We might also imagine

---

71 *Sails were in use at the time but many ships such as the Nydam preferred to rely on oar power and make better use of the space taken up by sails.*

that, then as now, many might have had to place their futures in the hands of middlemen more intent on profit than safety.

Bede reported that the 5th century exodus into Britain had caused a severe depletion of the population of Angeln in Denmark. An extra motivation to move may have been the proneness of this low-lying Danish coastal area to flooding, silting and erosion, making living there precarious. This is echoed by excavations near the mouth of the River Weser, on the adjacent north German coast, indicating the abandonment of a timber village in about 450, apparently because of rising sea levels. But even a damp and empty Jutland might have offered a more favourable habitat than harsher parts of Sweden, where other dangers also lurked. Excavations revealing buried hoards and burnt farms on islands off the Swedish Coast, apparently destroyed in the late 5th or early 6th centuries, suggest good reason for local residents at that time to seek a future elsewhere.

Those who thought that moving down into Frisia might be the answer would have found a land even more at the mercy of the North Sea tides and storms. The artificially raised mounds (*terpen*) used by many Frisians to keep their houses above the flood level were unable to support more than a limited number of newcomers. All the more reason to press on to Britain, especially if family or other connections had already settled there and could offer a relatively safe haven. According to Bede (see Map 4):

* the Angles settled in East Anglia, the Midlands and the North-East,

* the East Saxons in Essex,

* the Jutes in Kent and southern Hampshire (especially the New Forest),

* the South Saxons in Sussex; and

* the West Saxons in Wessex.

Although these broad locations seem realistic, there is less certainty that anything was so clear cut. There may have been another factor, too – a change after 450 in the situation across the Channel. Untypical place names south of the Pas de Calais, such as the major trading port of Quentovic near modern le Touquet, may indicate that some Saxon groups may already have settled along some northern coasts of Francia. But as the aggressive Franks advanced north of the Loire from about 460, their encroachment might have led some Saxon forces to relocate and seek their fortunes in Britain.

And what of London? There are few records at this time, but the sense is that the newcomers, seeking pastureland even within the city walls, simply made what they could of the old Roman town. The amphitheatre, for example, was likely to have been used for large social gatherings, while the nearby commercial port centre came to flourish as Lundenwic.

New kingdoms

Kent – Kent today is blessed with fine rolling hills, rich fruit orchards, hops for beer, and now increasingly with vineyards. The encircling North Downs and South Downs are the remains of a great horseshoe-shaped ridge from past geological action. In the middle, the Weald area shares its etymology with the German *Wald,* meaning wood. The forest, however, has been much reduced since Anglo-Saxon times, not just in the quarrying of underlying rock and stone, but also in supplying great quantities of timber for English fleets and fuelling furnaces for iron production. The *Cantiaci* or *Cantii*, the Celtic people believed to have been living there since the Iron Age (from whom Kent takes its name), remained close associates of the Gauls and Belgae across the Channel. Bordered by the Thames Estuary, the North Sea and the Channel, Kent also has islands, notably the Isle of Sheppey, named for its sheep, and the Isle of Thanet, then separated by the wide Wantsum Channel (now silted up to a small stream.) To the south lies Dover, the key cross-

Channel harbour. It was in these areas that the Romans had landed four centuries earlier, where the Jutes and Saxons first made major inroads in the mid-5th century, and where the Vikings were first to over-winter in Britain some 400 years later.

East Kent especially was fiercely contested for much of the late 5th century. After a fight back by native Britons and series of engagements at which the Britons' leader and Horsa both lost their lives, the Jutes were confined to Thanet by around 460. But within five years they had broken their bonds and started to lay waste to Kent. The natives resisted until a strong attack led by Aesc (reputedly the son of Hengest) put the Jutes and their allies in control of a wide beachhead for further landings. In 488 Aesc became king of Kent and was to reign for 24 years until 512, signalling the effective Jutish conquest of the area.

Sussex – Around 477 (or possibly earlier), *Aelle*, a probable warrior chief from southern Jutland, landed near Selsey Bill, a headland peninsular between Chichester and Portsmouth, with 'three sons' and 'three ships' of warriors. But 'three ships' is a much-used phrase which probably just means sufficient numbers to secure a beachhead.[72] Accounts that it took 14 years for the invaders to move just over 60 miles along the south coast suggest years of bitter struggle. The somewhat biased Chronicle also states (almost with relish) that when, in the late 400s, the Saxons captured the shore fort of Anderida, near Pevensey/Hastings, they massacred the locals. Bede asserts that, once their beachhead was established, up to 7,000 Saxon families settled in that area, an enormous number of people for the time.

Wessex – The north of Wessex may have been relatively stable for longer. A villa owner laying down new mosaic floors in the Cotswolds between 425 and 450, for example, hardly shows panic, even if that

---

[72] *Marc Morris (2021) goes so far as to describe three ships as a 'common trope.'*

THE 'DARK AGES'

came later.[73] The Wessex-orientated Chronicle claims that, probably around 495, a chieftain called *Cerdic*, with *Cynric* (possibly his grandson), landed near Hamwich (close to Southampton) with 'five ships'. The defending residents were again beaten back, with Cerdic's progress steady but inexorable. Possibly absorbing a Jutish settlement around the New Forest to the west of Southampton Water, the West Saxons pressed on north to Winchester, which soon became the central town of Wessex.

Here again, the truth may be more complicated. The name Cerdic has a British, possibly Celtic, ring which raises questions as to whether Cerdic really had Celtic ancestry (and all the implications that might bring) or whether he adopted a Celtic name and, if so, why? Another view is that Wessex at least partly originated with the *Gewisse*, who had settled the Upper Thames Valley with a possible base at Dorchester-on-Thames.[74] Sometime later, when the Gewisse spread south-west, they merged with groups of West Saxons heading up from the south coast to form the kingdom of Wessex. The more heroic creation myth (see next chapter) of Cerdic may subsequently have been established for what was then becoming the royal house of England.

Wessex became aggressively expansionist, but also met fierce Brittonic opposition. In 577 (according to the Chronicle) Wessex forces took Cirencester, Bath and Gloucester, killing several local kings in the process. At that stage there was still some refuge further west. Wales and the West of England provided areas of Brittonic refuge, where Celtic Christianity and ancient learning hung on. Some uncontested areas seemed to have remained vibrant, continuing to trade and produce valued exports, but many others in the 'firing line' were faced with a threadbare, hand-to-mouth existence, and some groups even returned to long-abandoned hill forts to eke out a living.

---

73 *Michael Wood (2023) p38.*
74 *Or possibly Old Sarum near Salisbury.*

East coast – Evidence so far suggests strong infiltration, mostly by Angles, along strategic areas of the long east coast from the Thames up to Northumbria. As in the south, Germanic foederati installed to repel earlier seaborne attacks might have assisted or resisted waves of newcomers in seeking a rapid foothold in their new homeland.

Either way, by the late 400s, Anglo-Saxon groups were firmly established along the south coast of Britain west up to Southampton, the main Thames Valley, the coasts of Essex, East Anglia, and beyond north up to south-east Yorkshire.

Where the newcomers did not overrun existing settlements, they seemed to have formed their own. Many homesteads started off small, some still bearing the suffix 'inga', shortened to 'ing', denoting a settlement by features such as stream, hill and wood, or the name of a leader.[75] Gradually these small settlements linked to others, coalescing around powerful warrior elites to produce some of the early Anglo-Saxon kings. But then came a concerted British fight-back.

Dark Years (500 to 550)

As the 5th century drew to a close, native Brittonic resistance seems to have checked the invaders. The turning point came sometime shortly before, around or even after 500, at Mons Baldonicus (Mount Badon). The Britons' victory proved enough to halt the Saxons in their tracks, and possibly to cause some of them to flee for the hills or the ports. Although there appears to be consensus about the result of the battle, neither its date nor its location is at all clear. This has not prevented both from being the subject of intense research and speculation, fuelled by possible connections with the legendary 'King' Arthur, as discussed in the next chapter.

---

75 *Much quoted are Hastings (the people of Haesta), Reading (the people of Raeda), and Wokingham (the farm of Wocca's people).*

THE 'DARK AGES'

Some years or decades later came two calamities. In the mid-530s there are reports of an extended period when the sky was dark, the sun disappeared, the winters were bitter and the summer harvests failed. A 2022 report of a team of archaeologists and glaciologists[76] put this down to a cataclysmic volcanic eruption, probably in Iceland, which deposited ash all across the Northern Hemisphere early in 536, causing summer temperatures to fall as low as 2.5°C.

Things were so bad that 536 has been described as possibly the worst year to have been alive. This led on to the coldest decade for over 2,000 years which brought widespread misery, famine and starvation across many parts of the world. Two more eruptions may have followed, in 540 and 547.

Those who survived to live in the most marginal conditions, especially along the coasts of the North Sea, would have faced enormous hardship. Some Irish monks chronicling the events of the times (not wishing to complain!) noted laconically that there was a 'failure of bread from the years 536–539.'

This was followed by the plague. The Antonine plague had hit in the second century, but the so-called Justinian plague, which spread from the middle east from 541 to 549, was devastating in its effects across Europe and the wider world. Estimates of deaths were up to 50 million people, perhaps close to half the world's population at that time. When the plague finally reached Britain by about 543 the death toll led to many villages becoming deserted as their populations were wiped out, especially those close to the ports through which the plague spread.

Some believe that economic and social degradation in Europe might have lasted for a hundred years until the 640s. In any event, the cataclysms would have left survivors battered and desperate for

---

76 *Including incredibly precise analyses from a Swiss glacier by a team led by medieval historian Michael McCormick and glaciologist Paul Mayewski at the Climate Change Institute of The University of Maine (UMO).*

a new life. It was a good reason to call this period 'the Dark Ages.' Residents and incomers, if they had taken the opportunity, might have had good cause to work together just to survive. But people, especially when frightened and exhausted, do not always do what is logical.

A short timeline for southern Britain 400 to 550

Note: The names of people and places who might be thought of as legends or creation myths (see chapter 7) should be taken as more representative than factual.

383   *Magnus Maximus* acclaimed and leaves Britain with his legions

Adjustment

407   *Constantine III* leaves Britain with his troops until finally defeated and executed in 411.
408   Britain is once again assailed by Scots and Irish[77] and possibly by some Saxons.
409/10   The *appeal to Emperor Honorius* for help. He replies that Britain is now on its own.
410/20   (Assumed) Britain relatively peaceful, but civil and social infrastructure starts to fail.
418   *Pelagius* excommunicated by Rome.
425/30   *Vortigern* becomes pre-eminent in southern Britain.
429   *Bishop Germanus* visits Britain to fight Pelagianism and the Picts – 'Alleluia' victory.
430/45   Further decay and renewed hostilities – probably Scots, Irish, Jutes and some Saxons.
446   Second visit of Germanus to Britain.
449   *Hengest and Horsa* become prominent in Kent.
441/50   Jutes rebel and attack Kent.

---

[77] *i.e. Picts and Scots! See chapter 5.*

THE 'DARK AGES'

Inroads

450/60	Jutes forced back into Thanet.
460/65	Jutes break out and lay waste to Kent.
465/70	Jutes held at bay for a time.
473	Kent – Counter-attack by *Aesc, new Jute leader in Kent*, leads to gradual conquest of Kent.
477	*Aelle*, Saxon chief, lands in Sussex with '3 ships' and steadily drives Britons back.
491	(or earlier) Sussex – Aelle attacks near Pevensey. 'Massacre' at Anderida; Saxons entrenched along a 60-mile stretch of coast between Portsmouth and Pevensey.
495	Hampshire – *Cerdic and Cynric* land near Southampton with '5 ships' and establish Wessex, with Jutish settlements in New Forest and nearby.

Dark years

500	One possible approximate date for the Battle of Mount Badon.
508	Hampshire/ Wessex – Cerdic and Cynric defeat the Britons near Southampton, from where they continue to press forward.
514	Hampshire/ Isle of Wight – *Stuf and Wihtgar*, reported as nephews of Cerdic,[78] land on the Isle of Wight with '3 ships' and claim an early victory.
516	Alternative date for Battle of Mount Badon.
534	Wessex – Death of Cerdic; Cynric *becomes* undisputed Saxon chieftain in the area.
536/9	Dust and debris from *volcanic clouds* hide the sun for years, chilling the climate and devastating successive harvests – with likely long-term effects.
537/9	Possible latest dates for the *Battle of Camlan/ Cammlan*.[79]
541-9	Plague of Justinian ravages Europe.

---

78 But stated by Bede to have been Jutes.
79 See chapter 7. Although others put the date later, this would have been at the peak of the 'dark years' following the volcanic fall-out referred to earlier.

Takeover (550 to 600)

By around 550 the Angles were firmly established down the north-east and eastern coasts, the East Saxons were embedded in Essex, and the Jutes across Kent, the New Forest and Isle of Wight. The South and West Saxons held much of the central south coast and hinterland. There are indications that, following the 'dark years' there were new levels of migration, with the period 550 to 600 seeing an almost relentless Anglo-Saxon expansion. This was both along the southern and eastern coasts and ever deeper inland to approach the new boundaries of the West Country, the Severn Estuary, the Welsh hills and the Pennine ridge. In the process, territories turned into kingdoms and kings battled for supremacy. One by one the leaders of the Britons fell by the wayside, leaving those in the future Wales and future Scotland to hold their ground.

The South – With Kent and Sussex now largely in Jutish or Saxon hands, Wessex was next in line. Capable, expansionist and aggressive in approach, the West Saxon kings' broad thrust after 550 was north-west towards Salisbury and north-east along the upper Thames Valley. This expansion inevitably brought conflict with other new kingdoms. In 568 the Wessex army triumphed over the men of Kent at Wibbandum, probably somewhere south-west of London.

The 570s saw Wessex pushing north of London through Aylesbury up to Luton and west through to the Severn Valley.[80] In the next decade it experienced some reverses, notably to the north and west around 584.[81] To the south-west was the Celtic kingdom of

---

80 *The Wansdyke is a great, and apparently incomplete, east-west earthwork running from Wiltshire to Somerset. It may be a boundary, but its real purpose and construction date remain a mystery. One idea is that it takes its name and mystic power from the god Woden – as Woden's ditch.*

81 *The genealogy of these times is a specialist study in itself, with events uncertain and many similar-sounding leaders' names: e.g. Cerdic, Cynric, Ceawlin, Ceol, Ceolwulf, Cynegils, Cwichelm and Cenwahl in succession to one another!*

Dumnonia, covering most of Cornwall and possibly part of Devon (opinions vary). The area came under progressive and repeated assault from Wessex, driving many survivors south to Armorica (Brittany) or deeper into Cornwall until the West Saxons were diverted by threats from its northern neighbour, the increasingly powerful Mercia.

East Anglia and Mercia – Moving north, the focus changes from coasts to rivers and estuaries, most notably the Thames to the south, the Humber Estuary to the north-east and the Severn to the west. (See Map 3.) These were vital supply lines and delineations in Saxon times, gateways for those with the craft and skills to navigate them, helping invaders access inland areas faster than by land. The incoming Angles, followed later by fresh waves from Sweden and Norway, were familiar with the ebb and flow of tides, sea surges along coasts, turbulent estuaries, and the uncertainties of marshland, silting and erosion, especially around the great rump still known as East Anglia after the Angles themselves.

Immediately to the west of East Anglia the land became first known as Middle Anglia, with the River Great Ouse (to be distinguished from the Ouse in Yorkshire) running north-east into the Wash and the River Trent broadly parallel to feed the Humber Estuary. But Middle Anglia soon fell to, and was largely absorbed by, the aggressively expansionist Mercia, which also extended to the River Severn in the west. (See Map 5.)

Further to the west lay the land of mountains and valleys now known as Wales, with three main kingdoms. Powys in mid-Wales and Gwynedd in the north came to share a border with Mercia, whilst Dyfed in the south faced a moving boundary between Mercia and Wessex. Throughout this history, these Welsh areas of distinctive Celtic Britons showed a fierce determination to defend their territory and maintain their independence.

Between Middle Anglia and the land north of the Humber another kingdom emerged for a brief period on the stage of turbulent Britain. This was Lindsey, roughly where Lincolnshire now lies. North-east of the River Witham, it lay hedged between the Wash and its nearby coast to the south and east, the upper Trent to the west, and the Humber to the north. Lindsey was destined to become another early casualty of its location between more powerful neighbours.

Northumbria and Northern England – The Humber, a name that may even pre-date Celtic times, is a wide tidal estuary which flows into the North Sea to the north of The Wash. It merges the waters of the Rivers Trent, flowing from the south-east, and Ouse, flowing from the north, forming a broad bay tapering to a beaked mouth emptying into the North Sea. Today its most striking feature may be the graceful span of the long Humber Bridge, but from early times its attraction would have been the clear approach from the North Sea into relatively sheltered waters, with access beyond through navigable rivers deep into the countryside to north and south. This wide estuary was a draw for the Anglo-Saxons and, much later, almost irresistible to the Vikings.

Like many other major rivers, the Humber created a natural boundary. Today this is between Yorkshire to the north and Lincolnshire to the south, with the dry chalk valleys of the Wolds bisected by the Humber's broad, shallow reaches. The river also gives its name to the land to the north, *Northumbria*, which was to play a major role in the emergence of England. A short distance north, up the River Ouse, lay the major former barracks town called *Eboracum* by the Romans, *Eoforwic* by the Angles, *Yorvic* by the Vikings, and ultimately *York* by the English. The ease of access through the Humber and Ouse, coupled with limited resistance, enabled the incomers rapidly to build up a strong presence in southern Northumbria.

Although most of the new arrivals were probably Angles, Nennius' claim that the early leaders in Northumbria were a son and nephew of the infamous Hengest of Kent is supported by the discovery of similarities in grave goods of the time. It may be that some of the early Jutish settlers did make their way north, or that some Jutish mercenaries employed to fight the Picts had stayed and settled there at that time. In any event, by the end of the 5th century, the Yorkshire Wolds and the Vale of York were heavily settled by Germanic tribes, who founded the kingdom of *Deira* (Deifr), with *Aelle*[82] as its king, from around 560 to 588.

Another major river, the Tyne, formed the next significant boundary to the north. Beyond that in turn was the Tweed, on which the long-term Anglo-Scots border town of Berwick-on-Tweed sits (just north of Lindisfarne). Further north again was the great inlet of the Forth, marked by the old Antonine Wall, which was the furthest extent of Northumbria's reach. To the east was the North Sea and to the west lay the Pennines, the great north-south spine of northern Britain. Aelle's kingdom of Deira initially held its ground as new waves swept in. This helped force the newcomers further north, towards the Brittonic Celtic-speaking people, the Gododdin, to take over the area of Bryneich after the Roman withdrawal. Accounts suggest that in 547 their centre at Bamburgh (just south of Lindisfarne) was overrun by Angles under *Ida*, who became the first Anglo-Saxon king of re-named *Bernicia*.

Brittonic control lasted longer in the north-west, where three kingdoms jockeyed for position with one another and with those around them. The northernmost, covering the area of Argyll (now firmly in Scotland), had since the 450s been progressively colonised by the Scotti from Northern Ireland. This was the new kingdom of Dalriada (alias Dal Riada or Dal Riata). To the south of Dalriada lay Strathclyde (Ystrad Clud), which covered much of what we now know as south-west Scotland, with its capital in Dumbarton. South of that (for a time) was Rheged, covering the mainly mountainous area of Cumbria up to (and possibly beyond) the Solway Firth. A lengthy period of struggle ensued as the Angles sought to expand into the

---

82 Not the same Aelle who landed in Sussex.

Brittonic kingdoms, with the latter fighting amongst themselves as much as against their common enemy. Then in 588 Aella of Deira died and his kingdom was united with the neighbouring Anglo-Saxon Bernicia when the latter's King Aethelfrith married Aella's daughter.[83] The stage was thus set for the combined kingdom to expand its remit.

Anglo-Saxon groups had now established a firm hold over much of southern, south-eastern, midlands and northern Britain. The peace after Mount Badon had certainly collapsed, and there was to be no going back.

---

83 *There will be much mention of names beginning 'Aethel' (with or without the diphthong Æ) which essentially denotes someone of (claimed) noble birth.*

CHAPTER 7

MEANING, MIGRATION AND MYTH

It's 600 CE, which is 99% of the timeline covered by this account, but only about half-way through the chapters and pages of this book. We've moved from ice to island through stone, farming, bronze and iron with cultures, Celts, Romans and now the Anglo-Saxons, who'll be with us to the end. It's a good point, before tracking the role of Christianity in creating England, to consider how the Anglo-Saxon influx had impacted the population and how stories and legends can become part of personal, regional and, ultimately, national myths.

Meaning and language

It's human nature to give meaning to whatever we see, hear and read. And we almost inevitably have some unconscious, as well as conscious, bias that will influence us. Consider Gildas the monk. Here is part of his graphic account of Saxon carnage among the Britons:

'A number of the wretched survivors were caught in the mountains and butchered wholesale. Others, their spirits broken by hunger, went on to surrender to the enemy; they were taken to be slaves forever, if indeed they were not killed straightaway, the highest boon.'

But how true was this? Some writers warn us to overlook Gildas at our peril, and there is certainly some evidence to support his account. But we should note both the historian and the circumstances in which he was writing. Gildas' mission was not to write objective history but to deliver a message about God's judgment on the moral depravity of the Britons. In looking for an explanation of disaster, he attributed to events the only meaning he could understand. Some 1,400 years later, echoing Gildas but writing in his own evocative style, Winston Churchill wrote of the Anglo-Saxon 'invasion' that:

'Even when self-interest did not preserve the native villagers as labourers on Saxon farms, we may cherish the hope that somewhere a maiden's cry for pity, the appeal of beauty in distress, the lustful needs of an invading force, would create some bond between victor and vanquished. Thus the blood would be preserved, thus the rigours of subjugation would fade as generations passed away. The complete obliteration of an entire race over large areas is repulsive to the human mind.' [84]

This is full of pathos, but Churchill too had an agenda – and a dilemma. In the troubled 1930s many in England and America saw the Anglo-Saxons almost as ideal progenitors. At the same time Churchill was more aware than most of the dangers of Nazi Germany and a possible existential struggle for Britain ahead. As such he was both confronting the evidence of a troublesome early English past and making a strident rallying call evoked in his later admonition to 'fight them on the beaches.'

We know that the Anglo-Saxons came, but not how many and precisely when. We know that they settled and came to dominate the native Britons, but we don't know exactly how and at what cost. We also know the Anglo-Saxons retained and refined their language, but we don't know quite how they did so. In reading Gildas, therefore, it's fair to note that he may be the only witness of the moment, but

---

84   *Churchill (1956) p 46*

in the matter of the Anglo-Saxons, he is clearly a witness for the prosecution. And in this case history was being written by one of its victims, not by the victors.

As we process this information, we too are often drawn towards what *we* can, or would prefer, to believe. Those who see history as a process of subjugation of the weak by the strong may see Gildas as reflecting an existential truth, just as those of Celtic sympathies might regard the Anglo-Saxons as early conquistadors. And those who abhor violence may shy away from believing accounts so far at odds with their personal values. To assess the evidence objectively we have to be very honest about our own inclinations. Even then, we are influenced by the views of our contemporaries and the ethos (and fears) of our times. Then there's the broader or collective view. We can't change what actually happened and is past, but we can (and often do) change our individual or collective view of that past.

Many centuries later, Bede still had to rely on much of what Gildas wrote, picking his way carefully between the mangled bodies of Gildas' account. But Bede too had his own Christian and Angelcynn perspective, as did the Anglo-Saxon Chronicle. The Chronicle records a relentless series of Saxon victories over the native British, but its accounts were written much later and from a staunch Anglo-Saxon viewpoint. And Henry of Huntingdon, who wrote *The History of the English* as late as the 12th century, clearly had his own flights of fancy. Hard evidence is, therefore, very limited.

One argument for the theory that the Anglo-Saxons annihilated the Britons is the apparent near demise of the native Brittonic language. Centuries later in Normandy the conquering minority Vikings adopted French, and in post-Norman England French finally gave way to English. Why did this not happen with the Anglo-Saxons?

The first point to make is that the near extinction of a language does not necessarily mean the near extinction of those who spoke it. Many place names, for example, were renamed by the Anglo-Saxons in the east with the change from Celtic to Saxon apparently slowing down as time went on and settlement progressed further west. One famous study[85] of river names indicated three main phases. In the first, nearly all rivers in areas taken over by the Anglo-Saxons were renamed, except for a few principal ones. In the second phase, many rivers, large and small, in areas in central Britain settled between 550 and 650, retained their old names. The third phase shows that in Wales and Cornwall, the last areas to be affected, nearly all rivers retained their Celtic names. Looking at this from another perspective, there was an acknowledged powerful 'Celtiberian' influence in western Britain for centuries. But we can't be certain what languages and dialects everyone else across Britain was speaking before the 5th century invasions. These may well have been varied and probably included Germanic languages from the strong pockets of existing Saxon settlement before 410.

There were also very good reasons for the Anglo-Saxons not to change. They were numerous, and predominantly farmers, with a detailed vocabulary full of farming terms which they understood and on which they depended for their livelihoods. Likewise, with the language of relaxation and merriment after hard work was done. It's not irrelevant that one fairly recent analysis showed that the hundred most common words in English, most of them severely practical, were all of Anglo-Saxon origin. The incomers had brought with them a rich language, accompanied by a mastery of heroic verse and speech which relished verbal tricks called *kennings* that audiences loved to pick up and enjoy.[86] The Frisians, Saxons, Danes, Jutes and others would probably have spoken related Germanic languages, even if with regional variations and different dialects. And they also liked to distinguish themselves from the natives, calling them *wealas*,

---

85 K.H. Jackson, *Language and History in Early Britain* (Edinburgh, 1953) pp 241-6 analysed by Fisher pp 46-49.

86 *Beowulf* (see below) is full of kennings, such as 'ring-giver' for a king, the sea as a 'whale-road', or a ship as a 'sea-plough'.

meaning *foreigners*, in their own land.[87] All would surely have found it far easier to coalesce around what they had in common rather than learn a wholly new language that their tongues and ears were totally unused to.

In short, the incomers had a language and culture that suited them well and preserved a continuity in times of upheaval. We might, therefore, ask the question the other way round. Why would the Anglo-Saxon settlers have changed the way they communicated if they did not have to?

A possible synthesis

We've seen that, after Saxon support changed to settlement, possibly sometime around 450, there was steady, and at times and in some places rapid, immigration. Some of those caught up in this first wave who did not flee soon enough may well have been killed or enslaved, especially in vulnerable areas within striking distance of southern coastlines. The world of that time was used to sporadic, and sometimes sustained, barbarity.

But as resistance grew, the invaders could (and evidently did) sometimes suffer the same fate themselves. Landing on foreign shores has never been without risk, and we know little of those lost on the way. Much may also depend on why, when, and how they came. There may have been some adventurers prepared and predisposed to strike hard, fast and ruthlessly. But others could well have been early 'economic migrants' seeking a better life, or refugees who had lost their homes. All these would be desperate for help, security, and a roof over their heads.

There is also the uncertain level of pre-existing Germanic presence in Britain, as highlighted earlier. We might recall *Carausius*, the bull-necked rebel admiral from chapter 5. He was originally from a Germanic tribe near the Rhine and operated from a Roman

---
87 *Later called Welsh.*

navy base in Boulogne, northern France. Yet he seemed to have no difficulty in establishing himself across the Channel in Britain. Would he have been able to achieve this so easily if there had not been a strong Germanic presence there already? And if so, would those people over many generations not have found some level of accommodation and integration with the native Britons, rather than a desire to wipe them out?

In support of the gradualist approach Stephen Oppenheimer, in his extensive analysis, maintains that there was no sudden replacement but rather a 'prolonged cultural and genetic interchange' between Britain and its neighbours. Francis Pryor, familiar with the East Anglian terrain, believes that archaeology does not support the Angles causing widespread death and destruction there. He considers that the signs indicate assimilation rather than conquest, and despite apparently higher rates of Anglo-Saxon 'intrusion' in eastern Britain, to date there has been scant evidence of wide-ranging brutal deaths or the overnight disappearance of native practices. Likewise, Marc Morris notes changes in burial and cremation practices along the east coast which suggest Saxon and other settlements co-existing there in late Roman times. All this could, of course, be questioned at any time by new excavations.

In his lively account, *Celt and Saxon*, published in 1993, Peter Beresford Ellis takes the other view, being especially eloquent in supporting Gildas. His account is worth reading for those of Celtic leanings or those seeking another perspective. It contains a vivid account of the flight of the native Celtic inhabitants of southern Britain, west to Ireland, south-west to Armorica (where strong Celtic traces remain) and south (back) to the Iberian Peninsula.

Like immigration, however, emigration does not have a single cause. Britons may have been driven abroad by factors other than the fear of being wiped out, with religion one possible flashpoint. In some areas, the invaders might have found devout Christian settlements, where inhabitants faced with being overrun by 'pagans' might have considered that the only way to preserve their religion was to flee. Faced with a sword, not everyone would stay to debate the merits of their faith.

The Chronicle, really a Saxon mouthpiece, suggests that the Saxons made steady progress north and outwards from the south coast, and north-west up the Thames Valley. Certainly, some of the Saxon attacks along the south coast in the years 440 to 500 do appear to have been violent. The Jutish break-out in Kent, the South Saxon inroads in Sussex, and the West Saxon push around Southampton and Portsmouth all apparently involved fierce fighting, with local resistance progressively driven back inland. In other areas, however, there is evidence of strong Brittonic resistance, with good reason to believe that, after the initial fury, some pattern of co-existence developed between incumbents and insurgents, even forming adjacent settlements in some places.

Religion and initial fear apart, incomers and residents would have had much in common in terms of day to day life and customs. Most Saxons had been kept at bay by the Romans and many Britons had lost any pre-Roman ways they'd had. Nor would money have been an issue; British coinage had by then disappeared and the early invaders had no use for one. Both groups would have relied heavily on farming, which might have needed more, rather than fewer, people to work the land, especially given the population depletions around 410 and 540. Indeed, in some places Celtic enclaves appear to have survived almost intact.

As the Christian church developed, embracing Britons and Saxons alike, closer integration could be expected, enhanced as inter-group marriage became acceptable at higher levels. And as time went on, common cause could be found by facing a new common enemy.

Seeking to balance these factors, here is one possible outline, with the usual caveats:

* *Resident Saxons* – For some time before 410, a significant number of groups from overseas,[88] collectively called 'Saxons', had been actively engaged as Roman foederati (effectively federal troops) in the defence of Britain's shores, possibly with extended families also in residence. While living as Britons, they might well have kept in touch with relations still on the Continent.

* *Generational change* – New generations growing up the other side of the Channel may have been keen for change, seeing Britain as a land of opportunity. If so, opportunistic characters like Hengest and Horsa (whoever they really were) might be expected to emerge, and it would not be unprecedented for them to seek benefit from opportunity and the perceived weakness of their hosts. Such groups tend to need ready cash, often achieved by a mixture of conquest and booty, including selling their victims as slaves.

* *Frisia and Francia* – The Saxons also attacked Frisia and the northern coasts of Frankish Gaul, where they had long had dealings, probing for the best opportunities. But when, around 483, Saxon detachments were beaten back by the Franks from the Loire and Angers, the Saxons may have switched their attention back to Britain (as the Vikings did later). The timing seems to coincide with major new landings on the south coast, notably Wessex.

* *The dark years* – After the standstill following the Battle of Badon, the cataclysmic effects of the Icelandic volcano and the plague of 541, Britain might still have offered better prospects than the devastated Continental North Sea coastal areas, encouraging a new surge of migrants, including many from Norway and Sweden.

---

88 Fergal Keane suggests these may have included settled Irish contingents in the west.

* *Emigration* – Rounds of immigration also induced a level of emigration, with some Britons fleeing across the Channel, especially to the traditional Celtic area of Armorica, later known as Brittany. These included Gildas himself, who founded a monastery in Morbihan in Brittany, where he wrote his history. Some émigrés even went as far as north-west Spain, another ancient Celtic homeland. Others crossed to Ireland and made their futures there, just as, at critical times in their island, many Irish sought refuge by fleeing east to Britain. There's also evidence that, later on, the roles were reversed; when the British fight-back did occur, some Saxons themselves felt compelled to retreat across the Channel.

* *Religion* – The paganism of the early settlers, especially the Saxons, would be likely to have caused some Christian Britons to flee to the far south-west or to Brittany.

Taken together, rather than overwhelming conquest and annihilation, these factors suggest periods and pockets of ruthless action interspersed with times of stand-off, integration, and assimilation.

The Power of Legend

Not all of our history is so extensively debated, and such is the power of a good story that many of the best remembered incidents of history may never have happened! The famous quote that 'When the legend becomes fact, print the legend' comes from a John Ford film,[89] but the variant from Tony Wilson may be even more apposite: 'When forced to pick between truth and legend, print the legend.' It's cynical, but may be justified by human nature; we are curious but also imaginative, and we often prefer the story to the truth. And while some stories start life as small embellishments to add 'colour' to the known facts, others take on a new dimension.

---

89   *The Man who shot Liberty Valance (1962)*

Take the case of King Alfred 'burning the cakes', which used to be the story most people knew about him. The original version seems to have Alfred sitting indoors by the fireside in a villager's hut, preparing his weapons. His hostess, meanwhile, knowing nothing of his real identity, was preparing to bake some loaves, known as cakes.

Alfred is described as helping turn the loaves, presumably to demonstrate his helpfulness. Sometime later, however, a storyteller in East Anglia, where Alfred was apparently less well regarded, changed the account to show the king negligently failing to prevent the cakes from being burnt, and being scolded for his neglect. Both make good stories, but inevitably burning the cakes has proved the more dramatic and memorable.

Another example of 'colour' is stating that invaders arrived in 'three ships' or 'five ships'. This may give an indication of how many men were involved, or may just be a device to help a listener envisage the scene. Similarly, with accounts that specify individuals. With Hengest and Horsa in Kent, or Cerdic and Cynric in Wessex, supposedly 'real' names give an added dramatic sense of apparent authenticity, especially in Anglo-Saxon verse and cadence, where alliteration was a regular and expected device. The same device is still used by many non-fiction writers today.

This takes us into the land of *myth* and *legend*, words often used synonymously. Technically, a *legend* is a traditional story, originally the written account of the life of a saint, but later used for a likely mix of fact, fiction and tradition describing the heroic exploits of a notable character. *Myth* is more often a spoken story about an incident, sometimes with an opaque meaning. The incident of Alfred burning the cakes is therefore a myth, but the story of King Arthur has become a legend. And if kings could not be central characters in their own histories, they could at least be the culmination of a glorious destiny, happy to have legends woven around their heroic forbears. Thus the 'creation myth', which royals loved to hear performed as epics in their honour by trusted court poets called *skalds*, combining entertainment for the many with glorification for the few.

And few creation myths carried as much apparent punch as those starting from Troy. The famed *Aeneid* of Virgil, for example, traces the flight of Aeneas from burning Troy through to the establishment of Rome by his supposed descendants, Romulus and Remus. In order to give glorious ancestry to the Celts of Britain, *Geoffrey of Monmouth* in around 1136 created a Brutus (not Caesar's assassin) as a supposed direct descendant of Aeneas, then settled in Italy. On reaching the fabled island of Albion, Brutus generously gave his name to Britain and its people, the Britons, from which start Geoffrey constructed a fabulous biblical-style genealogy.[90] And it was Geoffrey who initially seems to have elevated, if not invented, one of the greatest heroes of them all – the fabulous 'King' Arthur.

Arthur and Mount Badon

The Battle of Badon links us to two powerful names from the late 5th century, the Roman *Ambrosius (or Ambrosianus) Aurelianus* and the British *Arthur*. On some chronologies it was Aurelianus who was long-term master of the British troops, possibly up to the crucial Battle of Mount Badon. Arthur may or may not have succeeded him and led his men to victory in a series of battles, but probably not at Badon. And neither appears to have been a king. The date and location of Badon are also problematic, much debated but never clearly defined. 500 seems a good guide as a date, with a range from c. 480 to 520. As for location, 'mount' suggests a possibly isolated hill, with some historians suggesting there was a siege.

While a variously named Arthurian figure seems to have become something of a folk hero in Wales, Arthur himself does not appear to be mentioned in Anglo-Saxon sources until very much later. This was around 830, when a 'leader in battles' called Arthur

---

[90] *Geoffrey did, however, seem to have some valuable sources with detail that has not come down to us.*

is mentioned by Nennius, the great 'compiler'. Nennius has Arthur rampaging far and wide across the land in a series of improbable locations which have provoked analysis and detective work from many sources, but without consensus.[91]

And what about the location of Mount Badon? The most aggressive group at that time were probably the West Saxons, which favours a clash in mid-west southern Britain, a likely area if the Saxons were threatening to drive west into Wales or south-west into Devon/ Cornwall. Analysis favours two possible sites, Solsbury Hill above Batheaston to the north-east of Bath, or Liddington Castle, a prehistoric hillfort on high ground adjacent to the Ridgeway in Wltshire. Whenever and wherever it was, Badon stands out as the pinnacle of resistance to the Saxons, and effectively the southern Britons' last major stand.

Here's also where legend comes in. If, temporarily freed from defending their lands against the Saxons, the remaining Brittonic forces fell back on fighting one another, it might give some context to link to the Battle of Camlann, when Arthur supposedly met his death. And if, as some suggest, the Camlann battle took place around 537 to 539, it would have been in the depths of the 'dark years' when everyday existence was hard and perilous.

Putting aside supposition, however, we are left with the legend of 'King' Arthur, quintessentially British, putatively English, and most strongly claimed by the Welsh. His exploits and character were set down some 600 years later by a 12th century writer of well-researched historical fiction. One writer who has studied the issue extensively is Geoffrey Ashe, who concludes in his Mythology of the British Isles: 'In the end it has to be faced that while Arthur might have a certain human reality, he is a human being mythified.'[92]

---

91   Although Michael Wood's analysis of the Solway Firth / Carlisle area for a probably unconnected set of 'Arthurian' battles is persuasive.

92   Ashe (1990)

Arthur is not alone. As patron saint, England has St George, also famed in many other lands. George is thought to have been a soldier in the Roman army whose heroics in Libya and martyrdom at the hands of the Empire are said to have inspired countless numbers to convert to Christianity. Yet his link to England appears largely limited to the adoption of his symbolic flag (also an early Red Cross symbol) during the time of the Crusades. Interestingly, his predecessor as patron saint of England was St Edmund, the king of East Anglia, martyred by the Vikings. He was dropped from his position on the instigation of Edward III in 1348 in favour of the international figure of St George – with dragon killing included to indicate robust action to defend the innocent.

This takes us on to the major Anglo-Saxon hero, whose character was then held up as a shining example in a troubled world but who, unlike St George, finally lost out to a dragon.

Beowulf

Before the late 9th century, Old English was celebrated in verse and song, through works like *The Wanderer*, *The Seafarer* and *The Ruin*, with their strong spiritual messages. Sometime around and after 550 there was also *Hrolf Kraki*, whose aura was enhanced both by an alleged incestuous parentage and by being a favourite of the god Odin. Hrolf drew around him a formidable band of warriors, but at this point his story becomes even more one of legend, primarily celebrating Hrolf's famous ride through the deep forests of Sweden to meet the Swedish king Adils in the Svear heartlands around Lake Mälaren. In the story it is the valour shown in the ride and the prestige of having powerful warrior supporters that was perhaps more important to the hero's reputation than the ultimate result of the ensuing battle, since the result might, after all, be decided by the whim of the gods.

Some aspects of the Hrolf Kraki mythology become entwined

with the great legend of Beowulf, also (probably) grounded in the troubled 6th century. While Arthur seems to have been unknown to them, Beowulf was very present in Anglo-Saxon/ Early English society for some 500 years. Beowulf then lapsed into the background as Arthur took the foreground. And if Arthur was a quintessentially Brittonic figure, Beowulf was the embodiment of Scandinavian heroic virtues. The Arthur story shows him as a leader surrounded by, and working with, his key supporters, who grew into the knights of the Round Table, whereas Beowulf – a warrior endowed with superhuman strength – preferred to act alone. But while St George slew a dragon to protect a maiden, Beowulf and his own dragon died together, locked in combat. And it was betrayal by those closest to him, rather than a dragon, that led to the death of Arthur.

Why was Beowulf so significant for so long? For a start, the poem's descriptions of some past events, current buildings, arms, armour, household goods and personal adornments can be treated almost as (what I'd call) 'literary archaeology.' For example, two of the three ship burials described in the poem closely mirror the Sutton Hoo ship interment (see chapter 10). In addition to the ship imprints, the treasure unearthed at Sutton Hoo has also proved an uncanny match with the treasures described in Beowulf. Then there is the language – Old English in all its redolence, cadence and complexity, so rich and textured as almost to defy fair translation. It is a summary of ideals of personal courage and leadership, even if the Anglo-Saxon leaders may often have fallen short of living up to those ideals.

The outlines are that Beowulf, a chieftain of the Geats from south-western Sweden, hears of the travails of the Danish king, Hrothgar, and feels obliged to help. He visits the king in his great hall at Heorot to hear tragic tales of a night-time monster called Grendel beating down the hall doors and devouring or carrying off the warriors inside. While the king retires to his chamber, Beowulf lies down with the other warriors to await the visitation. When Grendel acts again, Beowulf grabs him in an armlock and then rips off his shoulder to disable him, leaving the monster to crawl back to die in his lair. But the lair is a deep pool in the mountains, where Grendel's mother lives, intent on revenge as her son lies dying. This time it's tougher for Beowulf, fighting a more powerful adversary deep underwater in the pool, until he locates the magic sword that can finally despatch her. Mission accomplished, Beowulf is lauded and loaded with treasure and returns to a long life back home as king of his Geats. Until finally he is forced, fatally, to confront a hoard-guarding dragon, a staple of Germanic lore.

To us today the Beowulf story is fantastical, based around great mead halls infused with the smell of fighting men and roasted meat, night-time slaughter by a monster, and the arrival of a super-hero with a great lineage and the undertaking of an impossible challenge. The unspecified locations and timelines that can confuse us today would probably have been well understood by those listening on the mead benches. And the verse is glorious Old English, with rhythm, assonance and counterpoint, to be memorised and performed by a favoured skald. To the listeners it might have been like hearing the rising and falling of a powerful symphony.

Like Arthur's story, the origins of Beowulf are hard to fathom and widely analysed, with only one (slightly charred) copy of the written work having come down to us. As a result, the basic composition (though not the writing down) has been variously attributed to many periods of early English history. One of many views comes from Bo Gräslund, a leading Scandinavian scholar who spent years analysing the work. He concludes[93] that there is good reason to believe that the framework of the poem was composed in Sweden in the mid-550s and brought over to the emerging England (probably East Anglia with its strong Swedish element) with settlers from Sweden. In other words, the essential story and background circumstances are, he suggests, Swedish in origin, possibly first put together shortly after the cataclysmic volcanic event which darkened Europe for years.

---

93 *'The Nordic Beowulf (2022) ARC Humanities Press*

On this basis, Gräslund suggests that the monster Grendel might represent the forces of darkness that had so clearly fallen on the earth at that time.

The poem does have a darker tone, despite the heroics. The audience would have known that Scandinavian power was then being contested between the 'Shield' Danes, probably based on Sealand, the Geats in south-west Sweden and, beyond the forests, the Yngling dynasty based near today's Stockholm. They would also have known that the Ynglings would later triumph to rule over all Sweden, with Beowulf's Geat line ending with his death. By Alfred's time Beowulf's lineage, with his heroic qualities, may already have seemed to belong to a bygone age. There is also the complex Christian perspective, with a higher divinity often invoked. Outside the glories of the great halls, the setting is a liminal world, with forces of dark and light battling it out in pits and caves on the edge of chaos. Beowulf continues to bear the burden out of duty and honour until his final and fatal heroics evoke more a sense of martyrdom than salvation. We are left with a series of dramatic impressions; of powerful but generous ('ring-giving') kings supported by loyal retainers, great halls for feasting and entertainment, violent clashes of armed warriors, heroic journeys and deeds, magnificent deaths – and spectacular funerals.

These events would have been topical in many respects in 550, with descriptions of wild times and violent encounters, bringing echoes of the Dark Ages. They may have celebrated heroism, but they hardly suggested a peaceful history. Against that background it is now time to chart the extraordinary rise of Christianity among the hitherto defiantly pagan early English.

CHAPTER 8

CHRISTIANITY AND NORTHUMBRIA

400 to 700

Given the limited practice of Christianity in Britain in the 5th century, few might have predicted the speed and extent of its impact over the next few centuries. From an uncertain start it grew to become an essential feature of life in many communities, a rallying call for Alfred against the Vikings, and a key building block of the future England. In exploring that transformation, time and context remain vital as earthly and spiritual power unsteadily come together. This time we can start in the west.

The background in Ireland and Britain

As the Roman legions withdrew from Britain, the pirates operating out of Ireland saw their chance by targeting the west and southwest coasts of Britain. On one of their raids, early in the 5th century, they captured the 16 year-old future *St Patrick* and shipped him off to slavery in Ireland.[94] Having spent six or more years there as a shepherd, he escaped and returned to Britain.

---

94 *The dating is unclear, although generally considered to have been (probably early) 5th century. Patrick appears to have been born into a Romano-British family of some standing in south Wales. His own short account, Confessio, leaves many issues open. The belief that he drove the snakes out of Ireland is generally now accepted as a myth in the absence of evidence that Ireland had snakes at that time!*

On his return, a vision impelled Patrick to go back to Ireland, where he spent the rest of his life spreading the faith, supporting learning, and influencing local leaders. As his encouragement of ascetic monasticism, missionary action and general popularity eclipsed most other Irish ecclesiasts of the time, St Patrick became revered as the primary patron saint of Ireland.[95]

Patrick was followed a hundred or so years later by *St Columba* (521-597), born in County Donegal, Ulster, then known as the 'land of the Scots'. After an argument, Columba left Ireland in 563 to settle on the remote island of Iona, off the south-west coast of Scotland. Here he encouraged conversion of the Scots (Scotti) and many Picts, while inspiring such luminaries as Aidan and Cuthbert. The Irish church itself generally followed Roman orthodoxy, but with some variations that later became significant, such as the form of monks' tonsure and the date of Easter.

Although Irish monks often lived austere lives, many ecclesiastical institutions grew to become major economic units in their society, with substantial land, tenants and income. These seats of learning helped extend links with Frankish and Anglo-Saxon courts, developing a reputation for their scholarship, which extended into researching and writing down laws on issues such as property and inheritance, often overlaying ancient customs with Christian principles.

The Growth of the Christian Church in Europe

Since the Christian Church plays a major role in the history of England from this point on, it helps to update the background. After Constantine in the early 4th century, Christianity had turned from a persecuted to an approved and, at times, compulsory faith in the Roman Empire. Initially at least, it was pragmatic enough to co-exist with native deities and beliefs, with many old 'pagan' feast days finding their way into the flexible Christian calendar.

---

95 *Along with St Brigid and St Columba.*

In fact, 'pagan' originally meant rural (and perceived simple) people or rustics, before the urban elite adopted the word as a derogatory term for an outsider.[96] *Only later did pagan come to be used by Christians to describe anyone who did not share their faith or – in some cases- their liturgies.*

As Christianity spread, so did its variants. One major issue of contention was the Holy Trinity, and the relationship between the Father and the Son. Was the Son, as leading bishops argued, of the 'same substance' as the Father (the *homoousian* principle.) Or, since God must have existed before the Son, was the Son necessarily of a 'similar', but not the same, substance as the Father, which was the Arian view? If this may seem abstruse now, it was an issue of life and death for many in the early Christian church. One reason for this was the belief that Jesus could only be regarded as redeeming the world, a fundamental of Christianity, if he was also God. If the Son is not of the *same* substance as God, then – so the argument went – the Son on his own could not reconcile man with God. Even within the Arian camp, there were diverse views on the issue.

The Christian church felt the need for common ground on such key doctrinal tenets. The Edict of Thessalonica in 380 therefore formally adopted the homoousian principle approved by the Council of Nicaea in 325 as the state religion of the Roman Empire. Differences continued, however, and in some ways the Arian-Nicene division could be seen as the forerunner of future (and highly complex) splits in the Christian church.

The relocation of the emperor's main seat to Constantinople in the 4th century had left a spiritual vacancy in Rome, which was soon taken up by the head of the church, il Papa – the pope. But as the western empire fell to invaders, the Church and its bishops with their wealth and influence struggled to maintain stability. With Italy in turmoil, popes needed the temporal support of powerful rulers to

---

96 *A familiar pattern!*

protect them. They also needed something to offer in return if they were to maintain some balance in the relationship. The papal answer was to link the ruler's military might with divine approval, conveyed through the Church. Being anointed by God's own representative would sanctify a ruler's reign from on high, making resistance to the ruler both treason and blasphemy. '[It] was far better that the Emperor be understood as God's deputy on earth, upholding divine justice, than as a tyrant whose position would be based on force.'[97]

One effect was to leave some popes as kingmakers, a decidedly temporal power that needed to be (but was not always) used wisely. And the church-state joint venture left open the thorny issue as to which of pope or king/emperor was the senior partner. The answer, as with many other relationships, might depend on the personalities of the two, as well as the events of the time. It was also unclear how far a pope's authority extended. Could popes interfere in matters of state; and could rulers see church organisation as within their remit? These were to become recurrent themes, resonating across Britain and other countries time and again, causing clashes between popes and kings that often became major flashpoints with dramatic consequences.[98]

For all its faults, the Roman Empire had provided structure and a form of justice, such that its demise left a huge moral and social vacuum, which the Church slowly sought to fill. Faith in better things to come, whether in this world or the next, provided comfort and helped motivation. Of course to achieve this it was necessary to have God on your side, and the Pope as God's deputy on earth would normally be best placed to confirm heavenly approval. Thus, in the centuries after Rome's temporal dominance fell, its spiritual power grew. Kings and emperors who claimed sovereignty in Europe,

---

[97] Linda Woodhead (2014) *Christianity – A Very Short Introduction* – Oxford University Press

[98] The clash between Henry II of England and Thomas Becket was just one, especially vivid, later example.

CHRISTIANITY and NORTHUMBRIA

and even would-be kings and emperors, therefore needed to think ahead, and might want to prepare their way carefully with the head of the Catholic Church before taking any fateful step. Gradually, but implacably, religious Rome took on much of the power of imperial Rome.

Augustine, Canterbury and the first royal conversion

We can now fast forward to 597 on the Isle of Thanet, the earlier temporary home of Hengest and Horsa (see chapter 6). It was here that Augustine (later Augustine of Canterbury) arrived with some 40 missionaries to start the conversion process that was to sweep across Britain.[99] York had been the key ecclesiastical location since Constantine's acclamation there nearly 300 years earlier, but its primacy now passed to Canterbury, just inland from Thanet. The Romans had built the Canterbury city walls and gatehouses, probably around the tumultuous years 270-290. The splendid walls that now stand in Canterbury mostly come from much later, but in a garden area just outside them two commanding statues today stand close to one another.

One figure represents the Anglo-Saxon *Aethelbert* (alias Ethelbert), King of Kent from approximately 560 to 616. The other is his wife *Bertha*, daughter of the Merovingian Charibert, king of the Franks, who were now the dominant force in former Gaul. The Franks had seen the advantages of a close relationship with the Christian church, and Bertha was herself Christian when she came to Kent to marry Aethelbert. She also brought with her to Britain her own religious retinue and secured her own path and gateway from the royal apartments to the church on the other side of the city wall.

Kent was then one of the strongest Anglo-Saxon kingdoms. The pope of the time, the wily and influential Gregory I, could see that a

---

99   *To be distinguished from the much earlier Augustine of Hippo, the arch opponent of Pelagius as explained in chapter 6.*

Christian queen there provided an ideal opportunity to spread the faith in Britain. Accordingly, he despatched Augustine as his emissary to Britain to seek conversion. King Aethelbert, initially suspicious of the missionary and his entourage, kept them at a distance until satisfied that he was safe from supernatural influences. We might also imagine vigorous discussions with his pious wife before the potential benefits to law, order and learning in his kingdom, as well as marital harmony, persuaded him. After the king overcame his reticence and converted, Augustine did not take long to establish his seat, known as a *cathedra*, at Canterbury, soon becoming Britain's first archbishop.

Briefed by Pope Gregory, Augustine appeared to respect old pagan ways, days and sites, steadily converting these to Christian use to smooth the path of the new religion. There were also benefits to Aethelbert and Kent. Supported by dynastic and religious links with the Franks, coinage developed and Aethelbert's control of increasing trade between Kent and northern France greatly benefitted the king's treasury. Riches from Byzantium suddenly surged into Kent via France, with flowing gold patterns and jewellery being created. All this helped Aethelbert to achieve his (temporary as it turned out) supremacy over other Anglo-Saxon kings.

Although Christianity was spreading, Augustine seems to have become impatient at the speed of progress. Reports suggest that, before his death in 604, he became increasingly arrogant and overbearing, threatening conversion by force if needed. In any case, faith does not necessarily pass to the next generation, as with Aethelbert's own son, Eadbald, who abjured Christianity in favour of pagan ways. North of the Thames Estuary the king of Essex remained pagan, and in East Anglia, King Rædwald equivocated. Although inclined to commit to the new faith, Rædwald seems to have had real concerns for himself and his people if they moved away from the old gods. The whole farming year, on which their lives depended, was infused with pagan significance with deeply held traditions and beliefs that many would have found hard to shake off.

One thing that might encourage conversion, however, was success in battle and the belief that the increasingly powerful Christian God was on your side!

Christianity in Britain takes root

Once King Aethelbert of Kent had converted, he treated Christianity as a 'top-down' religion. Realising that it also sanctified his own rule on earth, he became an active and strong supporter of the faith. One of his acts was to endow the early St Paul's church in London, where the cathedral of that name now stands. He also, shortly after his conversion, issued a set of laws, the first of their kind in Anglo-Saxon, as later acknowledged by King Alfred. These mainly set out fines to be paid for various offences, with those against the church incurring the highest penalties.

The message for those whose lives were far from the court was that, even if this world was one of sin and suffering, the right actions in this life (including loyalty to the lord) could give access to a glorious afterlife. Gradually rules were imported and adapted which progressively empowered the church, enabling it to give guidelines for people to follow to achieve salvation. Given the events of the previous two hundred years, this message of divine order may have seemed reassuringly straightforward for many people.

The nobility could have their sense of place and destiny reinforced, and the common people could see their impoverished existence as a passport to an eternal heavenly future. Augustine's missionaries encouraged the establishment of churches, monasteries and their entourage of priests and clerics. But churches also needed land. As Christianity took hold, therefore, kings could be seen to be acting generously by providing grants to support the work of the church on the basis that the king's reign was sanctified by God.

Many years later the Venerable Bede commented on the fleeting nature of life on earth in a famous passage in his history, where he puts a metaphor into the mouth of a chieftain talking quietly to his Lord. The chieftain likens our life on earth to the flight of a sparrow through a bustling mead hall, flying in from a stormy night through the hurly-burly of the hall and then out again the other side. We know nothing of what went before the flight through the hall, or what is to come after.

Humility, however, was one Christian virtue which some landed elites found problematic, especially if it involved giving away their worldly goods! The early Church accordingly offered a compromise whereby the wealthy could keep their estates, but pay for good works, either in the form of physical buildings or by way of endowment of a religious institution. Christianity thus became a worthy cause for 'investment', even if the return on capital employed in building a new church might be more in the next life than this – perhaps a form of afterlife insurance. It was an arrangement which encouraged something of a building boom, with church and religious building requiring contractors and specialist trades, smiths, stores and merchants.

Even so, not all were convinced. In Prittlewell in Essex, sometime around 600 CE, a man of some rank, possibly a senior member of the Essex royal family, was buried. In his coffin, inside a sealed chamber, were over 100 objects, including personal items alongside emblems of status and leadership – a huge feasting cauldron, a finely decorated sword, a flagon from Syria, gems from Asia, gold coins from France, a lyre to sing him into another world, and food to sustain him on the way. What especially attracted archaeological attention was that, although all the signs were of a pagan burial, two gold crosses over the eyes suggested at least tentative Christian beliefs or a Christian intervention.

Another type of figure has attracted a different sort of attention. For centuries the outlines of the Cerne Abbas giant in Wessex appear to have lain dormant beneath long hillside grass, unrecorded until the late 17th century. And the figure, braced against the hillside with an erect phallus and a raised arm wielding a huge club, would have shocked many when finally exposed. Recent OSL (Optically Stimulated Luminescence) technology surveys under the auspices of the National Trust then surprised many by indicating that the figure was probably created in 7th century Anglo-Saxon times. One theory is that it was a highly visible protest at the constraints of Christianity, with the dating perhaps coinciding with a period when Wessex reverted to paganism, either around 635, or between 676 and the mid-680s. Christianity's meteoric rise does indeed seem to have stalled somewhat during this period, especially during and just after the supremacy of the overbearing pagan Penda, king of Mercia from c 625 to 655 (covered in the next chapter).

Some years later, when the Archbishopric of Canterbury fell vacant, Pope Vitalian selected the outstanding cleric, Theodore of Tarsus. The choice was surprising in that Theodore, though experienced and erudite, was already over 65 years old by the time he was consecrated in 668. And despite his fluency in classical languages, he had never been to Britain and did not know the language. Just as surprising was his equally accomplished companion in the venture, the self-styled 'man from Africa', Hadrian from Libya. It was even more remarkable that Theodore lived for another 20 years and Hadrian 40. They proved to be a succesful double act, based in Canterbury but travelling and spreading the word together throughout the land. Their work contributed to a Carolingian renaissance on the Continent, led a Christian resurgence in Britain, and supported the great religious foundations and seats of learning at Wearmouth and Jarrow in Northumbria. By the time he died in 690 (aged 88) Theodore, with Hadrian's help, had contributed to the widespread dissemination of key Christian texts and education.

Increasingly well-funded, many religious institutions became centres of learning and education, the most respected drawing in scholars from other countries. Communities grew around them, many becoming major landowners and food producers in their own right. These new seats of piety and learning in turn gave considerable opportunities for those seeking to combine education through the church with good connections for civil life.

Northumbria

Although his analysis is now considered over-simplistic, Henry of Huntingdon,[100] followed by Bede and others, identified seven major early kingdoms, which he named 'the Heptarchy'. (See Map 5.) These were Northumbria in the north, Mercia and East Anglia in the Midlands, and Wessex, Sussex, Kent and Essex in the south. The 7th century was especially contested in the north, drawing in combatants from Wales, the Midlands and East Anglia. There were clashes with the Picts, leadership battles, unlikely alliances, surprising loyalties, and bewildering changes of fortune. As the conflicting kingdoms battled for control and hegemony, the remaining Brittonic kingdoms gradually fell to larger and more powerful Anglo-Saxon confederations.

The next major stage in the development of Christianity in this period takes us up to what for a time became the northern powerhouse of Northumbria.

Today's Northumberland, which covers the area just north of Newcastle upon Tyne up to the current Scottish border, is a fraction of the area of Anglo-Saxon Northumbria, which at its peak included today's Northumberland, Newcastle, County Durham, and the extensive county of Yorkshire. Around 650 two main kingdoms occupied this whole area. Bernicia in the north included the hallowed precincts of Jarrow and Wearmouth, the great castle of Bamburgh and the remote island of Lindisfarne. To the south was

---

100 See chapter 7.

Deira, with a base at York. When the two came together it was as *Northumbria,* the land to the north of the Humber.

The eastern boundary of Northumbria was the immense tapering coastline of the North Sea. Immediately north of Bernicia was the land of the Gododdin, covering what are now the eastern Scottish Lowlands up to the Firth of Forth (site of today's Edinburgh). North-west lay the growing power of Dalriada, land of the Scotti, spreading across from northern Ireland. South of Dalriada was the Brittonic kingdom of Rheged, broadly straddling the Solway Firth (the western end of Hadrian's Wall) and Cumbria.[101] To the south lay the small Brittonic kingdom of Elmet, whose boundaries are less certain and whose future was also limited.

Battles for supremacy

Aethelfrith – The spotlight now falls on *Aethelfrith,* Anglo-Saxon King of Bernicia (the northern kingdom) from 593 to 616, who steadily pushed its borders out to the west. He also faced the threat from further north which came to a head in 603 when the Bernicians fought a major battle against the Dalriadans (at an unknown location). Despite being outnumbered, suffering severe losses themselves, and Aethelfrith losing a brother in the fighting, the Bernicians won a comprehensive victory. After this, Bernicia and Dalriada were reluctant to engage in further major confrontation, which might have checked Scottish moves further south. To strengthen his hand against Dalriada, Aethelfrith sought an alliance with Deira to the south by marrying the daughter of its King Aella. Not content with this, in 604 Aethelfrith ousted Aella and annexed Deira itself to create the vast kingdom of Northumbria.

Aethelfrith does seem to have been one of those leaders

---

101 *The history of this area was later much contested as the land of the former Damnonii became Alt Clud or Ystrad Clud and then Strathclyde, with its southern neighbour of varying extent as Rheged or Cumbria.*

constantly on the move. In 613-6 he campaigned against, and defeated, an army from Celtic Gwynedd (North Wales) at Chester, according to Bede laying waste large areas of territory. Although the Welsh borders were far from York, the real target might have been someone the Britons of Gwynedd were suspected of harbouring. This was Edwin, the son of Aelle, whom Aethelfrith had ousted from Deira and regarded as an ongoing threat.

Edwin – In fact, rather than remain in Gwynedd, Edwin had sought the protection of Rædwald, king of East Anglia from c. 599-624, at whose court Edwin lived for some time. But Rædwald ('power in counsel') must have been in a quandary.[102] If Rædwald supported Edwin, and Edwin succeeded, he would expect the younger man to acknowledge his over-lordship. But Aethelfrith, desperate to see the back of the Edwin threat, was offering increasing bribes (and perhaps some threats) to Rædwald to surrender Edwin to him. Rædwald himself, uncertain of Christianity but reluctant to antagonise an aggressive near neighbour like Aethelfrith, may increasingly have become minded to accept Aethelfrith's pressure. It was Rædwald's wife who is rumoured to have intervened to remind her husband of the traditional Germanic duty to honour and protect his guest. Finally, Rædwald decided to support Edwin and trust in God – or the gods of war. He marched north in 616 to meet Aethelfrith on the banks of the River Idle in Lindsey (today's Lincolnshire), the small kingdom between Deira and East Anglia.

The battle and its aftermath – The day was a bloody one with mixed fortunes, ending with the defeat and death of Aethelfrith, but also the loss of Rædwald's own son. With his way now cleared, Edwin took the throne of Deira. But once in power, Edwin had his own ambitions. Constrained by his debt to Rædwald not to move against East Anglia, he conquered the small Brittonic kingdom of Elmet

---

102 *Rædwald is also connected with the spectacular burial at Sutton Hoo, as described in the next chapter.*

and removed its king. This period also highlighted the role of 'wide-ruler' or *bretwalda,* an acknowledged (if titular) over-king. This was a position held by Aethelbert of Kent, succeeded by Rædwald, with Edwin as his effective under-king. After Rædwald's death, Edwin himself was for a time recognised as bretwalda, with a major influence over the north of Britain.

Cadwallon – Possibly seeking to expand to the west coast and the grain-rich Isle of Anglesey, Edwin now set his sights on Gwynedd, north Wales, ruled by its Celtic king, Cadwallon. The first round went to Edwin, with Cadwallon fleeing the scene and seeking refuge in Ireland. Significantly for the future, Cadwallon's next move was to make an alliance with King Penda of Mercia. The second round went decisively in favour of Cadwallon and Penda, with the defeat and death of Edwin at the battle of Hatfield Chase near Doncaster in 632. Ostensibly to 'enforce peace', Cadwallon and Penda systematically ravaged Northumbria and destroyed Edwin's family, one of the many vicious reprisals the area was to suffer in the course of its history. But, as so often happened, there was another branch of the family ready to emerge.

Oswald and Oswy (alias Oswiu) – Just as Edwin had sought to avenge his father, Aelle, by removing his antagonist, so Aethelfrith's sons, Oswald and Oswy, sought their own revenge. Oswald surprised and killed Cadwallon in 634 at Heavenfield, near Hexham, a victory often ascribed to the Christian God. Oswald then set out to extend his new domains, only to meet his own grisly end in 641 or 642 at Maserfield (near Oswestry in Shropshire) at the hands of another combined Brittonic and Mercian army under Penda.[103] In the light of this, Oswald's brother Oswy (r 641-670), changed course and turned north to renew the offensive against the Scots and Picts, who, Bede tells us, acknowledged his supremacy and paid tribute.

---

103 *See also next chapter.*

Once again the pendulum swung back when Oswy's son and heir, Ecgfrith, headed north to attack Pictish lands, only to die in 685 at the battle of Dun Nechtain (or Nechtansmere). In retrospect, this battle has been seen as cementing the power of the Picts and contributing to the establishment of the future Scotland.

We return to Oswy in the next chapter, but meanwhile need to rewind slightly. After their father, Aethelfrith, was defeated and killed by Edwin, Oswald and Oswy had taken sanctuary on the Isle of Iona where they were brought up by Irish monks in Christian ways. Despite his warlike history, Oswald became regarded as a highly Christian ruler who did much to encourage the spread of the Christian faith throughout his domains, later becoming venerated as a saint.[104] Oswald's achievements included promoting the Irish monk and missionary *(St) Aidan*, who founded the Lindisfarne Priory and became its first bishop. Travelling tirelessly through the kingdom to spread the word to all classes of people, Aidan's life was chronicled by the Venerable Bede with a quality of research and style that set a new standard for biography. And it was Bede who, basking in the glory that was Northumbria at the time, wrote his acclaimed ecclesiastical history.

Oswy, however, had a religious schism to address – the alleged heresy of Pelagius, summarised in chapter 6. After a determined campaign by the official Church to impose its doctrinal orthodoxy, Oswy convened the Synod of Whitby in 664. With a decision on vexed issues such as the dating of Easter and the style of a monk's tonsure awaited across Britain, discussion ran on without consensus. Finally, the king was reminded that it was St Peter, first bishop of Rome, who held the gates to heaven. Had he not said that he would build his church on the rock of *Rome*? The Roman Catholic view triumphed as a result and was to remain ascendant in England for over 800 years.

---

[104] *Especially in Mercia – despite Mercian responsibility for his death.*

Saintly highlights

Having opened with St Patrick, this chapter concludes with some other, possibly less well-known, saintly figures, starting with one remarkable queen who did much to progress the faith.

St Seaxburh[105] – Earlier we saw the influence of Queen Bertha of Kent in persuading her doubting husband to convert. She was not alone. Other extraordinary women forged their own paths, with some recognised for their contributions and others showing how hard it could be for women to match expectations of femininity and saintliness. One such was Seaxburh (later St Seaxburh) of Ely (c.636 – c.700), a daughter of Anna, then king of East Anglia. She became the wife of King Eorcenberht (king of Kent 640-64), the mother of two later kings of Kent, and mother-in-law of the powerful Wulfhere of Mercia through her daughter, Ermenilda. Having brought up and acted as regent for her elder son after his father's death, she then left royal life to become a nun, founding a church (now Minster Abbey) at Minster-in-Sheppey in Kent,[106] where her daughter Ermenilda also became a nun after her own husband's death. Seaxburh then moved to the double monastery at Ely in East Anglia to take over the role of abbess there on the death of her sister in 680. In this case the sister, Æthelthryth (alias Etheldreda and Audrey), had chosen to retain her virginity during two marriages, the latter to the young King Egfrith of Northumbria, before leaving her marriage and establishing the monastery.

Above all, Seaxburh had set a clear precedent for queens and their daughters to have the option to stand back from their royal duties to choose an alternative life, even after motherhood. In the process, she was also able to inherit the position of abbess from her sister and have it to pass on in turn to her daughter and granddaughter.

---
105 *Presumably pronounced 'Saxburh'.*
106 *Where – coincidentally – I was married!*

Even if women were as yet unable to be monarchs in their own right, they established in the south-east a form of matrilineal succession in their own religious foundations.

The Venerable Bede lavishes praise on Æthelthryth for her piety and virtue in remaining a virgin through two marriages, whilst glossing over the achievements of her sister who had borne and supported her children.

St Frideswide – Also known as *Fritha,* Frideswide is the accepted modern version of Saint Frithuswith (old English *Friðuswiþ*). Born possibly in 650 (or somewhat later), she either founded or ran a religious order which many centuries later was incorporated into Christ Church in Oxford. Known for her dedication, piety and ability to perform miracles, Fritha was the daughter of a sub-king, *Dydda* (alias Dida or Didan), who ruled part of what is now West Oxfordshire.[107] Not only did Fritha inspire people by her piety; she also attracted a reputation for beauty and wealth, such that her fame soon spread. Enter the inevitable powerful predatory male! This time it was *Aelfgar,* alias Algar, sub-king of Leicester, then within Mercia, who seems to have been thoroughly undeterred by Fritha's commitment to church and celibacy. When she refused his offer of marriage, he decided to carry her off by force. On hearing of his intentions she fled from the town and hid among swine.

At this point the stories differ. In some versions the overbearing Aelfgar is said to have been struck blind by lightning, or to have fallen off his horse and broken his neck (or possibly both). Notwithstanding her plight, Fritha, overcome with compassion, immediately used water from a holy well to restore Aelfgar to full health and sight. Not just that. The holy water also purged the royal body of his desire for the lady, whereupon he galloped away, never to be seen again.

---

107 *Dydda's Cottage lives on as the fast-growing town and major railway interchange of Didcot.*

CHRISTIANITY and NORTHUMBRIA

Fritha remained abbess of the nunnery in Oxford until her death around 727, centuries later becoming the patron saint of the city. Miraculous properties were later ascribed to her in relation to the well at St Margaret's Church, Binsey, just upstream. Maidens of later centuries were reputed to bring their beloveds there for what might be described as 'trial by toad'. If the resident toad spat at the young man, the man was not to be trusted. Whatever the strength of evidence for Fritha's miracles, the toad test does seem from a different era. Indeed, the accounts of Fritha's life are limited[108] and, whilst there seems evidence of her piety and dedication as a role model for others, the arrogance and travails of Aelfgar do have the ring of a later morality tale. As with legends, the line between miracle and myth may be a fine one.

St Cuthbert – Cuthbert was born around 634 on what are now the borders of Northumberland and Scotland, living his early years at Melrose Abbey. Switching from Celtic to Roman Catholic Christianity after the Synod of Whitby in 664, he lived a simple life, concentrating on preaching and conversion. Already associated with miraculous powers, Cuthbert became prior of Melrose before retiring to live the life of a hermit on the nearby desolate Farne Islands. He was finally persuaded to accept appointment as Bishop of Hexham in 685, but preferred to have his seat on Lindisfarne. Not long afterwards he returned to seclusion on the Farne Islands where, after a painful illness, he died in March 687.

Known as a man of utmost integrity and saintly qualities, Cuthbert (known affectionately as Cuddy) continued to be associated with miracles long after his death. His (allegedly undecomposed) body and relics were so valued that they were later removed on an epic journey from Lindisfarne, to avoid falling into Viking hands. His remains were finally installed in the new Durham Cathedral, and the story of the

---
108 See especially Blair, John. "Saint Frideswide Reconsidered." *Oxoniensia* 52 (1987), 71-127.

carrying of his body through the northern hills now has the ring of legend.[109]

St Wilfrid [110] – Wilfrid was of a different mould, a hugely influential figure in northern Britain in the mid-7th century with a fluctuating career. Born at about the same time as Cuthbert, which was also around the time that Cadwallon defeated and ravaged Northumberland, Wilfrid grew up in the relative peace of Lindisfarne with its links to Iona and, through Bishop Aidan, King Oswy. Well-connected, and with high expectations, Wilfrid arrived in Rome in 653, where his head may have been turned by a papal blessing and sight of the wealth so clearly on show. When he returned, his brashness repelled some but attracted others, including King Oswy's son, Alchfrith, who gave him a monastery and lands at Ripon. At the Synod of Whitby Wilfrid was chosen to present the Roman Catholic position, but alienated many by speaking contemptuously of those of different persuasion.

Overall Wilfrid appears to have been a divisive character, whom many thought an unsuitable choice when he was finally appointed as Bishop of Northumbria. Wilfrid, however, took his elevation as licence to interfere wherever he chose. Matters came to a head in 678 when he was deposed, and – with an armed retinue – took his case to the pope in Rome. After being reinstated, Wilfrid was imprisoned, released and shunned before making his way to Sussex, where Cædwalla from Wessex was causing havoc. It's alleged that, when Cædwalla set about exterminating the population of the Isle of Wight for being heathens, Wilfrid gave him his spiritual blessing in return for a quarter of the resulting profits. Again restored to his bishopric in Northumbria, Wilfrid was banished by the pious new king, Aldfrith, only to set off to Rome once more and be partially restored. His unbending combative nature and willingness to support forced conversion remained at odds with the views of most

---

109 *See, for example, Cuddy by Benjamin Myers (2023) Bloomsbury.*

110 *Marc Morris devotes much of a complete chapter to Wilfrid's career.*

CHRISTIANITY and NORTHUMBRIA

of his contemporaries. Even if Henry II much later never actually said it of Becket, the description 'turbulent priest' might well have suited Wilfrid.

The Venerable Bede – In some ways Baeda, known as the Venerable Bede, created (or extended) the vision of an English, or at least an *Anglish*, people. A monk based at Jarrow, on the south bank of the River Tyne (between today's Newcastle and South Shields), Bede was, then aged twelve, one of the few local survivors of the plague in 685. He was later content to spend his life in Jarrow as a polymath who also enjoyed coastal walks and cooking. He laboured faithfully on many works, notably his *Ecclesiastical History of the English People,* finally completed in 731, since published and read widely in Europe and beyond. Written in a time when few wrote down current or recent events, it remains one of the key reference works for the period.

Despite being a passionate Christian, Bede was much exercised about those who were not. Chief culprits were 'the Britons', to whom in chapter 23 of his history he ascribes a 'national hatred for the English', but who, being 'opposed by the power of God and man alike', were 'powerless to obtain what they want.' But who were Bede's 'English'? Writing in Latin, he refers to *gens Anglorum*, seemingly based on the Angles, whom Bede saw as the dominant people in Northumbria. But the scope of his work clearly covers the many others whom we think of as Anglo-Saxons. Translating Bede's history as being 'of the English People' may therefore be anticipating the English who were not really to emerge for another two hundred years.

In many ways Bede's overall theme seems to have been deterministic, based on the belief that his people were sent by God into a new land to be converted to Christianity and rule over the people there in harmony and, eventually, peace. His underlying message of ineluctable progression from paganism to true faith, and diversity into unity, gives a strong sense of the biblical journey of the chosen people. Secure in his lodgings, based firmly in the north and close to its king, he may well have seen Northumbria as the intended unifying force. In the event, as we'll see, this was a role that might have been taken by Mercia, but which ultimately fell to Wessex.

The Saints' Ways to Lindisfarne – Northumberland today remains a special place. With its rugged moorland, craggy outcrops, rippling streams, huge sky, seascapes, and spirituality, it has a remote beauty of its own. And set just off its coastline, few places stir the senses like Lindisfarne, the Holy Island south of the border town of Berwick-upon-Tweed. Two long-distance footpaths make their way to the causeway that links island to mainland, both celebrating the movements of 7th century saints. One route is attributed to St Oswald, whom we met earlier progressing from a religious upbringing on the Isle of Iona to avenge his father and bring Christianity to Northumbria. But it was Oswald's death near Oswestry in 642, at the hands of Penda of Mercia, that made his religious reputation. Although his body was mutilated by the victors, the spot and Oswald's remains soon attracted attention for their miraculous powers, later recognised by his sainthood.

The St Oswald's Way, commemorating him, runs for 110 miles (including the extension to Berwick) from the Roman wall and battle site at Heavenfield, to cross a mix of rolling country, heather moorland, dramatic outcrops and peaty rivers to the coast at Warkworth. From there it heads north via dunes, sandy beaches, tidal estuaries, and rocky edges to the dramatic site of Bamburgh, where Oswald had his capital in the 7th century.

Starting further north, at Melrose, now in Scotland, the *St Cuthbert's Way* is one of its finest mid-length walks, a winding 62-mile west to east pilgrimage across some of the most glorious and remote parts of the north-west. The route takes in hills, valleys, the high-level moorland of the Cheviots and the bleak openness of Flodden Field before reaching St Cuthbert's Cave, believed resting place of the monks carrying the saint's body to Durham. From the crags behind the cave Holy Island becomes visible across the tidal salt flats with Bamburgh Castle rising, almost mystically, above the horizon to the south.

Lindisfarne developed a reputation for learning and scholarship that attracted donations from far and wide and was later to manifest itself in the magnificence of the Lindisfarne Gospels. For over a century Lindisfarne continued its work while different kingdoms battled it out for supremacy. But it was not to last. Just before the end of the 8th century, religious sanctity came to a shattering end as the lure of gold in a remote location proved an irresistible attraction for the early raiders we know as the Vikings. Lindisfarne was about to become known for something far darker. That story is picked up again in chapter 11, but before then we need to head down to the Midlands to follow progress there.

A short timeline for early Christianity in Britain

400 to 410 ?	St Patrick enslaved, escapes and returns to Ireland.
429	St Germanus visits Britain – later secures 'Alleluia victory'
563	St Columba leaves Ireland for Iona
597	St Augustine arrives in Kent
600 ?	Aethelbert of Kent converts – 'Prittlewell man' in Essex
636 – 700	St Seaxburh – Kent and East Anglia
604 – 641/2	St Oswald – Northumbria
634 – 687	St Cuthbert – Farne and Lindisfarne
633/4 – 709?	St Wilfrid – Northumbria, Kent etc

650 – 717	St Frideswith – Oxford
650 – 680	Possible reaction against Christianity – Cerne Abbas giant?
664	Synod of Whitby
669	Theodore arrives in Britain, followed by Hadrian
673 (?) – 735	Venerable Bede

CHAPTER 9

EAST ANGLIA AND MERCIA

600 to 825

Chapter 6 saw the take-over of Kent and the Anglo-Saxon expansion into Sussex and Wessex in the 5th century. Chapter 8 charted the Christian mission after 600 through to the consolidation of Northumbria. This chapter turns to the geographical middle ground, ranging from the Humber in the north to the Thames in the south, and from the Welsh borders in the west to the North Sea in the east. The eastern area gradually consolidated as East Anglia while the middle became the 'borderland' or Mierce, later known as Mercia.

One significant element of later Mercian power was its seizing control of London, with its fast-growing and valuable mercantile connections. The port's burgeoning economy was subsequently enhanced (in economic rather than human terms) by the Mercian trade in captured slaves, often destined for foreign ports and an uncertain servile life abroad. This was a time of emerging, competing, and occasionally cooperating, monarchies, when the concept of bretwalda or 'over-king' remained largely undefined and fragile. Although it was Mercia that was to become the dominant kingdom in this period, the battle for wealth and supremacy ranged far into the north and south, with sudden and largely unpredictable changes of fortune. It's a complex story with a summary chart for 600-700 set out at the end of the chapter.

Early Mercia

Icel – One early East Anglian power group appears to have come from the Angeln-Schleswig area of south-central Jutland, possibly in the early 6th century. They were reportedly led by a man called *Icel* (or Icil), son of Eomer, allegedly the last king of the Angles in Jutland. Unless this was another foundation myth, a new king deciding to emigrate with most of his people suggests a pressing need to leave the homeland in Jutland. From an initial base in East Anglia the Icel appear to have moved steadily inland, across from the fens and main rivers towards the heart of Britain, building up a coalition of sub-kings who supplied men and tribute in return for a degree of self-rule. This domination gave Icel a claim to be the first king of Mercia.

For the next 50 or so years after Icel's death in c.535 his successors sought to maintain their hold over this central area, in addition to East Anglia, where new factions were challenging. Eventually, perhaps in the late 6th century, Icel's heirs appear to have concentrated their resources in the new, inner kingdom of Mercia, while the Wuffingas (see below) consolidated their hold on southern East Anglia.

Penda – The first well-known king of Mercia is *Penda*, who had a forceful 30-year rule (c. 625 to 655). With his origins obscure, Penda may have been one of the British sub-kings who proved able to persuade other 'tribal' rulers to accept his authority.[111] At least initially, he also seems to have built alliances with Welsh leaders by treaty and marriage. Aggressive expansion then took him south to the Cotswolds, south-west to the Severn Valley, and north (with his Welsh ally, Cadwallon) to defeat and kill Edwin of Northumbria at Hatfield Chase in 632. As seen in the last chapter, after further

---

111 *A document called the Tribal Hidage dating from around this time, seemingly centred on Mercia but also covering areas further south, mentions some 35 tribes and their number of hides (a measurement of land – see chapter 10).*

years of conflict Penda also defeated Oswald of Northumbria (and ritually cut him to pieces) at Maserfield in 641/2.

The reason for this antagonism is unclear, although Cadwallon had reason to seek revenge against Edwin. For Penda, the excessive Christian zeal of the Northumbrian kings, keen to expand both territory and faith against the 'heathen' Mercians, may also have been a factor. Bede certainly saw the conflict in terms of Christian versus pagan with his account very selective in favour of the Christians. For him, the Northumbrian brothers, Oswald and Oswy, could do little wrong. There must therefore have been great Christian relief and rejoicing in Northumbria with the defeat of Mercia and death of Penda at Winaed in 655. This also turned out to be the effective death-knell of royal paganism in Anglo-Saxon Britain.

Winaed may, however, not have been quite the triumph of Christian values it had seemed. The Mercians and their allies, having laid waste much of Northumbria, had reached Oswy and his supporters far to the north. Faced with probable defeat, Oswy appears to have sought to buy off Penda with treasure. Despite Bede's reticence on the issue, it seems quite possible that Penda did accept Oswy's offer of treasure and a truce. But when Penda's booty-laden and partially dispersed army trudged back south through late autumn rain to find itself trapped by flood water near Leeds, it was destroyed in a surprise attack by Oswy's men at Winaed.

Whatever had, or had not, been previously agreed was now irrelevant; with Penda dead the Northumbrian victory was comprehensive. Oswy adopted direct Northumbrian rule over half of Mercia with the other half in the hands of his son-in-law, (Penda's son) Paeda, as a client king. The 2009 discovery of what became known as the 'Staffordshire Hoard' inside a former Mercian royal estate has increased suspicion of Oswy's actions. The hoard's stunning contents appear to be consistent with exactly the kind of 'war loot'[112] that

---

112 *Michael Wood's term (2023) p 91.*

Penda would have collected from Oswy if a deal had been struck. Perhaps some of Penda's men did make it home, hid the treasure underground – but never came back to recover it. The story is only missing a hoard-herding dragon.[113]

Wulfhere and Aethelred – Paeda himself did not last long, supposedly murdered by his own wife during Easter festivities. But Penda had left other sons. The first, *Wulfhere* (659 – 675), managed to combine diplomacy with warfare. Having converted to Christianity, he was readier to delegate practical control to subservient kingdoms, perhaps recognising that he simply did not have the resources to do otherwise. His brother *Aethelred* (675 – 704), a resonant name in later English history, was more religious. Despite being less expansionist than his father, Aethelred subdued Kent and fixed the northern Mercian-Northumbrian border at the River Humber following the Battle of the Trent in 679. This largely ended Northumbrian ambitions to the south and restored the embattled small kingdom of Lindsey to Mercian control.

By then Aethelred was married to Osthryth, the daughter of Oswy of Northumberland, which made him the brother-in-law of Oswy's son and successor, Ecgfrith. But rather than encourage amity, the union caused inter-kingdom and inter-family hostility, factors which may have led to Osthryth's murder in 697. Her death seemed to hit Aethelred hard. He struggled on for another seven years before retiring to live out his remaining years in one of the monasteries he and Osthryth had founded together. Mercia's star had waned temporarily, but was soon to rise again.

Mercia, Wessex and Sussex – The advance of Wessex in the 6th century did not continue long into the 7th as expansionist Mercia merged with (or perhaps absorbed) groups such as the *Hwicce* (south-west in the lower Severn Valley), the *Magonseatan* (south in

---

113 *The hoard included one gold cross with a folded arm, suggestive of a Christian artefact deliberately altered for reasons that can only be guessed at.*

Hertfordshire) and the *Middle Angles* (to the east). To add to this, when Wessex sought to expand south-east, Sussex unwisely sought the protection of Mercia. The result was that the rulers of Sussex were demoted to sub-kings, and then ealdormen (nobles owing allegiance to the king), of Mercia.

One possible cause for Sussex's concern might have been the nature of the king of Wessex from about 685. This was Caedwalla, whose reign was nasty, extremely brutish and mercifully short. Having been ousted by Mercia from Sussex he attacked Kent and briefly claimed kingship there before being removed. His infamy was, however, assured by his invasion of the Isle of Wight. Here, as seen in relation to St Wilfrid, he sought systematically to exterminate its inhabitants and claim their land, even executing local leaders after forcing them to convert. Having been badly wounded in the process, Caedwalla retired to Rome where he died.

East Anglia and Sutton Hoo

The land – East Anglia covered the lands of the North Folk and the South Folk, now Norfolk and Suffolk. For a time it also extended west into Cambridgeshire. To the south lay Essex, the land of the East Saxons, and to the north, between the Wash and the Humber, was Lindsey. But the biggest factor in East Anglia's geography was, and still is, the great curving, and constantly eroding, shore of the North Sea and the ports that thrived and died with silt, storms and longshore drift. Much of northern Norfolk is low fenland country crossed by rivers, streams and general wetland. If, as suggested earlier, many from the low-lying Angeln area of Denmark had first settled here, the terrain would have been familiar to them. Suffolk to the south is more varied and hilly in landscape terms, with better protected points of access to the sea.

As suggested earlier, initial settlement in East Anglia seems to have been relatively peaceful, with communities settling around great halls at such places as West Stow in Suffolk and surrounding areas.

Elsewhere there are signs of some early Christian and pagan Germanic residents living close to one another in relative harmony.[114]

The incomers did adopt some new place names, such as Icklingham from Icel's people, progenitors of the Mercian royal house. Many other settlements were named after their new occupiers or their former homesteads. And, as it was repopulated, much of the area was drained and turned to arable use or pasture (especially sheep), or dug for peat to provide heating.[115] Beyond that, apart from the evidence of Sutton Hoo covered below, little is known of the early development of East Anglia, with such records as did exist largely being destroyed by the Danes when they overran the area in the 9th century.

The Wuffingas – Various East Anglian groups appear to have fallen under the sway of the Wuffingas, who benefited from a considerable period of dynastic stability. It started with a man known as Weha, the first recorded king of East Anglia, possibly around 550, whose son Wuffa ('the wolf') gave his name to the royal line around 575.[116] If, as commonly believed, the Wuffingas came from Swedish royal connections, they may have overcome, or pushed west, the earlier Anglian settlers, notably the Icel dynasty which went on to found Mercia. The Wuffingas might even have moved from Sweden into the abandoned lands of the Angles in Jutland before following the Angles in moving west.

The new royalty probably based themselves around Rendlesham, close to Sutton Hoo and the Deben Valley in Suffolk.[117] Here,

---

114 *See Michael Wood (2023) p 35.*

115 *Some of these excavation channels much later formed the basis of the waterways of today's Norfolk Broads.*

116 *Wuffa + ingas = people, in this case descendants, of Wuffa – or, more dramatically, sons of the wolf.*

117 *If it still existed, the royal hall, probably at Rendlesham and very much in the mould of the great hall of Heorot in Beowulf, was probably burned down by the Vikings in 869 when the East Anglian royal line ended with the death of King (later Saint) Edmund.*

later on, was the stronghold of Rædwald, the grandson of Wuffa (encountered in the last chapter equivocating about both his faith and his duty to Edwin of Northumbria). And it is Rædwald, king of East Anglia from 599 to around 624, who is the prime candidate for the missing body at Sutton Hoo (see below).

Christianity was apparently contentious enough in East Anglia at that time for Rædwald's son, Eorpwald, to be murdered for his faith. After this, East Anglia reverted to paganism until Eorpwald's brother (or step-brother), *Sigeberht*, succeeded to the East Anglian throne in 630. On his return from exile in France during Eorpwald's reign, Sigebehrt enlisted the help of a priest from Burgundy called Felix. It was Felix (later St Felix), consecrated as Bishop of Dunwich, who encouraged the founding of schools and steady Christian conversion in East Anglia.[118]

The biggest threat at that time, however, was Mercia. After defeating Northumbria and killing Edwin, Penda of Mercia turned against Edwin's former protectors, East Anglia, leading to the death of Sigeberht in battle around 640. Sigeberht's own successor was his cousin, King Anna, whose piety left no one in any doubt, and whose four daughters (mentioned in the last chapter) became famous for their sanctity. Unfortunately for Anna, Penda was still in power in Mercia, and with the minor kingdom of Middle Anglia becoming a bone of contention between them, the Mercians made repeated attacks on East Anglia. In 653/4 they finally defeated and killed Anna, after which East Anglia effectively ceased to be a major power.

Sutton Hoo – The discovery of the stunningly rich artefacts at Sutton Hoo has increased the apparent connection between the East Anglian Wuffingas and the Yngling Swedish royal line; in fact the excavations there led to an almost immediate claim by Swedish authorities that the artefacts originated in Sweden. Archaeology also suggests Sutton Hoo as a probable royal burial ground in

---

118 *And after whom the port of Felixstowe appears to be named.*

East Anglia until Christian times, While we cannot be certain that the Sutton Hoo ship burial did originally contain the body of Rædwald, the links to Sweden raise intriguing questions as to the extent of Swedish immigration into Britain in Anglo-Saxon times. That said, those visiting Sutton Hoo today should not expect to see the remains of a huge ship and royal graveyard. Even the burial mounds (18 to 20 in all) are shadows of their former selves. The informative exhibitions and spacious open site itself do, however, carry echoes of the past. And the modern replica skeleton of the 89 foot long ship that was buried there gives some sense of the effort that must have been required to pull it up from the nearby river. This is the *Deben*, meaning *deep river*, possibly true once but not so now, with heavy tidal mud flats lining the banks below the town of Woodbridge opposite.

The challenge of kingship

What then did it take to become, and even more to remain, a king in those times? Strength and military prowess were critical; followers needed to believe in their leader, and battle was still the ultimate test. Key supporters needed to be rewarded for their effort and the huge personal risks entailed in every fight. They therefore expected generosity from a leader, stylised in verse as 'ring-giving'. But to be a generous ring-giver, a leader needed to be, or become, rich enough to share sufficient spoils to satisfy his followers. Failure to do this would lead to desertion of support, and the risk of friends suddenly becoming enemies. And it was not all glory. Booty needed to be fought for, with warring factions feeling free to ravage the lands of their enemies.

Royal succession was an especially tricky time, and even the best laid plans of a king might go awry if his appointed heir died too soon. In some kingdoms, such as Wessex, the eldest son had no automatic right of succession. Thus the concept of the *aethelings* (or athelings), princes of royal blood from whom the next king would be chosen.

This might have reduced the risk of the worst person succeeding, but it also created major uncertainty until the last moment.

The death of a royal father, or even a brother, could be a dangerous time to be around if there were other, more ruthless, contenders for the throne. Behind the scenes, relatives, including some queens, were not immune from helping their own son's prospects by clearing the way, most notably of step-sons who might otherwise take precedence.

Loyalty, or the lack of it, is one of the great themes of the time. Rædwald of East Anglia, for example, had been about to fall under the sway of Aethelfrith's pieces of silver to betray Edwin. He held back, only then to lose his own son in the ensuing battle and have his protégé rise to dizzy heights. Some kings clearly chose to rule by fear. Indeed, all successful Anglo-Saxon leaders seemed able to instil some fear in their enemies – and perhaps in their supporters. And a king needed not just many followers but also palatial halls in which to feast and entertain them, as so clearly evoked in Beowulf. As time went on, however, with battles bloodier and the outcomes less predictable, trade might be seen as a more effective way to build or maintain fortunes.

Near to Sutton Hoo and the possible royal seat at Rendlesham, a trading settlement grew up at Gipeswic in Suffolk (today's Ipswich), probably controlled by the Wuffingas. Trading links with the nearby Rhineland appear to have brought in many luxuries, matched by exports of local goods and products. This success may even have rubbed off on Norwich to the north, whose star rose in the future as that of Ipswich fell. Rædwald certainly appears to have been ready to take advantage of the boom times, but other kings found force faster and more effective, reaping the double reward of fame and bounty.

Another factor was guile, a quality which the court poets might secretly admire but whose attribution to their ruler would have to be handled with care. As Oswy of Northumbria had shown, knowing how and when to wrong-foot an enemy could be all important, as well as how and when to dispose of a threatening friend. There were no rules of war, and advantage had to be taken where it could be. Alliances were formed out of expediency and then broken, as they've always been. And even if only one party had breached the terms of an accord, hostages might be killed or mutilated, simply as a sign that peace was at an end.

Battle involved huge risks. Kings were expected to be in the thick of the action, so that defeat in battle often meant sudden and violent death. And a royal death might itself cause an army's defeat. The risks had to be worth taking, but there was not always a choice. A king who was not prepared to defend his territory and people, revenge the death of one of his family, or respond in kind to an insult or challenge, could soon lose the support that kept him in power.

And so, a vicious circle ensued, with battle and success needing more battles and success, meeting growing defence, envy, apprehension and retaliation. And when kings fell, unless their kin or enemies got to them first, their sons would soon plot and exact revenge on those they held responsible. Whether it was the territorial aggression of Wessex or Northumbria, or the vengeance of Cadwallon, or the attempt to keep honour with Rædwald in East Anglia, the period was one of recurring struggle. Victory would lead to excess, and devastation was likely to follow. Overall in this process the increasingly Christian Anglo-Saxons proved highly successful, gradually pushing back to the extremes the Brittonic areas unprepared to accept their over-lordship.[119]

It is less clear why the Anglo-Saxon armies ultimately overcame the Britons. It was far from one-sided, even when hostilities restarted after Badon. The forces of Cadwallon proved able to give as good as they got, but seemingly only once they had allied with a ruthless

---

119 *The level of violence in these times does raise the question of whether the later Vikings were really that much worse! (A point picked up in chapter 11.)*

Mercia. But gradually the remaining Britons were overwhelmed, or driven back to the margins, leaving the 7th century as a time of restlessness and fluctuating boundaries before the main kingdoms emerged from the maelstrom. And, as more settled economies started to bring income and produce through the system, the 'opportunity cost' of cross-border war as a means of raising revenue and profile may have become too high. Kings still came and went, but over time there was more stability. At least until the Vikings changed almost everything.

The Supremacy of Mercia

A late starter, the central kingdom of Mercia consolidated the earlier gains of Penda, steadily building up its power and range during the 8th century to achieve a position of dominance in Britain south of the Humber. Once again this was largely down to two powerful kings, each with lengthy tenures: *Æthelbald* who reigned from 716 to 757, and *Offa*, king from 757 to 796. Although not without its travails, this unusual 80-year period of continuity enabled Mercia to pursue an aggressive path of enlargement and influence, backed by control of key trading centres. At one point Offa was even in direct negotiations with Charlemagne (the Great), who recognised the Mercian king (perhaps with a degree of judicious flattery) as a brother ruler.

Expanding south and with fluctuating relationships to the west and north-west, the Mercians may have been building towards a Greater Anglia, with the process aided by a common language and, after Mercia's conversion to Christianity, a common religion. Its initial weakness, of having neither natural boundaries nor coastline, became a strength as Mercia carved out resilient trade routes to and from the east and south coasts. They were so successful in this as to drive back the rulers of Essex and take over the thriving port of Lundenwic (London). Not content with that, they also beat the kings of Kent into submission to ensure trading routes through

Canterbury to the south-east, and forged routes through Wessex to Hamwich, the predecessor of Southampton.

Æthelbald and Offa – Æthelbald, who became Mercian king in 716, was the grandson of Eowa, brother (and possible co-ruler) of Penda who had done so much to build up Mercia in the previous century. Æthelbald's forceful but headstrong character saw Mercian influence extended south, but his allegedly lascivious life and later military reverses came to an end in 757, when he was assassinated, allegedly by his own bodyguards. After the ensuing confusion, Offa, possibly also a descendant of Eowa, became king. Even more ambitious than Æthelbald, Offa's aim seems to have been not merely to dominate other kingdoms but to annex and absorb them in a greater empire. Sussex and Kent were subdued, giving Offa control of Canterbury and its mint, leading to rapid coin production after 785. This was a major factor in boosting trade – and the king's income from it.

Like many other rulers of the time, Offa was an itinerant king, travelling where he could and moving his court around his domains. This meant that his chief supporters would be expected to provide board and lodging, not just for the king but also his retinue (many in tents in the manorial grounds), for as long as the king chose to stay. This must have been especially challenging in the extreme winter of 763-4, when there were months of thick snow, a time of impromptu log fires and many buildings being burned down as a result. Later, the king had a royal seat created at Tamworth, then Mercia's principal town, whose buildings may have included a huge mead hall, Beowulf-style.

Unusually for royalty of the time, Offa elevated the status of his wife, *Cynethryth,* whose image appeared on some of his coins. Thinking ahead, he sought to secure the throne for his sole legitimate son, *Ecgfrith*. To smooth the path, and help protect his son as effectively anointed by God, he sought to have the boy consecrated by an archbishop in the manner of Charlemagne. But the Archbishop of Canterbury, having seen Offa bully Kent into

EAST ANGLIA AND MERCIA

unwilling submission, refused to go along with the king's plan. Undeterred, and having provided suitably generous donations to the church, Offa secured the Pope's authority to establish a new, third, archbishopric at Lichfield. This meant that bishops north of the Thames were now answerable to Lichfield in Canterbury's place, and enabled the newly-appointed Archbishop of Lichfield to officiate at the consecration ceremony.

Offa's ambition at that point seems to have been to emulate Charlemagne. There were even inter-family marriage proposals, until Offa's presumption seems to have irked the Frankish leader, leading to tense moments before the rift was healed. Nor had Offa finished using his power elsewhere. In the words of the Chronicle, in 794 'Offa, king of the Mercians, had Æthelbert (the then king of East Anglia) beheaded.' We might guess, but don't know why. What seems to have mattered is that Offa had the power to do so.

Death finally reached Offa himself – in his bed – in July 796. Despite all his precautions, his son Ecgfrith died shortly afterwards. The respected *Alcuin of York* reflected that the blood the father shed for his son was not 'the strengthening of his kingdom but its ruin.' Perhaps divine judgement was still a force to be reckoned with. Cenwulf, who followed, continued Offa's aggressive path, especially in Kent, before his own death in 821. The initiative now passed to Wessex when its king, Ecgbert (alias Ecgbehrt), defeated Beornwulf of Mercia at *Ellendun*, near Marlborough in Wiltshire, in 825. Mercia's long supremacy was at an end, and the progress of Wessex is picked up in chapter 12.

Offa's Dyke

The origins of, and real rationale for, *Offa's Dyke* are unclear. Although some of its physical features remain, the first known *documentary* reference to it is by King Alfred's biographer, *Asser*,

179

some 100 years after Offa's heyday. In practical terms, the wall aimed to deter raiding and cattle-rustling from Wales, using the contours of the landscape to make the barrier highly visible and intimidating from the Welsh side. Up to 25 feet high, it was not so much a border as a clear defensive line not to be crossed without consent. Even if the religious divide by then largely came down to liturgy and the date of Easter, the dyke was a clear boundary between the English and the 'strangers' to their west – the *wilisc*.

The rampart and ditch are much now reduced, but the dyke's reputation is maintained by the Offa's Dyke Path walking trail that runs about 170 miles from Chepstow on the Severn Estuary through to the north Welsh coast. In many places the path runs close to a steep slope, sometimes following the bank, sometimes the ditch, and at others following a raised area between fields. The walker is rewarded, especially on the southern section, with standout views of the River Wye below huge cliffs, Tintern Abbey, the Hatterall Ridge, and the wonderful unfolding countryside between Kington and Knighton.

Yet the effort of walking the route is as nothing compared with the dyke's construction, probably by subject peoples each building a section to an agreed specification. It's been estimated that the process may have involved 4 million human hours – a figure which ignores the lives lost in the process. Today's path is at least some memorial to that immense effort – and the vision, or arrogance – of the man who used his power to bring it into being.

A summary chart for chapters 8 and 9 (part) – 600 to 700

(B = Brittonic: AS = Anglo-Saxon)

Far north		
West	**Central / East**	**Summary and dates**
Dalriada (B) (Scotti)	**Picts** (B)	*Dalriada – pushed out of Ireland by Irish High King, advance through Argyll against Picts*
North (and North Wales): 600-650		
Rheged (B) (Cumbria area) absorbed by Northumbria during later 7th century **Gwynedd** (B) – North Wales Cadwallon – 633: defeats Edwin 634: killed by Oswald	**Bernicia** (AS) and **Deira** (AS) merged into Northumbria (604) – recreated and reabsorbed **Elmet** (B) – defeated and absorbed by Northumbria from 625 **Northumbria** (AS) supreme in north from 634 on; monks and monasteries flourish (Bede and St Cuthbert)	*604 – Aethelfrith unites Bernicia with Deira to create Northumbria* *617 – Aethelfrith killed fighting East Anglia; his sons Oswald & Oswy seek refuge in Iona* *617 – Edwin king (+ over-king)* *625 – Caradoc – last king of Elmet defeated* *633 – Edwin killed at Hatfield Chase* *642 – Oswald killed at Oswestry* *664 – Synod of Whitby under Oswy* *670 (to 685) – Ecgfrith Northumbrian king* *679 – Mercia defeats Northumbria (Battle of the Trent) and dominates it for 3 years* *681 – Jarrow founded; Bede enters monastery* *685 – Ecgfrith attacks Picts, is defeated and killed*

Midlands			
Gwynedd (as above)	**Mercia** (AS)	**Lindsey**	*Mercia slow to develop but then expands fast and aggressively Battles with Northumbria Lindsey absorbed into Mercia*
Powys (B) Wales	**East Anglia** (AS)	**Essex** (AS)	*624 – Death of Rædwald (Sutton Hoo?) 630 – Accession of Sigebehrt; missions by Felix 653/4 – Death of King Anna*
	Mercia dominant		*655 – Penda killed at Winwaed Field 658 – Wulfhere king of Mercia 675 – Aethelred king of Mercia*
South			
Dumnonia (B)	**Wessex** (AS)	**Sussex** (AS) **Kent** (AS)	*Aethelbert of Kent as over-king c 600 Wessex expands west and north-east Sussex dominated by Mercia and then Wessex 628 – Wessex held at Cirencester by Mercia + by Welsh in west 688-705 – Wessex under Ine limit Dumnonia to Cornwall; Kent becomes Wessex client kingdom*

CHAPTER 10

LIFE IN ANGLO-SAXON ENGLAND

In some ways the 8th century had been an extension of the 7th. Mercia became even more dominant, Wessex moved on from the wildness of Cædwalla, East Anglia lapsed from glory to subservience, and Northumbria, with its own crises, largely held the line in the north. The Channel and the North Sea seem to have seen more trade than raid, and the worst of the incursions from Ireland had passed. The Welsh border continued to be contested, especially when power changed hands within Wales, but with less effect elsewhere after Cadwallon – for a time. The Christian church, with its supporting monasteries, nunneries and acolytes, was expanding its holy writ and coordinating its practices.

While this chapter pauses to consider something of the life of the people at that time, an overview is far from easy over such vast timescales and distances. Life in York, for example, would have similarities to, and major differences from, life in Wessex, Kent or East Anglia. The basics may have been similar, but much would have depended on the when and where, and who was then in the ascendancy.

The land and the seasons

We've seen that the great Roman towns of Britain, decaying through lack of upkeep, held few attractions for the Anglo-Saxons. Grand senate halls and temples were not why they had come to Britain. But the physical evidence here is scanty because, whereas Romans built mostly in stone (and brick[120]), of which some remains survive, Anglo-Saxons largely built in wood which has long since decayed. Houses were, by now, larger and typically rectangular, sometimes sunk into the ground, with sturdier walls of upright wooden planks or wattle and daub, and thatched roofs. Some would have the animals behind screens at one end, providing some level of security and extra warmth – with all that went with it! Some would house extended families; other buildings might be used as workshops and store rooms.

For the most part, therefore, archaeologists are left with just fragments as clues, such as burial grounds, cremation pots, kitchen middens, grave goods, and shards of pottery. Buildings might be deciphered from hard foundations or post-holes, the indentations in the ground into which upright supporting timbers were fitted. And improved aerial-based survey techniques are now giving us greater insights into possible land layout and use.

The Anglo-Saxon preference was to settle outside towns where roads or drove trails were at hand, or in fertile river valleys. Strip fields were introduced close to small clusters of housing, some of which grew into nucleated villages.[121] The key unit of measurement was the *hide*, the amount of land deemed necessary to support a household. Initially assumed to be around 120 acres, a hide was often later measured by its expected income, which changed from being paid in kind by produce and/or services to a monetary value when reliable coinage made this practicable. The elites would rely on the physical work or income from those who occupied and farmed the land, but would be expected to account to their lord or the king for their own dues.

---

120 *The art of brickmaking appears to have been lost in Britain for centuries after the Roman exodus.*

121 *i.e. Formed or gathered around a central area.*

As the population increased and cultivation became widespread, some lords built up large estates which then split into smaller units and parishes, often with their own churches. In the process, parish boundaries became important, with the religious aspects of settled tenure being celebrated in the annual procession of 'beating the bounds'. Place names with suffixes like *-ham* and *-ton* became common to indicate settlements, along with *-stead* for a subsidiary farm, *-ley* a clearing in the woods and *-stoke* for a dairy farm.

A rudimentary land law developed. A king with land at his disposal might grant a formal charter of a number of hides to a church or monastery, or to an individual in return for service or some form of rent in money, specified produce or service. For the most part, land was transferred with what was on it, including the buildings and the people. In effect the hides were transferred as a 'going concern' – complete with their occupiers. The free remained free to move, the slaves were owned by, and tied to, their masters, and the peasants were tied to the land. But a landowner wishing to move on was limited in what could be taken, and was obliged to leave the land fertile.

From the 8th century onwards (until the Norman Conquest, when some fundamentals changed), land became more of a market commodity – to be bought and sold in its own right, increasingly without reference to the king. This was still not absolute *ownership* as we now think of it, but a right of possession with some benefits and subject to certain conditions. These conditions varied, but might require army service, hosting the king and his retinue, being obliged to build bridges, or having to construct fortifications. Land possession was thus a privilege with potential major costs, from which many religious foundations sought exemption.

The early Anglo-Saxon preoccupation with farming was reflected in the agricultural calendar. January was the *After-yule* month and February marked the return of the sun. March, named for the Roman god of war, indicated the start of the fighting season. Anglo-Saxon April was linked with *Eostre*, goddess of the radiant dawn, later adapted as Easter. By then it was spring, time for the first ploughing with teams of oxen, sowing of crops and digging out ditches. May was the *month of three milkings* a day (following the lushness of the grass) and June the time to set out on travels, with July the second travelling month. August saw hedge-laying, repairing and weeding, followed by the holy month of September to bring in the harvest, plus threshing, thatching, more ploughing, and sowing of wheat. October's full moon might be a 'hunter's moon', giving enough light to track and catch well-fed deer for the winter larder. Then preparations would be made for winter, including bringing in the livestock before choosing animals for the winter sacrifice (the 'blood month' of November), or for salting down in readiness for the months of cold and damp. December was *Before-Yule* with 'Mothers' Night' to celebrate the birth of the new solar year.

Between times cats, dogs, geese and chickens ran free with the children, while pigs grazed in woodland glades. But this was no rural idyll. Deeper in the woods bears, wolves and wild boar could still be encountered, and in the fields rustlers could be a constant menace for owners of livestock. There was always the risk of a bad harvest and consequent failure to pay the rent, quite apart from the lack of food and nourishment needed to live on. And as ever, farming was hard work, with its effect on human health. About 20% of the population did not make it to eighteen and only about 6% beyond sixty. For women there was the huge risk involved in childbirth, especially for girls marrying young, and for men the risks of death or disfigurement in battle. But when they did survive childhood, by now the average age at death for women was around 31 and for men 38.[122]

---

122 *A major improvement from centuries earlier, and not dissimilar from many industrial areas in early 19th century England.*

Social structure

Even if the term *feudalism* is contested today, we can fairly say that most Anglo-Saxon settlements were based on *hierarchical* principles, with higher-status individuals firmly in charge. By 550 such tribal dynasties had developed in many areas in the country, even some in walled towns, with the overlord of large groups being expected, if need be, to lead his people in battle. They were his *cynn* (pronounced 'kin') and he became their *cyning* or king.

The lord was the centre of everything, literally 'the provider of bread' in Anglo-Saxon times. His hall would normally be the hub of the community where local roads would meet, the focal point around which churches were built and markets held. Centred on his hall, the lord dispensed land, weapons and justice, committed to share food and drink with his chief retainers and to provide protection for the rest of the community. Nearby would be the smiths, craftsmen and craftswomen who would provide the necessaries to enable the farms and workshops to operate and the markets to flourish.

The bond between lord and his people, deeply embedded in the Anglo-Saxons' Germanic roots, carried through into Britain. A slave had almost no rights. Next above the slave, the *ceorl* ('churl') would hold land under a lord, and above the ceorl *freemen* could hold land in their own right. Most freemen, however, had the obligation to fight for the lord and provide him rent, food, ale and livestock.[123] In each case the loyalty was personal to the lord, but once established, that loyalty was absolute, with men expected to give their lives in the lord's service. As the Roman Tacitus had observed, possibly with some degree of approval, the chiefs fought for victory and the followers fought for their chief. And there were no half measures. An individual who was lordless was an outcast,

---

123 Only men with some status would fight in the army. There is no (current) evidence that women did.

at best shunned by all, and at worst someone to be hunted down. Being an outcast was regarded as the most miserable state anyone could reach.

A lord's chief companions would expect weapons, horses and other armour (known as *heregeat* or *heriot*) on loan in return for their service, along with the right to feast in the lord's hall. The companions would be expected to avenge their lord if he were killed or injured, which might lead to feuds lasting generations. Equally, if the lord were exiled, his chief companions might be expected to share that exile. And if any retainer turned against and murdered his lord, as sometimes happened, the offender could expect to be hunted down and killed mercilessly in turn.

Outside the settlement, as time went on, heavier work might leave lasting visible traces, such as barren land after peat removal, silver and iron ore extraction and smelting, or major pottery kilns. While seeking self-sufficiency, most communities had to import basics. These included metals for tools and salt for preserving foods, such that saltpans became estates of value and salt-pedlars essential middlemen. Likewise iron had to be sourced and traded, for anything from basic tools and agricultural equipment up to high quality weapons. A range of ordinary smiths to specialist craftsmen might then gather around larger communities.

Trade exchange brought in items unavailable locally while, higher up the social scale, luxuries were traded internationally, as far as the Mediterranean and beyond. This attracted local kings keen to extract taxes from the process. Internationally, people might trade with Merovingian coins from France, or small, thick silver coins called *sceattas*[124] (often known as pennies), minted around key North Sea trading areas. Subsequently, kings like Offa of Mercia moved to control the mints and imprint their own stylised images on the coinage.

---

124 *Generally pronounced without sounding the 'c' – e.g. 'see-at-as' or perhaps even 'see-dars'.*

Law, Religion and Art

The Anglo-Saxons brought with them many of their old laws and traditions. Some of these were detailed and prescriptive, with rules often designating people's rights and obligations by their class or occupation. Many of the early kings, often with a Christian subtext, then issued charters or law codes on specific subjects. Although many royal charters survive, most law codes have been lost, with limited clues as to their contents. But other laws were customary and largely unrecorded, making experts who actually knew the law highly valued.

Even so, early Anglo-Saxon justice tended to be rough and ready, based on feud and vengeance as a means of maintaining loyalty and keeping the peace. As the Christian Church grew, however, it encouraged a more formal approach, geared towards compensation rather than retribution, especially for church property and people. This encouraged physical retribution to be gradually replaced in many, but not all, cases by compensation payments called *wergild*. But the cost of atonement depended not just on the type of injury caused but also on the status of the victim. Valuing the lives of the poor at a fraction of those of the rich thus reinforced the power of those who already had it, and could afford to pay.

The early pagan Anglo-Saxons were highly conscious of the power of their gods, a pluralistic group who could be as wayward as their Roman counterparts. There was a wide-ranging pantheon of divinities and half-divinities who might need to be placated, and many varied tales of their powers. Their principal gods were *Odin* (in Old Norse and *Woden* in Old Saxon) and *Thor*, both associated with war. The muscular Thor, seen as similar to Roman Jupiter or the Greco-Roman Hercules, was most famous for his hammer, the infamous *Mjölnir*. Thor was associated with everything from wisdom and learning to war and frenzy, with his protection seen as vital to protect the lord's hall, his warriors and, by extension, his people. His main creatures were the wolf, raven and eagle, often used in poetry and sagas to represent their master. His symbols included the spear and whetstone, with occasional human sacrifices still made to honour him. *Freyr,* symbolised by horse and boar (and not to be confused with his twin sister *Frejya*), was the god of fertility, marriage and children, while *Loki* was the purveyor of mischief.

This range and unpredictability might in time have made Christianity seem an attractive alternative belief system to some! It was simpler, its God had, at times, been shown to be very powerful, and faith carried the hope of salvation and the joys of a peaceful eternal life. Even so, many were reluctant to abandon the old ways, preferring not to change or hedging their bets by following both ways. But once a king converted and ruled in the name of God, it would have become increasingly hard for his subjects not to have followed suit, however reluctantly.

As Christianity grew, it needed churches and those churches needed land and income. Land not given by the king was often allocated by the lord or his thanes, but income needed some new approaches. One such, alongside a fee for burial in church ground, was the *church-scot*. This was a Norse term for a payment, often in the form of grain or other crops, calculated by reference to the number of hides possessed by each landowner in the relevant area.[125] There was also the church *tithe*, perhaps voluntary to start with, but becoming compulsory from about the 10th century, with severe penalties for non-payment. The major religious growth, however, seems to have been in monasteries and nunneries, which flourished from the 7th century onwards.

For all the talk of the Dark Ages, the Anglo-Saxons were remarkably creative, notably in the richness of their language and poetry, and in their artistic designs. Patterns symbolised connections and

---

125 *Exempt estates would be 'scot-free', i.e. free of any cost, a term later applied to criminal cases where someone escaped without penalty.*

LIFE IN ANGLO-SAXON ENGLAND

movement, with and between people, the current and the past, the real world and the mythical world, the human world and the animal world, the world of the living and the world of the dead. Whether on stone, manuscript pages, jewellery or even swords, patterns added ornament and meaning. Moulded by its new situation, the Anglo-Saxon language adopted more versatile speech patterns, progressively dropping much of the harsh grammatical formality of its Germanic roots. Religious themes inspired people to bring to life a more radiant vision of God's creation, helping them think and feel beyond their daily travails. A faith in heavenly justice, exemplified in the majestic order of the sun, moon and universe, could all make sense, as did the need to keep at bay the devil's brew of sin, pride, and manifold other human evils.

For those brought up on Beowulf, with its emphasis on selflessness and fairness in the face of evil, one might almost imagine the glory and power of the mead hall transferring to the rafters of the parish church in a new blend of secular and spiritual consciousness.

As they adapted, from the challenge of dealing with imagined monsters to the themes of light transcending darkness that resonate in church, rural people might have grown in their faith. They could start to believe that the sun *would* rise again the next day, that summer *would* return, that sadness *can* be mixed with joy and that a good life lived with faith *could* be repaid many times over. Such a sense of enlightenment would help fuel education, notably for those able and prepared to commit themselves to the church. With many fine scholars honing their skills in Latin, poetry and linguistic imagery, there was a surge in biography and religious philosophy. Wide-ranging correspondence encouraged debate and the sharing of ideas internationally. In the late 9th century King Alfred declared, with some pride, that many in his day could read what was written in English – even if they might not be able to write it.

London – Having declined after 410, the revival of London may have started with Mellitus, consecrated first bishop of London in 604,[126] when he used old Roman stone to help build his new church at St Paul's. Next to spot the opportunities were the traders, who appreciated the Thames as a valuable and well-connected shipping route. They saw the shoreline to the west on the curve of the river, around today's Charing Cross and the Strand[127] to Temple, as an ideal trade harbour. This became known as *Lundenwic*, which developed quickly from the mid-7th century, soon matching other key cities across the northern Continent, fuelled by internationally accepted coinage.

At Lundenwic new wharves were built, with roads to carry goods to and from them, around which homes, shops, streets, lanes and alleys grew up haphazardly. Just outside this bustling trading area, farmers and monasteries alike produced a rich surplus of crops and animals, helping the local population rise to around 7,000. Inevitably such a prize attracted the attention of the kings whose competing territories lay all around the vibrant new market. Essex, Mercia, Kent and Wessex by turns sought pre-eminence there. And with control came the ability to take a royal cut of the benefits, whether by tolls on connecting roads or on trade within the area. Steadily, kings began to realise that control of Lundenwic might afford them not just the financial advantage of direct access to the sea lanes and international trade routes, but also valuable political and economic power.

Proto-England in 800

Although in 800 Mercia was near its peak, it proved unable to build on, or even maintain, its ascendancy. As with Northumbria in Bede's time, past success was no guarantee of future performance. Nor could anyone have predicted what was to come. At the risk of indulging

---

126 *And, later, Archbishop of Canterbury.*

127 *Strand remains German for beach.*

in so-called *counterfactual* history, we might ask if it was inevitable that the Anglo-Saxons would become supreme in southern Britain. If *everything* else had been exactly the same, there is no reason to expect any different result. But a change in just one critical factor might have shifted the balance entirely. For example, the forceful Franks, although well ahead of many of their neighbours, were minimally engaged in the battle for Britain in this long period. But by 800 Charlemagne was at the height of his power as Holy Roman Emperor. Had Britain in 800 been in the same parlous state as it was in 550, Charlemagne's ambitions might have been very different, as the future Danish and Norman invasions were to show.

Two other factors might be mentioned here. The first was human, in the form of kings. Those who achieved power seem to have done so by force of character and ruthlessness. But when a king died, or a new king arose in a neighbouring kingdom, much might change – very quickly. The second factor was ecclesiastical, as Christianity spread erratically but implacably through the land. That caused its own conflicts, whether Christian versus pagan or Celtic versus Roman or ascetic versus overbearing and indulgent. But as it spread, Christianity provided a support system, almost like a spiritual suit of clothes, for the downtrodden. It was also taken as a God-given right to rule for kings whose legitimacy might otherwise be questioned.

In many ways, as it was imposed and adapted, Christianity helped underpin a new hierarchy that lasted for a millennium. This was a system which many people today might consider unequal and unfair. But that risks imposing today's values on times that were completely different, while undervaluing the framework and support which the religion must have given to individuals and society.

Meanwhile a significant new force was growing in the wings – the Northmen.

CHAPTER 11

ENTER THE NORTHMEN

790 to 900

We need to remember that, as with the initial Anglo-Saxons, much of the history of the Vikings in Britain was written by the victims, not the victors. But before describing their attacks, this chapter goes behind the scenes to try to understand who the Vikings really were, why they came, and why they came when they did. This will make it easier to follow the succeeding phases of activity which interleave both with Britain's neighbours and the rise of Wessex described in the next chapter. For that reason the timeline is set out at the end of that chapter (12).

The 'Viking Age'

The start point here is that *viking* – or a'viking as they called it – was an activity, not a race or people. Nor was there a neat 'Viking Age' (commonly defined as 793 to 1066) which tracked the later Anglo-Saxon Age. The reality was that 'Viking' attacks and settlements affected many countries over long periods with different phases of activity and intent. This meant that the participants, objectives and results might change from one period and area to the next. And the two regions most directly affected were themselves in the course of transition – the Franks into French and the Anglo-Saxons into English.

ENTER the NORTHMEN

And as to dates, the Viking inheritance lasted well beyond 1066 in Ireland, parts of Scotland and the northern islands. Nor was the attack on Lindisfarne in 793 the first; it was more that Lindisfarne was the event which first brought home to people the power of the Northmen.

Today, when we start to think about the Vikings, we feel their enormous gravitational pull in terms of history and legend. 'Viking' conjures up a vision in the way 'Anglo-Saxon' or 'Norman' simply doesn't. This highlights a basic duality. On the one hand, the Vikings are seen as bloodthirsty adventurers ready to murder, rape and pillage with abandon. On the other, we seem unable to get enough of them! Indeed, some people aspire to the cachet of part Scandinavian DNA to claim some Viking heritage. How do we reconcile these conflicting senses of outrage, decency and identity? Do we really empathise with the Vikings as bold adventurers while hating their brutality?

And how might the emerging English have felt at the time? As archaeologist Neil Price puts it: "The Anglo-Saxons knew that this Viking world-view was not so far removed from what theirs had been not so long before, and maybe, under the surface, still was."[128] Were the Vikings holding up an uncomfortable mirror to the Anglo-Saxons' own basic nature?

The successive Viking invasions from the 9th century onwards inevitably added to the Scandinavian bloodline in Britain. Those who dropped their swords and harnessed their ploughshares became settlers, often marrying local women, with successive generations contributing to the great diversity of English DNA. The Viking blood that ravaged France as much as England at this time was also diluted by Frankish blood as the fearsome Northmen became the implacable Normans. What is less clear is the point at which the Vikings who settled could be said to have become English in England or French in France.

---

128 *Quoted by Thomas Williams (2017) p 142 fn 32.*

In 2022[129] the results of cutting-edge DNA sequencing from more than 400 'Viking' skeletons caused great surprise when published. The findings from archaeological sites across Europe and Greenland indicated that many 'Vikings' had brown, rather than blonde, hair, with considerable numbers coming from outside Scandinavia, even before the 'Viking Age.' Some had origins in Asia and Southern Europe and others came later from Scotland and Ireland. As one report's lead author noted: 'Scottish and Irish people [had] integrated into Viking society well enough for individuals with no Scandinavian ancestry to receive a full Viking burial, in Norway and Britain.' Viking influence may have been immense, but just as not all Vikings were Scandinavian, not all Scandinavians were Vikings. 'Viking DNA' is therefore really an illusion.

Viking ethos and society

Accordingly, it now appears that the people who went *a'viking* came from a wide area of Scandinavia and beyond. Initially they seemed to act in autonomous and semi-amorphous groups, coming together and splitting apart as opportunity or need arose. What brought them together was the drive for adventure, the readiness to fight, and the lure of riches. They were of their time, and in that time they fundamentally changed the world they impacted.

But timing is again important. The early Viking forays were in the late 8th century, just as the Carolingian Empire was reaching its zenith. The Franks had a head start in nation building, but the other national identities affected were mostly in their infancy; *England* itself would really only come together later, partly in opposition to the Vikings. The future *Ireland* and *Scotland* were, like England, also shaped by Viking (especially Norse) activity.

In many ways it was the Vikings who helped to mould many nation

---

129 *The six-year research project, published in* Nature, *was led, or supported, by the Universities of Cambridge, Copenhagen and Bristol.*

states, and those nation states that were ultimately to make the Vikings redundant.

The term seems to have originated from the old Norse 'vik', meaning a bay or creek from which people set sail.[130] Thus *'viking'* in Old Norse became the action of embarking on a sea voyage. This was originally as traders, before the lure of potential riches and targets encouraged them to turn raiders. In Old Norse, their main language, *vikingr* described someone away from home on some type of active service. Those involved included outcasts from their homelands, perhaps banished for crimes or family rivalries. But their return home with new fortunes, a band of associates and growing reputations, could transform them into heroes, whose exploits might be fostered in folklore and polished beside Norse firesides.

Nor did those they attacked call them *Vikings* at the time, but *Danes* or *Norsemen* in England, or *Danois (Danes), Northmen* or *Normanii* in France (from whom Normandy takes its name). Often to Christian communities they were just *heathens* or *pagans*. It was only in the 19th century, when the Victorians were casting round for old-style heroes, that 'the Vikings' were reinvented as fearless marauding raiders with long red hair and beards, and falsely endowed with horned helmets to enhance the image. Since then, 'Viking' has become a brand which sells books, brings in sponsorship, and draws crowds to *Viking* events. Marketing today seems as powerless to resist the Vikings as their original victims.

Being a Viking meant adopting a way of life. It involved strength and courage; the ability to be part of a longship crew tossed around in rough seas; to wade in through the rocks and shallows to unknown territory; to roar, fight, feast and drink with the best and the worst; and

---

130 *The old Norse 'vik' appears to have similar origins to the old English 'wic', meaning a camp or trading place. Examples include Aldwych – old-wic – the ancient port in London, Sandwich in Kent, and Anglo-Saxon Eoforwic (later Viking Jorvik or York.)*

to kill or be killed at almost any time. They were drawn by adventure and the pursuit of wealth, with determined leaders keen to grow their own power and influence.

In addition to a mastery of water and navigation allied to strength and fearlessness, Vikings were mostly well briefed and highly tactical. Learning where dissention existed, they were always ready to exploit divisions among others to their own advantage. Bolstered by a team ethos and untrammelled by Christian consciences, they were powerful people bound together through thick and thin. They played by their own rules, and needed no pretext other than the pursuit of glory and wealth. Although their superstition and heroic beliefs drove them to extraordinary feats, they also weighed the odds, often listening carefully to their spiritual advisers. If the runes were bad, action might be delayed or even avoided. But their runecasters were also men of the world, and this was no blind faith. It could be unwise always to counsel caution, or too often to encourage attack which might lead to defeat.

For young men coming of age, going *a'viking* could be a rite of passage, like a 'gap year' abroad. There was the added hope of returning rich, famous and more powerful, able to settle and farm where they liked, an especial lure for younger sons with limited prospects. For others, the gap year was an apprenticeship that turned into a career. As men on the make, Vikings could be as fierce with their friends as with their enemies. Brothers might kill one another but any outsider trying his hand against a father, son or even brother could be pursued relentlessly by the rest of the family. With multiple unions and interbreeding, the bloodlines became difficult to keep apart, causing feuds that could reach over wide areas.

Over time, some of the raiders stayed longer, where their prizes, human or economic, drew them to enjoy what they had taken. For others, wanderlust and a taste for adventure kept them exploring further afield. Iceland was settled, not without accident and hardship, and even Greenland for a long time, but Newfoundland proved a bridge too far, with a combination of sickness and Native Americans driving the intruders away. The Scottish Islands were colonised, and the explorers forged seaways round to Ireland, where *Dublin* became established as a major Viking base and European slave-trading capital.

The east coast of England had been raided and well settled by the Anglo-Saxons, but that did not prevent successive Viking attacks down the coasts and up the rivers. Huge sums were raised in threatened areas to try to buy off Viking raids, often serving only to encourage the marauders to return. France was at least equally attractive, its major rivers being easily navigable by the longships. With most settlements initially unprepared for attack from the water, riverside monasteries proved grist to the Viking mill. And as the raiders moved down the Seine, Rouen and then Paris were attacked and burnt, sometimes being torched again when the attackers came back down river.

Then there was religion. The Scandinavians were deeply imbued with their old ways and Norse gods. Time and again they were confronted and counter-attacked by Christian forces on the coasts of Britain and the rivers of France. Christian sites therefore became almost an extra incentive. But gradually, for the raiders who chose to accept terms and settle, conversion might give them a legitimacy that centuries of raiding and pillaging would not. And when they converted, being Vikings, they would not wish to be less fierce in their Christianity than anyone else. Like the Franks before them, the ex-Viking, now Christian, rulers came in time to enforce the faith that they had adopted with the zeal they had previously shown in massacring its adherents. Especially as, in north central France, these Northmen became Normans, they continued many of the Viking traditions of their Viking forefathers in new, Christian, clothing.

Although their lives were typically centred round the home and farm, some Scandinavian women may have had more independence than in many other societies of the time. The moment the man of the family left on an expedition, the woman was expected to take over, in addition to her many other responsibilities. Even so, women were generally not treated as equal to men. They could not appear in court and, although they could divorce, remarry, and receive inheritances, these rights were limited. They were also unable to pass on their property by will, and few women had any real political power. While in theory women were able to choose their marriage partners, their fathers often took charge of the selection, with a contest between father and daughter always likely to cause trouble. Where there was a shortage of young men, however, a degree of competition between several women might not be uncommon. And they would have been very young, often marrying at twelve to fifteen years old.

It now seems that some women may also have joined Viking parties as so-called shield-maidens, female warriors who fought alongside and shared the responsibilities of male fighters. Researchers from Uppsala University used chromosome analysis on a set of 10th century remains from Sweden to discover that the presumed male figure buried with full military accompaniments was actually female. This must have been someone with enough strength and authority to be accepted on board. But, given Viking values, and until research reveals otherwise, we might assume that women on raiding expeditions were very much the exception.

Viking ships and crews

From early ash-wood canoes with ox-hide outers, Scandinavian ship design progressed rapidly, with different types of ship for different uses. The marauding longships that developed were light, narrow and fast, with a shallow draught that enabled them to make lightning raids on shores and into river estuaries, and to depart again as quickly. Trading and cargo vessels tended to be broader and slower, geared to handling goods. The later warships of the Viking fleet might range from 50 to over 100 feet in length, hulls being clinker-built with overlapping planks. They were steered by a single oar on the right-hand side near the stern – known as the 'steering board' or 'starboard'. In warships, martial figures adorned the bows and stern, giving a clear impression of warlike intent. Sails and oars could be used according to circumstances, enabling a considerable turn of speed when required.

In the absence of reliable navigation systems, especially for longitude, navigators preferred to follow a visible coastline. If in open water, however, such as crossing the North Sea, they would aim to sail on a west/east axis to gauge their position. Straying too far north or south could lead them far astray, with the risk of being carried into the unknown. There was typically little or no shelter for a longship crew from the elements, though rudimentary coverings might be made for a chieftain. Each of those aboard, at least in raiding ships, would double as crew and warrior, bringing on board helmet, drinking horn, axe, blanket and a sea chest containing a few personal belongings. If there were no built-in benches, these sea chests could double as seats for the crew to man the oars. Shields, removable when the ship was at sea, could be placed along the vessels' sides, both for protection and to inspire fear.

Crew numbers varied, as did the number of ships in a fleet. The men near the bows were often particularly adept at hand to hand fighting, either in combat against other ships, normally close to the coast, or in making rapid sorties onto land. When engaging enemy ships, the intention would be, where advantageous, to capture rather than destroy, with both ships and their occupants being potentially valuable commodities.

When not fighting, the Vikings could, of course, excel at feasting and drinking, adding another challenge to their leaders! Such men were best not left idle for long, so that their leaders would be constantly alert for the next opportunity. To retain leadership it would be necessary to keep fighting and have gold and silver to distribute; the leader who had no battles to fight might have no men to fight when he needed them. In Beowulf terms, the ravens, wolves and eagles beloved of mythology needed to be fed – and fed again and again. As a result, violence might perpetuate itself until there was a more powerful reason to stop.

This culture was supported by the belief that those who died bravely in battle would be rewarded with a place in Valhalla, where a future of fighting and feasting might have seemed more attractive than some eternal, but uneventful, after-life. And Vikings were brave, but rarely stupid. They liked to fight, but not at any cost. If the opposition could be cowed into submission, especially to surrender land or pay large sums of money or valuables, this was likely to suit a Viking leader well. But if threats did not achieve their objective, then what followed could be a grisly way to spread the message, so that next time, in theory, it would be easier for all. But, as with leaders anywhere, if the red mist of anger came down on them, the results could be horrifying.

Warriors were expected to own their personal weapons, with their local chief providing for those who could not. The main weapons – spear, sword and battle-axe – were used both for fighting and to display the wealth or renown of their owner with intricate decorations of silver, bronze or copper. Spears had varying lengths and blades, capable of being used to deadly effect in trained hands. Some highly skilled spearmen were said to be able to catch a spear in flight and hurl it back, almost in one movement. More expensive to make, swords could be up to three feet long, with blades initially of wrought iron and mild steel twisted and forged together, often with a highly decorated and individual hilt. Battle-axes were short, capable of being used whilst holding a shield, or long-handled, requiring both hands to wield in hit-and-run raids from behind defended positions. Shields themselves, mostly decorated with simple patterns or perhaps mythological scenes, were initially round, measuring up to three feet across. They were made of leather or occasionally metal, with a handle riveted inside and protected by a metal boss outside.[131]

---

[131] *Kite-shaped shields seem to have come later, from around the millennium, being designed to give more protection to the legs.*

Hand to hand combat was the norm, with numbers varying, typically up to thousands on each side. As things became serious, warriors would stand together with shields interlocked to make a shield wall, starting an engagement by throwing missiles and firing arrows before engaging in hand-to-hand fighting. Frequently, a heavily armed phalanx of men would seek to drive a wedge through enemy lines, typically aiming at, or close to, their opponents' leader.

The Berserkers, those normally in the forefront, might go into battle in bearskins, believing that Odin would protect them and give them superhuman powers. They would drive themselves into a frenzy before an attack, biting into their shields and being able to withstand great pain whilst the frenzy was upon them, giving us the modern word berserk.

Fighters had to look the part too, and inevitably tastes in hairstyles and facial hair changed with the times. We can get some idea from the descriptive nicknames, taken seriously, of some kings and chieftains. Harald Bluetooth could then be distinguished from Harold Finehair; and Sweyn Forkbeard (indicating a pitchfork beard) might mark him out from the many other Sweyns of his time. In the east, while many Swedish Vikings (Rus) were clean-shaven, others grew beards long enough to plait like the tails of groomed horses.

Some Scandinavians clearly built up a degree of wealth, as evidenced in caches of valuables, either buried for safekeeping or interred as grave goods. In extreme cases, such as with major chieftains or their close relatives, a complete ship with valuable contents might be buried, Sutton Hoo style. This accentuated the deceased's wealth, along with the spiritual image of the ship sailing into the afterlife, carrying the body of the deceased complete with armour, helmet, and richly embellished sword. Buried treasure, however, as every child knows, attracts pirates, and archaeologists in Sweden have detected that burial mounds from the 5th and 6th centuries seem to have been robbed much more than those from the 7th and 8th centuries. If this pattern holds true overall, it suggests periods – as in Britain – of relative anarchy being followed by a degree of order and stability from 7th century onwards before things deteriorated again.

Britain and Europe in 800

Charlemagne – While Mercia was asserting its dominance in Britain, much of western continental Europe had been falling under the sway of the Frankish Merovingian dynasty, culminating with the rise of *Charlemagne the Great* (c. 747 to 815) and his Holy Roman Empire. When Charlemagne became King of the Franks in 768, he led a series of campaigns to unite most of western Europe under a sole emperor for the first time since the fall of the Western Roman Empire. Even if, as the prolific French wit and writer, Voltaire, remarked, the Carolingian Empire was neither holy, nor Roman nor an empire, it held sway over an enormous area. This included German Saxony and a border on the neck of the Jutland peninsula, a near existential threat to the Danes at that time.

Much of this was down to Charlemagne himself: imposing, energetic, courageous, capable and determined. His Carolingian Renaissance introduced major advances in administration, education (building schools and standardising curricula), inspired a boom in architecture, contributed to the preservation of religious and literary works and the advancement of writing, and standardised currency. He also found time for family, with five wives in succession and, reportedly, at least eighteen children. This inevitably raised issues of succession, where, despite prior experience, he followed the precedent of the Merovingians in dividing the empire between three sons.

Denmark – Of Denmark after 800, apart from some rich archaeology, little is known for certain. Charlemagne's muscular Christianity may have been counter-attacked by King Godfrey of Denmark around that time. Soon after that, having had his Danes raid the Baltic shores and then Frisia without recognising the dissent he was creating, Godfrey was murdered by his own people. Denmark, having had an over-mighty ruler, then seems to have suffered decades of internal strife and even civil war with many sons of contending royal and would-be royal families vying for supremacy.

This early 9th century anarchy in Denmark would have created ideal conditions for contenders excluded from power to launch alternative Viking careers. It is probably therefore no coincidence that Viking activity in Britain and France surged in the mid-9th century. It was to take another 100 or so years before a single royal dynasty emerged in Denmark, with authority over Jutland and the Danish Islands. And when that did finally happen, it turned out to have even more serious repercussions for England.

Viking inroads: Phase 1 – c 790 to 850

Lindisfarne – Just one report of undefended wealth reaching the wrong ears might have been enough to set in motion events that were to shatter the small religious community at Lindisfarne. If the monks who gazed out over the North Sea had any idea of what was happening across the waters, they may have believed that any threat was too far away and that their faith would see them through. We should recall, however, that most 'English' history of that period was written by Christian monks or scribes, appalled at the descent of their land into nightmare. What we would now see as atmospheric events or Northern Lights were interpreted after the event as heavenly signs of impending disaster. The Chronicle for 793, for example, refers to sheet lightning, whirlwinds, flying dragons and famine. The respected prelate Alcuin, like Gildas before him, saw events as God's retribution against one of the holiest places for the sins of society.

What happened was that, in 793, a small fleet of Viking ships landed out of the blue on Lindisfarne, ransacked its treasures, killed some of the monks and others they encountered, and fired the buildings. They then made off with all the precious objects they could find, probably with some hapless captives as slaves. Even if the details are dramatic, the onslaught was devastating to people, property and the sense of heavenly protection. There is still discussion as to whether the attack was in June or early in the year, perhaps from an existing base on or near Orkney, the ships hugging the British mainland coast as they went.

Lindisfarne was not the first Viking attack on Britain. There had been a (possibly isolated) Viking-type raid on Thanet in the 750s,[132] and again against Weymouth in 789, when the local reeve went to remonstrate with some unruly mariners only to find sudden death at their hands. Many other attacks had already taken place elsewhere, especially around the Baltic.

Despite the savagery, Lindisfarne continued after the attack to operate much as before. It was nearly a hundred years[133] before the bones of St Cuthbert were threatened enough to be moved from the island and taken overland on an epic journey to sanctuary. Nor was Lindisfarne the only holy site to be desecrated. Two years later, in 795, Vikings raided monasteries in Ireland and on the remote Scottish island of Iona. Further raids in 802 and 806 finally impelled the monks of Iona to move to an inland site at Kells in County Meath.[134] By that time the Vikings had found that attacks on monastery feast days were likely to be especially effective in securing maximum booty and slaves.

Horrific though they were, the attacks at this stage were only occasional, with no indication as to what might follow. And the

---

132 *In 826 Thanet was devastated and its community largely wiped out by Vikings.*

133 *Considered to be 875 when the Lindisfarne monastery was actually abandoned.*

134 *From which the famous beautifully illustrated Book of Kells takes its name.*

ENTER the NORTHMEN

evidence of actual atrocities in terms of archaeology is still limited. The message that resistance was likely to be futile would soon have been passed on, but whether death was often better than slavery might be a matter of chance. And it was not always one-sided. The marauders came to know that not all their attacks would succeed, and they needed to be ready to accept the same brutality as they meted out to their victims.

Scandinavian groups appear already to have colonised the islands of Orkney, about a day's sail from Norway's West Coast.[135] And the raiders themselves varied. The Norse were mostly more active around the north coasts, the Scottish islands and Ireland, with the Danes a stronger presence in south and east Britain. Around the coasts and islands either side of the Irish Sea, Norse-led and Danish-led Vikings sometimes cooperated and sometimes competed. For the next century or more this constituted a combustible mix with sudden changes of direction, unpredictable action, and unexpected alliances.

After a time, a pattern began to emerge. The element of surprise, warships crewed by fierce warriors suddenly appearing over the horizon and onto the shore, meant that lightning raids could be stunningly successful. Initially the raiders could kill and plunder as they chose, making a fast escape before meeting any major resistance. Attacks then spread from the coast, where people might be more wary, up rivers and estuaries where raids might be less expected. The shallow draught, speed and manoeuvrability of their ships gave the attackers great advantages. Further inland, they could spread out quickly as a land army, supported by fast horses (often captured), using their fleet as a moving supply base.

830 to 850 – In the anarchy after Godfrey's death, many Danish renegades went on the rampage. Closest to them was *Hamburg* on the River Elbe, just beyond the Danish border. By the time they attacked

---
[135] *And possibly Shetland, maybe even before the main Viking arrivals.*

the port there in the 830s, the Danes already had a fleet of several hundred ships. Next was *Frisia*, former homeland of many Anglo-Saxons, where, alongside the vital commercial route of the Rhine delta, lay the important trading and financial town of *Dorestad*, near modern Utrecht. Near its peak when the Danes arrived in the 830s, Dorestad's heyday turned out to be short-lived before the raiders progressed along the coast to France.

After passing the mighty chalk cliffs of the Pays de Caux (modern Dieppe and its neighbours), the Viking leaders must have relished sight of the huge mouth of the River Seine, which soon became one of their favourite hunting grounds. After their first incursion in the early 840s, the navigability of the river and its bankside treasures brought them back time and again in the following years. In 843, having rounded Finisterre ('the end of the earth') in Brittany, one Danish fleet reached the Atlantic mouth of the mighty Loire. In many of these areas, after the initial surprise, they met with resistance but returned, with sickening regularity for the inhabitants, their forces often swelled by followers of one of the petty kings who had held sway in Denmark, or new renegades from ruling Norse families.

To give some idea of the intensity of Viking attacks in this second period, following a lull after 800, south-east England (mainly Kent and around the Thames Estuary – a prime target) was hit at least six times in the thirty years after 835. The Solent was attacked in 840 and 861, the West Country southern coast in 838 and 840, the Severn Estuary three times between 836 and 850 (and far inland up the Severn itself in 855), and Anglesey in 850. France fared no better, with its great Northern rivers, the Seine and the Loire, attacked constantly from about 841 onwards for over 50 years. These rivers enabled the Vikings to move deep into the hinterland from a mobile base with few of the impediments of a standing land-based army. Further south, the Gironde was also penetrated, giving a route deep into the south-west. For those for whom this was not enough adventure there was the even bigger trip, round Spain and through the Pillars of Hercules into the Mediterranean itself.

The scale was massive. From the 'three ships' of armed warriors of early Anglo-Saxon attacks, some of the coastal skirmishes in the 830s and 840s could have involved 1,500 or more men on each side in hand-to-hand combat, numbers which then grew. In 836 when a Viking war band landed at Carhampton on the Somerset coast, a force led by the previously undefeated Wessex King Ecgberht was beaten back by the invaders after intense and bloody fighting. Two years later the Danes showed new tactics. Recognising the animosity between Wessex and Cornwall, the Danes joined forces with the Cornish (alias the 'West Welsh.') The two groups met (probably in 838) at a place then known as Hengestdun ('Stallion Hill'). Now called Hingston Down or Kit Hill, this is a high (1,000 feet plus) natural feature overlooking the Tamar Valley in Cornwall. This time it was Ecgberht who won a resounding victory, enough to bring to an end a near century of warfare between Cornwall and Wessex. But it turned out to be no more than a temporary setback for the Danes – and a reminder of their adaptability.

Ireland – What then of Ireland, land of kings, mystics, saints and lakes? From 811 onwards Viking raids on the island were mostly contained by local forces. But still they came. In 836/7 Vikings with fleets of 60 or so ships were raiding deep into the island via its plentiful estuaries. Then in 841/2 Viking groups over-wintered in Dublin, literally 'black pool' in Old Norse. Here they barricaded themselves against counter-attack behind ship enclosures they called *longphorts*, triangular-shaped sections of land between a major river and its tributary. These provided protection for ship docking and repair, accessible by water and easily defensible for manufacture and trading. From this base, Dublin grew as a key port and a major Viking-led European slave market. With their maritime activities extending to Wexford and Waterford in the south-east, substantial amounts of gold and silver soon accumulated in Irish Viking coffers.

Phase 2 – c. 850 to 900

The Great Army – In the 850s, disturbing reports came from France of even larger fleets, up to hundreds of ships, involving thousands of fighters. It seems that the war bands, led by a mix of Scandinavian sub-kings, earls and chiefs, each with their own group of retained followers, had absorbed a new generation of recruits. For a long time the French had no answer other than to offer their attackers money to go away, which often seemed just to encourage the next demand. When the French finally managed to find a way to hold back the raids, the Viking fleets, not wishing to suffer needless losses, revised their tactics. With France resistant and the Anglo-Saxon kingdoms divided, Britain now became their chief target.

Although one group had spent their first winter in England in 851 (on the Isle of Sheppey in Kent), it was not until the 860s that the longships began arriving on eastern British shores in great waves, involving some 350 ships sailing into the Thames Estuary. This huge force was (in the language of the time) 'se micel here' (literally 'the great army') – known to those in their path as 'the Danes' and to Anglo-Saxon writers of the time as 'the Great Heathen Army'.

Returning to assemble in East Anglia in 865, the Great Army now became an invasion force, which within ten years was to control East Anglia, Northumbria and much of Mercia. York, the key to the north of England, fell to the invaders in 866. This time, as these destinations suggest, it was predominantly the Anglian, rather than the southern Saxon, areas that fell so quickly. Bernicia in the north of Northumbria remained largely independent, but the bulk of eastern Britain now lay at the Vikings' very limited mercy.

The Vikings in France – The next stage of the story in Britain, charting the near fall and then rise of Wessex, is covered in the next chapter. But events in the emerging England of that time were still closely linked with what was happening in Ireland and France. As Alfred's Wessex fought back, the Viking leaders needed to keep their followers occupied. While some now chose to settle in Britain and farm the land they had taken, many of those who preferred to continue a'viking returned to France. This resulted in a succession of attacks along the Seine, further devastating Rouen and Paris. The French rulers tried everything to stem the tide and save their cities and people. Heavy river defences seemed to work at first. Like paying tribute, however, they were only effective for a while before the Vikings came back with new stratagems. Even the attempt to pay some Viking leaders to turn against their fellows (itself a good Viking ploy) failed.

Although the Vikings had reached Paris several times before, in 885-6 there was a particularly desperate battle to save the city, when supposedly just 200 French knights kept back 30,000 Danes from 700 ships. After months of attrition, the French emperor finally arrived, managing to lift the siege by diverting many of the raiders to turn south against Burgundy. Other Vikings not yet ready to settle down set off on prodigious world travels, leaving the rest to consolidate their bases along the lower Seine around Rouen. This last group, led by the formidable *Hrolf* – alias *Rollo 'the Marcher* – then turned from poachers to gamekeepers by entering into the Treaty of St-Clair-sur-Epte with the French leader. The treaty gave Rollo and his people the obligation to protect the lower Seine area in return for the right to settle there. This became known as the land of the Northmen – *les Normands* – and thus *Normandy*, an initially modest area which Rollo and his fiery descendants steadily enlarged to something much greater.

One irony is that it was Alfred's success from 878 onwards that enabled a nascent England not just to survive but to drive many Vikings back to seek their fortune in the new Normandy of 911. It was a move that was to have major repercussions for England just over 150 years later!

Ragnar Lothbrok and sons

We have limited knowledge of most of the Viking leaders of this period, but there are some exceptions, plus glimpses from archaeology, travellers' tales, sagas and poems. Here again, fact is often embellished by legend, leaving us with some figures who may have been real in themselves, but whose names may have been invented and their exploits carefully embellished. Chief among these were *Ragnar Lothbrok* (alias Lodbrok) and his 'sons', whose careers evidence just how mobile some of the Viking leaders were.

Ragnar – Believed to have died in the 850s, Ragnar is often seen as a main driving force behind the initial attacks on Britain, France and Ireland in the early 9th century. He and his sons, some by different mothers, became so ubiquitous as to suggest that they may have been part of a Viking foundation myth. The sons are variously named as Björn Ironside, *Halfdan* (alias Healfdeane), *Ubba*, *Sigurd* (*Snake-in-the-eye*) and *Ivar* (alias *Ivar the Boneless* and many similar names). There is also *Olaf*, who may have been a brother. All seem to have been involved at some time in raiding along the coasts of Britain and dragging away captives – the rich for ransom and others for sale as slaves.[136]

One story is a snake-dragon killing episode, a familiar theme. Hearing of the beast, Ragnar fashions a suit of bulky crystalline armour that is impenetrable to the serpent and its poison. Having slayed the beast, he leaves his spearhead pinning the serpent's head to the ground, but takes away the spear shaft with him. When the deed is discovered, people marvel and call out to find whose spear shaft fitted the spear point. The prize was, of course, the beautiful daughter of the local Jarl or Earl who, seeing Ragnar stride forward

---

[136] *Working out who did what and when, however, is complicated by different details in later Icelandic sagas, by confusion between Sigurd and Siegfried, by operatic fantasies and Tolkien inventions and, more recently, by films and TV dramas which add both Viking colour and pure fiction.*

in his baggy suit still covered with the beast's bile and blood, acknowledged him with the title 'hairy-pants.' Here are echoes of so much folklore, evoking everything from Arthur, Beowulf and St George in the battle between light and dark, with Ragnar on this (rare) occasion representing the light.[137]

The Ragnar of mythology, and possibly of fact, was the son of Sigurd Ring (alias Hring), himself a semi-legendary character, who overthrew his uncle Harald Wartooth (not to be confused with the later Harald Bluetooth!) to become king of Denmark. This gives Ragnar and, by extension his sons, a royal lineage – with the ruthlessness to go with it. It also gave Ragnar's sons an apparent justification for their later treatment of Anglo-Saxons generally, especially the Northumbrian king Ælla, who is alleged in 865 to have thrown Ragnar to die in a pit of snakes. If this deed ever happened, it might have been seen to justify extreme revenge, but other stories have Ragnar – after years of mayhem – dying sometime in the mid-850s. If so, Ragnar would have died many years before his alleged murder, leaving Ælla innocent of his death.

To a Viking intent on bloodletting, however, Ælla's innocence was probably immaterial. Even if imagined, the story gave the brothers the right of vengeance against Ælla when they finally cornered him in York. But they showed no less mercy to King Edmund of East Anglia who, after his army was defeated, refused to renounce his Christian faith. Both added to the infamy attached to the Lothbrok 'brothers', loathed and feared in Britain for their apparently gratuitous violence, but lauded among many of their Scandinavian contemporaries.[138]

Edmund's fate was, with some attendant miracles, enough to make the holy king a sanctified martyr with a shrine at Bury St Edmunds, the

---

137 Thomas Williams gives an extensive account of these and other such legends in his chapter 7 – Dragon-Slayers.

138 Ælla was rumoured to have been subject to the 'blood-eagle' treatment, where the lungs are pulled out from the victim's back. Edmund was used as archery practice for the victorious Danes, martyred like St Sebastian.

burh named in his honour. There are other echoes here too – of human sacrifice and other martyrdoms. The Norse god Odin hanging on a tree for nine nights evokes Christ's crucifixion, and Odin's trading of body parts for wisdom suggest an extreme version of 'no gain without pain.' When the time did come for conversion to Christianity, therefore, it may have been in a form initially well-tailored to the Norse mind and spirit.

Halfdan – Ragnar's 'son' Halfdan also had an intense career. Along with brother Ivar, Halfdan seems to have been one of the leaders of the Great Army that invaded East Anglia in 865. It then moved on to Northumbria, taking York in 866 and defeating Ælla and his fellow king the following year. After being held up in Mercia by a combined Wessex-Mercian force, the Viking army returned to York to regroup. In 867 they came back to, and this time conquered, East Anglia, martyring King Edmund in the process. Brother Ivar then appears to have moved on to Ireland, becoming king of Dublin before dying around 873. This left Halfdan in charge with a colleague called Bagsecg, of whom little is known, to lead an attack on Wessex. They were supported by major reinforcements from Scandinavia, including another group led by *Guthrum*.

Bagsecg died fighting Wessex in the Battle of Ashdown in 871, leaving Halfdan sole commander. Having agreed truce terms with Alfred, the Viking army withdrew to London. The next year it moved again, either to quell a revolt in Northumbria or to renew the attack on Mercia. Having overwintered at Repton, the Vikings largely conquered Mercia in 874. At this point the Great Army split; Guthrum led a renewed campaign south and west against Wessex while Halfdan headed north to engage the Britons and Scots of Strathclyde. Diverted to Ireland, Halfdan led a campaign to regain the throne of Dublin that had previously been held by his brother, Ivar, shuttling back and forth between Dublin and York .

In 877 Halfdan faced a force of 'Fair Heathens', probably a rival group of Scandinavians, who had long settled in Ireland and might have resented the newcomers. The confrontation led to the Battle of Strangford Lough in Ireland, when Halfdan's luck finally ran out. After his death there, his followers fought their way back to Northumbria via Scotland. Then in York in 883, a man called Guthfrith (or Guthred), whom it was rumoured had been nominated by a visitation from the blessed St Cuthbert, was chosen as the new king of Northumbria. Guthfrith himself died in 994/5 after defeating a large invasion force of Scots.

Ivar – Things became even more complex with the activities of Ivar the Boneless,[139] another of Ragnar's supposed sons. Ivar (also Imar and variations) was probably with Halfdan at the deaths of Ælla of Northumbria and Edmund of East Anglia, managing to be active both in Ireland and Northumbria as well as points in-between. He is named as a possible founder of a royal dynasty in Dublin, being called co-king of Viking Dublin from 857 and allegedly to have styled himself 'King of the Northmen of all Ireland and Britain' shortly before his death, reputed as 873.

For decades Ragnar and sons seemed to carry all before them. It would evidently need something and someone remarkable to stop them.

---

139 *There seem to be several different possible interpretations of the soubriquet 'Boneless.'*

CHAPTER 12

WESSEX FROM DISASTER TO TRIUMPH

825 to 939

In many ways King Offa of Mercia in the 8th century had established a model state by unifying a series of divided tribes into a single kingdom with a common language, common coinage and a firm, centralised control. It could therefore have been Mercia, rather than Wessex, that created a nation. But fortune, a different style of leadership, and events all played their part in the changing fortunes of the 9th and early 10th century. Map 6 covers the outlines of what followed. The dark grey indicates the emerging Scotland, the Brittonic kingdom of Strathclyde, and the kingdoms of Wales. The mid-grey highlights the Danelaw, the Five Boroughs plus York and Northumbria. The Norse Settlement shown hatched was of uncertain (and sometimes contested) status. The light areas cover the essence of Wessex and Mercia in the early stages of the recovery under Edward and Æthelflaed, which then extended under Athelstan to the mid-grey areas.

The Assault on Wessex – January 871

The end of chapter 9 saw Mercia defeated and subdued in 825. Wessex success under Egbert was, however, soon reversed by Mercia under Wiglaf before both kings died in 839. They were replaced by *Aethelwulf* in Wessex and, after an interim period, *Burgred* in Mercia. When Rhodri ap Merfyn, later Rhodri the Great (r. 844-77), came to the throne of Gwynedd and extended his rule from Anglesey in the north to the Gower in the south, a threatened Mercia had to change focus to defend itself. Finally, Mercia and Wessex started to cooperate, supported by marriage in 855 between Burgred of Mercia and *Æthelswith*, the daughter of the Wessex king, Aethelwulf. In retrospect, it was a crucial moment of alliance. No children are known to have come from the union, and Burgred and Æthelswith were later to be driven by the Vikings into exile in Rome. But Æthelswith's youngest brother was ultimately to turn the tide of English history.

Alfred – This youngest brother was Alfred (or Ælfred with the Anglo-Saxon diphthong), the youngest of the five sons of King Aethelwulf of Wessex and a mother of possible Scandinavian origins. Alfred was born in 849[140] at Wantage, north-west of Reading, with four elder brothers limiting his prospects. In 868, not yet twenty, Alfred was married to *Eahlswith* of the royal house of Mercia, renewing the inter-kingdom bonds started by his sister. But these were hazardous times, not least as Saxon tradition encouraged kings to lead their armies by way of example – from the front. As a result, after their father's death, Alfred's elder brothers become kings of Wessex in turn, before successively dying.

This left Alfred, still in his late teens, campaigning against the Danes with his only surviving elder brother, Æthelred. When Æthelred later died of battle wounds, leaving a young son, the choice in Wessex between the æthelings (princes of the royal blood) lay with the Witan, a council of the senior figures, the ealdormen. After they had elected Alfred, who had already shown his promise, as the next king, they might have questioned their choice when the start of Alfred's reign saw the nadir of the fortunes of the House of Wessex.

---

140 *Although some sources state 847 or 848.*

Against all odds, however, Alfred's recovery from extremis enabled him to keep the Danes at bay while he coordinated a fight back. Despite suffering from a recurrent illness, Alfred turned out to be a man of many talents, from scholar to military tactician, sustained by an extraordinary faith, fulfilling his royal duties by leaving capable successors willing and able to continue his work. It was also Alfred who laid down many of the principles of English law and ecclesiastical practice that were to survive future invasions, even when the reigning rulers did not.

Ashdown – As we saw in the previous chapter, the Anglo-Saxon kingdoms had faced a continuing onslaught from the Viking Great Army since 865. One by one the kingdoms had succumbed, leaving just Wessex under Æthelred. In December 870, the Danish leader, Halfdan, moved to create a fortified camp at Reading, on the Thames about 40 miles west of London. In the first of a series of raw encounters the men of Wessex, having tried but failed to dislodge the Vikings from Reading, pulled back into the hills to the west.

Here, at the *Battle of Ashdown* on a bitter early January day in 871, the Anglo-Saxons defeated the attacking Viking army, a rare victory in what had become a procession of defeats at the hands of the invaders. One account of the battle suggests that, while King Æthelred sought divine reassurance in a nearby chapel, Alfred, just 22 years old at the time, saw a window of military opportunity and led his troops to a resounding victory. Although the exact location remains uncertain, the main conflict is believed to have taken place around the Berkshire section of The Ridgeway, in the hills to the west of the Thames.

Victory though it was, the Anglo-Saxon advantage at Ashdown was short-lived. Two weeks later the Vikings were victorious at Basing to the south, followed by Marlborough and Wilton to the south-west. With many of its ruling ealdormen now dead, it seemed close to the end for the House of Wessex – and for the Anglo-Saxons. The end was a hair's breadth away. But it did not come.

The Emergence of Alfred (reigned 871-99)

Alfred's fortune, or misfortune, was to become king when Wessex was the last kingdom south of Hadrian's Wall under true Anglo-Saxon rule. England still did not exist; in many respects it emerged out of opposition to the Vikings, and because it had a highly capable leader able to evoke the vision of an English people. Yet, even if many elsewhere in the country longed to see the back of the Vikings, they were not necessarily ready to accept a single Anglo-Saxon overlord, especially from Wessex.

With limited other evidence, our history is largely reliant on Alfred's own words, the sometimes laconic, and not always reliable, Anglo-Saxon Chronicle,[141] and the words of a monk based originally at St David's in the southern Welsh kingdom of Dyfed. This is the man known to us as Asser, perhaps a biblical name meaning 'blessed.' Once asked to join the circle of learned and literary men at court, he quickly progressed to become Bishop of Sherborne, spending much of his time with Alfred, and coming to know him well. In 893 Asser wrote in Latin his *Life of Alfred, King of the Anglo-Saxons*, a key work for historians.

Whatever his spiritual qualities, however, Asser is frustrating as an historian. As Christopher Brooke puts it: 'Asser often informs in order to tantalise: the curtain is lifted only to be dropped again; Asser is devoted, wordy and clumsy.' The balance and accuracy of Asser's work is also questioned. One concern is that the work is hagiographic, designed to show Alfred's saintly qualities, both heroic in the mould of Charlemagne and also ascetic, possibly afflicting Alfred with an illness more severe than he actually had. Like many others, Asser may well have added some dramatic colour, and on matters of detail, such as dates, he can also contradict himself. Then

---

141 Alfred himself may have strongly influenced the Chronicle at this point.

there are the missing five years – the last five years of Alfred's life which are oddly absent from Asser's *Life of Alfred,* even though the author survived the monarch. Yet, while Asser's history should be read with caution, it does help to fill out an otherwise limited picture of Alfred and his time.

The cause of Alfred's recurring illness or disability remains uncertain. He suffered, as he thought of it, from healthy male desires and prayed for his lust to be abated. But his real affliction may have been more physical, such as severe haemorrhoids or Crohn's disease – or even both. Whatever it was, it did not seem to diminish his desire for knowledge or wish to administer his kingdom virtuously.

Retreat and fight back

Renewed Danish assaults – Despite defeating them, the Danes would have noted that the West Saxons did not simply buckle under pressure. Accordingly, when Alfred offered a truce after Marlborough and Wilton, the Danes were ready to accept. Likewise, in buying off the Danes at this point, Alfred was being pragmatic, securing much-needed breathing space. At this point, in 876-7, the Great Army divided. Halfdan, seeing better prospects or more pressing issues elsewhere, headed north, leaving a faction led by Guthrum and others to renew the pressure on Wessex.[142] In 876 Guthrum's forces seized Wareham on the Dorset coast as a strategic location. The West Saxons again defended fiercely. In the midst of negotiations, a large Danish group broke away to the west and took Exeter, hoping to link up with a major Danish fleet in the Channel. As happened many times in Britain's maritime history, the weather took a hand, and a violent storm scattered the Danish fleet. Guthrum accepted terms and withdrew north to batter Mercia again.

Ignoring the truce, Guthrum's army returned unexpectedly to Wessex in late 877. Acting covertly in the depths of winter, they

---

142 *Guthrum was accepted by the Danes as a king and may have been a failed candidate for the Danish throne.*

surprised the festive Anglo-Saxons by overrunning the royal town of Chippenham on Twelfth Night in January 878, the Christian feast of the Epiphany. Many senior West Saxon supporters were killed, and the loss of such a strategic stronghold would have been like a hammer blow. Such of the Wessex fighting men as could escape fled to their homes or abroad.

To the marshes – Miraculously, as it might have seemed, Alfred and those closest to him slipped through the Viking net at Chippenham.

With much of the surrounding area held by or submitting to the Danes, Alfred withdrew to the marshes of Athelney in Somerset with a few supporters. As the Danes pillaged Wessex, Alfred's position was desperate. Much of this area of Somerset was – and still is – very low-lying, hardly above sea level.[143] *It was excessively marshy, with limited and changing tracks through to marsh-fringed islands and few patches of higher ground known only to the locals. All too well aware of the dangers of such places, the Danes held back. Alfred took about six weeks to plan; his next move would be critical and fraught with risk.*

Alfred would have been bolstered by news that Odda, ealdorman of Somerset, had engaged and stopped a Danish force which had landed in Devon with 23 ships. For good measure Ubba, one of the Lothbrok brothers, had been killed in the fighting. Knowing his enemy, the Wessex king would have calculated that his only hope of securing the advantage was by a decisive victory. Anything less would only lead to a further round of truces and renewed fighting, with the element of surprise lost and potential Danish reinforcements arriving. The Danes were, when circumstances advised, fully prepared to be bought off for a time, but were hardly accustomed to surrender. They had had also shown that agreeing a truce gave no certainty it would be honoured. With the rest of the country

---

143 *Alfred seems to have known the area fairly well from his boyhood.*

effectively in Danish hands, Alfred needed a decisive victory from which he could dictate terms.

First, he had to let his supporters know he was alive and well, and then to summon them to an agreed meeting point at a stated time. To carry the message he needed people whom he could trust, and who were brave and capable enough to get through. And he had to rely on the leaders to support him by turning up at the appointed place and time. Even after receiving pledges of support, he could not have been certain until the last minute that his messengers had got through, that his troops would not be intercepted, and that his supporters would stay to fight. Alfred would have prayed hard in the days before the appointed hour, and it's a huge testament to the loyalty he had already inspired that his call was so resoundingly answered.

Edington and aftermath – The chosen rendezvous was Egbert's Stone, near Selwood in Somerset, close to the borders with Dorset and Wiltshire, a point of high ground then crested by a great forest. Here the men did indeed come from the counties around, seemingly in great numbers. Alfred's plan was to draw the Danes out into the field rather than attack them in one of the towns they had taken and fortified. For their part the Danes, initially unaware of how many men Alfred had been able to raise, were keen to crush him before more rallied to his cause. Two days after the rendezvous at Egbert's Stone, in early May 878, the armies of Wessex and the Danes came face to face at a place named by Asser as Ethandune, now generally believed to be *Edington*, near Westbury in Wiltshire. This was a fortified royal estate, about 15 miles south of Chippenham, a place of significance to the Saxons, who attacked vigorously, with little quarter given.

The Chronicle records laconically that Alfred won the day. Asser is more expressive, describing the deployment of the Saxon shield wall and writing that: 'He [Alfred] overthrew the Pagans with great slaughter, and smiting the fugitives, he pursued them as far as the fortress.' Whatever else, Edington soon acquired near mythic status, suggesting resurrection and potential divine favour.

The fortress to which the Danes retired was Chippenham, where they barricaded themselves in. Having been decisively beaten and denied the chance to re-provision, they sought peace after just two weeks. This time they did surrender, unconditionally, leaving Alfred to take hostages and dictate terms.[144] As usual, the Danes agreed to leave Wessex, but now Alfred had the chance to insist on other key requirements. In demanding that Guthrum accept Christianity, Alfred would have acted both out of religious conviction and a belief that converting the Danes gave the best hope that they would honour the peace. He may even have hoped they could later be integrated into some early vision of a broader Christian kingdom.

For his part Guthrum, long curious about Christianity and seeing apparent proof of its power in Alfred, was ready to convert if that was the price he needed to pay. With Alfred as his sponsor, he was baptised at the Somerset village of Aller three weeks after the battle, taking the baptismal name of Athelstan. It was a major triumph for Alfred but, even so, he was wise enough to know that Guthrum was only one leader of one Viking army; even if he did not return, others almost certainly would.

A year later the Danes retired to East Anglia where Guthrum was allowed to rule as king. He did find a pretext to attack Kent in 884, but when he was again defeated, he entered into fuller treaty terms with Alfred which recognised an agreed boundary between Wessex-Mercia and the area under Danish rule, known to us as the *Danelaw*. The Danelaw boundary varied over time, but initially ran

---

144 *The initial terms were an oral and personal agreement between Alfred and Guthrum, only later enshrined in the written Treaty of Wedmore, probably in 884 or 886 (see below). It's notable that the treaty terms seek to align compensation for murder at the same level between the English and the Danelaw, and also contain an early reference to the testimony of 12 witnesses prepared to swear to the truth of events (as witnesses, not as jury.)* .

along the northern bank of the Thames Estuary, turning north-east of London along the River Lea to Bedford. From there it ran broadly north-west to the Wirral peninsular on Merseyside. The Danelaw specifically included the so-called *Five Boroughs* (prosperous towns of which future mention will be made) of Leicester, Nottingham, Derby, Stamford and Lincoln.

In the event, although there were new Viking attacks in the 890s (though not from Guthrum), these were beaten back. By 896 the Great Army had dispersed, some settling in East Anglia or York, while those who wanted to keep going took ship for Normandy, where another future awaited them. There were still restless areas, incursions from Dublin and conflict between bands from Denmark and Norway. But Edington had been a major turning point.

Consolidation and assessment

It was Alfred's holistic approach to kingship and the development of his realm that showed his true greatness. Learning well from others, including adopting some Viking stratagems, he took a series of measures to protect Wessex and consolidate his kingdom.

Army – When on the move, living off plunder, the Danes had large groups ready to strike hard and fast at short notice. A key issue for Alfred was how to maintain enough armed forces to counter them without draining the labour needed to work the land and essential industries. Alfred accordingly reorganised the *fyrd*, the system of calling up men for battle, so that he had a strong force available to take the field at any time. By rotating his forces, he had men ready for active duty for periods and available to work their settlements at others.

Navy – To counter the Danes' dominance at sea, Alfred commissioned a fleet capable of intercepting the raiders before they reached the English shore. This proved powerful enough to seize a small group of ships in 882, but not to prevent a large Danish fleet from landing in Kent in 884. Alfred's ships may have been over-engineered, too long and heavy to manoeuvre well enough in muddy estuaries. Nevertheless, a strong navy was to become a cornerstone of the future defence of the kingdom.

Garrisons – Another key act was to establish the system of *burhs*, fortified and permanently manned garrisons in strategic locations, which were capable of acting as fortresses for attack and defence. In time, with the security they offered, these burhs, later known as boroughs, also became the natural centres for trade and production.

Law, trade and economy – Alfred consolidated laws from Kent and Merica with those of Wessex into a single law code, which not only brought consistency but also helped break down old barriers between kingdoms. Strong trading links backed by relative peace and a sound currency were also key principles. Coinage minted in London shows Alfred progressing as *King of the Anglo-Saxons, King of the Saxons and Mercians* and, from about the mid-870s, *King of the English* (perhaps then seen as the combined people of the enlarged Wessex and Mercia).

At the same time, Alfred avoided becoming too distant from his subjects. He also preferred to treat wealth as facilitating the royal ability to provide for prayer, labour and – where necessary – war. That he was devout seems certain, having a piety mixed with restless curiosity and a growing wish to make learning accessible to his people. He had been an avid learner from his youth and capable of great feats of memory. And twice in his early childhood he'd visited and been influenced by Rome, once with his royal father, meeting the Pope, staying long enough to absorb a deep sense of Latin tradition and many aspects of old Rome. These early days in Rome, especially when he was dressed by the pope in the style of an early Christian warrior, retained a lasting influence. Though he did not seek to emulate their opulence, he had certainly seen the learned magnificence achieved by Charlemagne's successors.

Alfred now aspired to a different type of kingship from his predecessors, believing that kings should be educated and educators, not just warriors. But first, having missed childhood education in reading and writing, he had to apply himself to major learning at the age of 38, including the Latin needed to understand the great works of the day as well as the past. It was around this time that Asser joined Alfred's entourage, becoming his Latin tutor. And once he had mastered the texts, Alfred wanted to convey and discuss the knowledge with others, seeking learned men around him to learn from and debate with. His involvement of archbishops, bishops, Mercians, Franks, Saxons, Frisians, Bretons, Irish and Scandinavians showed Alfred's huge intellectual curiosity.

His drive also extended into having many of the leading texts of the day translated from Latin into Old English, possibly managing some translations himself. This was an almost revolutionary approach at the time; by ensuring these works were open to more than the clerics, Alfred was way ahead of his time. Well into the Middle Ages some who dared publish the Bible in their native language could be, and were, put to death for their pains. Alfred's motivation was that he saw a common English language as a unifying force for the people of Wessex and Mercia, whom he called his *Angelcynn* (with the *Angle* or *Angel* element perhaps especially appealing to the Mercians.)

Alfred's achievements were a vital stage in the establishment of England, but could easily have come to nothing if he had not had highly capable family successors ready and able to consolidate and build on what he had gained. These included one of the great female figures of the time (and possibly all time) – his daughter and first child, Æthelflaed.

Æthelflaed[145] – To set the scene involves going back to 874, four years before Alfred's great victory at Edington. With East Anglia

---

145 'Noble beauty'.

WESSEX FROM DISASTER TO TRIUMPH

by then an effective Danish colony, the Vikings had returned to Mercia, strengthening their hold around Repton, near Nottingham. Using the River Trent as a highway to subdue much of north-eastern Mercia, they removed the Mercian king, Burgred, who retired to, and soon died in, Rome. He was followed in western Mercia by *Ceolwulf II*, very occupied with wars against the Welsh and much disparaged (perhaps unfairly) by the Chronicle. The history then is obscure. Ceolwulf disappeared from the scene and a new leader, *Aethelred*,[146] took power. Danish pressure, combined with a Welsh reversal, then encouraged Aethelred to align with Wessex in 882.[147]

This alliance had given Alfred the chance to follow the precedent of his sister, who had married Burgred, by a marriage between the much older Aethelred, Lord (and de facto king) of the western Mercians, and Alfred's daughter. Æthelflaed herself, perhaps 15 or 16 at the time, would have had little choice, but was to find a role in a man's world in which she could flourish as a woman. One early product of the alliance was the recovery of London, a valued Mercian outpost before it was absorbed by the Vikings. Having aided its recovery, Alfred returned the city to Mercia, with Aethelred's formal acceptance of the overlordship of Wessex perhaps being linked. Once their only child, a daughter, was born a year or two later, the Mercian first couple set about recovering the rest of their kingdom, with Æthelflaed prominent in the process.[148]

Attacks renewed – More Viking attacks erupted, which might have been stimulated by Danes seeking better fortunes in Britain after a failed harvest in northern France in 892. Two fleets landed separately in Kent, established defences and set about pillaging.

---

146 *Probably a senior ealdorman and general, and possibly Ceolwulf's chosen successor.*

147 *The 'Watlington Hoard' (see Introduction) includes coins of the 'two-kings' type, featuring Alfed and Ceolwulf and, later, Alfred and Aethelred.*

148 *London was later 'absorbed' by Æthelflaed's brother King Edward, with the port of Lundenwic being abandoned in favour of a new fortified harbour at Lundenburh, the site of the old Roman Londinium.*

Alfred positioned his forces between them, ready to attack any who emerged. This frustrated the Danes, with the larger Danish force reacting by striking west through the Wessex heartlands of Hampshire and Berkshire. Here it was intercepted by an army led by Alfred's eldest son, Edward, who drove the raiders back. In north Kent Alfred paid for peace from a force led by Hastein, who accepted funds and selective baptism and withdrew to Essex. At that point, a new Viking fleet of 100 ships sailed round from Northumbria and East Anglia to attack Devon from the south-west coast, prompting Hastein to break out again from Essex with a combined force and attack Mercia from the east.

Alfred elected to tackle the menace in the west while the Mercians came to grips with Hastein's forces, with some success. The Vikings regrouped and returned twice before being pushed back to Essex via a circuitous route. In the process the burhs created on Alfred's model proved vital in defending Mercia and Wessex, making the raiders increasingly frustrated at their lack of ability to do as they had done before. Almost a year passed before, in late 894, the Viking army left its base on Mersea Island on the Essex coast. Having sailed along the Thames, they carried on up the River Lea to a position close to Hertford.

This was technically within the Danelaw territory ceded to Guthrum, who had died a few years earlier, but too close for the Londoners to ignore. When their assault in summer 895 failed, Alfred returned with his army and commissioned two new burhs, either side of the Lea, to guard against any escape by ship. Seeing this, the Danes swapped their ships for horses and rode for the upper Severn where they overwintered at Bridgnorth in Shropshire. Viking groups from Northumberland and East Anglia now took up the battle. After sailing down the east coast and along the south with fairly free rein on the shores of Wessex, they suffered reverses. Finally, in summer 896, after some further significant losses, both they and the Bridgnorth contingent departed, to leave Wessex in peace – for a time.

Death of Alfred – King Alfred died in 899, with little acknowledgment from the Chronicle and none from Asser, whose biography ends in 893. In fact, Alfred only became known as 'the Great' centuries later, when the Tudors were looking for an English hero from the past. He had reigned 28 years, united the major part of the main southern kingdoms, and turned apparent disaster into at least provisional triumph. Alone among the Anglo-Saxon kingdoms, he had reversed the Viking juggernaut by a consistent strategy supported by clever planning and tactics. By accepting the existence of the Danelaw, probably more populated than Wessex and Mercia combined, he had shown his respect for treaties and given himself space to consolidate his own kingdom. Above all, he had shown a rare combination of courage, belief and wisdom. Alfred had started the emergence of England; he may not have completed it, but he certainly saved the project from death by a thousand cuts.

For a country to have freedom and a sense of national identity it needs a common purpose and values that hold it together. Creating this was Alfred's genius. In many ways the heathen Vikings were a perfect opposition against whom he could rally his Angelcynn. And where he extended his territory, he emphasised control rather than retribution, seeking to live in harmony with difference rather than fomenting xenophobia and racial stereotyping. What Alfred sought was not based on conquest for the sake of conquest, but for a greater purpose – in his case a distinctive 'Angelcynn' culture held together by the spiritual glue of Christianity.

Edward 'the Elder' (reigned 899 to 924) and Æthelflaed (ruled 911 to 918)

Edward and Æthelwold – Despite the custom in Wessex, Alfred did his best to ensure that he was succeeded by his son, Edward. And Edward himself (still young, but now called 'the Elder' to distinguish him from the later short-lived 'Edward the Martyr') shared with his father the vision of a united nation, and had already proved himself in battle. From the start, however, Edward's accession was contested by his nephew, his brother's son, Æthelwold, who had been bypassed when Alfred was elected king. Although Alfred had been chosen by the Witan, had more than proved himself – and had let his nephew live – Æthelwold had long nurtured a grievance. This erupted on Alfred's death, when the nephew, resenting his limited share of his royal uncle's estate, seized lands in Dorset, including Wimborne where his royal father lay buried.

Edward rapidly convened an army, causing his cousin to bolt to the Danelaw and offer his services to the Scandinavian warlords there. They agreed to accept him as titular king and join him in an attack on Mercia and then Wessex. The year was 902. Edward responded by mustering an army to drive the invaders back. But part of Edward's army lingered too long pillaging Danelaw territory, leading to the Battle of The Holme, somewhere in East Anglia. In the resultant fighting many senior figures on both sides perished, including Æthelwold himself. This removed the succession dispute, but not the Viking attacks.

Edward and Æthelflaed – The situation was further complicated in 902, when the native Irish rose against the largely Norse Vikings and expelled them from Dublin and surrounds. The eviction created an exodus of marauders ready to settle or raid across the west coasts of Britain and the northern isles. One flashpoint was Chester, just across the sea from Dublin for Irish Vikings. This was a strategic town on the north-west border between Mercia and the Danelaw, refortified as a burh around 906/7. When, probably a year or two later, the Norse, having been given land to settle and in breach of their truce, attacked the town, the Mercians used Viking-style guile to trap and butcher their besiegers inside the city. To add to all this turbulence, early 10th century Britain appears to have been in the grip of a serious climate downturn, with deep cold and cattle epidemics adding extra pressure on struggling settlements.

Edward had immediately shown himself as willing to work with his sister, Æthelflaed, and her husband Aethelred, in re-fortifying key towns such as Gloucester and Worcester. But, having been ill for some years, Aethelred of Mercia finally died in 911. At this point Æthelflaed took over the reins of power on her own. Becoming known as the 'Lady of the Mercians', she had probably already led the Mercians to a substantial victory over the Danes at Wednesfield near Wolverhampton in 910, with major loss of life among the Danish leaders.[149]

Expansion – While Æthelflaed progressed through north-west Mercia to Tamworth and Stafford, Edward was expanding Wessex control through to East Anglia and Essex. This time it was the Danes who lacked coordination, with the armies of individual towns being easier for the English to defeat. Æthelflaed had backup teams of engineers and builders ready to build or improve fortified burhs as her armies advanced, such as at Runcorn where the River Mersey narrowed enough for a powerful fort to be built to deter Viking river raids into the interior.[150]

Edward's expansion of his northern and eastern frontiers prompted several Danish leaders to submit during 915 and 916, a trickle which grew into a flood as Edward progressed and Æthelflaed captured Derby, though not without the grievous loss of some of her senior lords in fierce fighting there. Realising its likely fate if it resisted, Leicester submitted, and by 918 the Mercians had reached the Humber. By this time the Norse Vikings had returned in force to Ireland and retaken the Dublin throne, but events were being closely watched by the Anglo-Danish lords of temporarily kingless York. Increasingly aware of the threat from the English to the south and the Norse from Ireland, the lords of York offered to pledge their allegiance – not to Edward, but to the Lady of the Mercians.

---
149 *The site of Wednesfield has also been attributed to nearby Tettenhall.*
150 *The River Mersey, meaning boundary river, shares the same 'border' name root as Mercia.*

This was a significant point, with brother and sister having laid the foundations for an expanded realm of a future England south of the Humber. But Æthelflaed was not to live to see her triumph, dying suddenly at Tamworth in June 918, aged around 50, just two weeks before her planned triumphal entrance into York.

As Lady of the Mercians, Æthelflaed seems to have achieved near universal acclaim for her vigour combined with wisdom, prudence and sense of justice.[151] She was queen of Mercia in all but name and had proved herself more than fit for the role in her own right. Indeed, she had restored Mercia and its self-pride to the extent that Mercia might have seemed to be at least an equal partner with Wessex. The relationship between the two kingdoms was still far from settled, but, given the parlous state of Mercia when she came to power and its huge role in consolidating the future England, Æthelflaed probably has as much a claim to be one of the founders of England as her more illustrious father, brother and nephew.

Once again, Æthelflaed is an example of the right person in the right place at the right time. Yet she may not have been able to achieve what she did anywhere else. Elsewhere, most queens at that time were required to be subservient, with the only way for Anglo-Saxon noblewomen to have authority largely limited to religious institutions. But Mercia, with different roots, was prepared to recognise the role of a woman as more than mother, household-manager and dispenser of food and drink to the nobles. It's even unlikely that Wessex at that time would have allowed Æthelflaed the role she had in Mercia, so much so that the Wessex versions of the Chronicle at this point largely disregard her contribution. Æthelflaed was a trailblazer, but it was to be over 600 years before England had a queen in her own right.[152]

---

151 Much lauded by Irish annals especially. And we can probably discount the idea of Æthelflaed having a fling with a Viking chief as pure fiction!

152 The Tudors, Mary and then Elizabeth I, though Henry I's daughter Matilda came close in the 12th century.

Mercia subsumed – Æthelflaed, however, had no son,[153] and Edward's willingness to work with his sister did not extend to his niece. Ælfwynn, daughter and short-term (6 months') successor of Aethelflaed, was soon ousted by Edward and persuaded to keep a low profile.[154] Although Æthelflaed seemed to have been grooming her daughter to take over, the change passed off peacefully. The untested young woman may have been seen as a risky option by the nobles and allied Welsh kings compared to her successful uncle. Aged about 30, Ælfwynn was also unmarried, giving Edward extra reason to avoid a possible brother-in-law with conflicting support and ambitions.

As added protection, Edward dissolved Mercia into the Kingdom of Wessex, consolidating all his sister's success into his own – and much of her history too. This left him effective master of England up to the Trent on one side and the Mersey on the other, acknowledged by East Anglia as well as Mercia and even several Welsh rulers. With new burhs and a new bridge at Nottingham he seemed in control up to Lincoln, which still tended to look to York. York's offer to submit to Æthelflaed, however, did not outlive her, and was not extended to Edward. The Norse warlord Ragnall (alias Rognvald or variants) rapidly took over the throne there, with many in the region possibly considering that a committed Viking was more acceptable than a remote king of Wessex.[155]

Death of Edward – The success of Edward and Æthelflaed was a huge advance on Alfred's start, with the combined forces of Wessex and Mercia now seen as more than a match for the Danes. Some kind of treaty seems to have been established with the northern kingdoms at Bakewell in Derbyshire in 920, but in 921 when Ragnall of York

---

153 *She may have experienced a traumatic pregnancy and/or delivery of her daughter – with lasting effects.*

154 *Probably in a nunnery.*

155 *Tim Clarkson's 'Æthelflaed' provides a detailed account of the whole of this period.*

died, his kinsman *Sihtric*, who had come from Dublin to take over, almost immediately started to raid Mercia. Chester too, on whose defence his sister had taken such pains, rose against Edward, causing another insurrection for him to put down.

Perhaps worn down, Edward died in July 924. He had been a man of action, who, alongside his military exploits, had found time to father at least thirteen legitimate children, including five sons from three different mothers. If that was not enough of a recipe for trouble, on the king's accession and marriage he had parted from his eldest son's mother, about whom little is known. The boy himself, the young Athelstan, was sent to grow up in the household of his aunt Æthelflaed in Mercia. Edward's new queen, Aelflaed, meanwhile, remained in Wessex and rewarded him with two more sons. After Aelflaed's death aged around 36, Edward married again, this time to *Eadgifu*, the daughter of the Ealdorman of Kent, fathering two more sons, *Eadred* and *Edmund*.

If the new union was intended to secure Kent's ongoing loyalty, it turned out to have greater implications and competition, both between sons of different mothers and also between stepmothers and kingdoms. Wessex supported the eldest son of the second union while Mercia supported Athelstan – and independence from Wessex. There was also uncertainty as to the future of the two latest aethelings! Much that Edward had gained therefore risked being undone by family rivalry and a succession dispute.

Athelstan (reigned 924 to 939)

This combustible mix was dampened, but not extinguished, when Aelfweard of Wessex, son of Edward's second union, died shortly after his father, from unknown causes. But with the way now apparently cleared for the Mercian-raised Athelstan, Wessex resisted. The situation was saved by a deal hammered out, possibly with the help of Edward's widow, Eadgifu, mother of the young Edmund and Eadred. Athelstan was accepted as sole ruler, seemingly on the condition that he would have no legitimate children of his own (a promise he appears to have kept) and that his young half-brothers by Eadgifu would be his heirs. Accordingly in September 925 Athelstan was crowned at a royal estate at Kingston on Thames on the border between Mercia and Wessex. It was a spectacular ceremony and occasion which sought to emphasise Athelstan's legitimacy.

York and the North – Athelstan's most immediate challenge was the north-west. In 919, Irish Scandinavians had seized York and now ruled down as far as the Wash. Athelstan accordingly resumed his late father's attempt to negotiate a treaty, backed by a marriage between his sister and the then Norse ruler, Sihtric. In early 927, however, just over a year later, Sihtric died, creating a vacancy for which there were several immediate bidders. Athelstan seized the opportunity (and considerable treasure stored in York), seeing off Sihtric's kinsman Guthfrith from Ireland in the process. In light of this, Ealdred, the ruler based at Bamburgh to the north, who had his own aspirations, fled to the court of *Constantin* (alias Constantine), King of Scotland.

By establishing a new national border close to Carlisle, Athelstan also encroached on the Kingdom of Strathclyde. He had thus made major territorial gains, but also many enemies in short order. And in Wales, where previous Mercian aggression had encouraged something of a national consciousness to develop, there were major divisions as to whether to support or fight the English. This was also the first time a king from southern Britain had ruled north of the Humber.

But it was not enough for Athelstan, who wished both to be, and be seen to be, supreme ruler in Britain. Accordingly, in July 927 he summoned all the powers around to Penrith to acknowledge his lordship – and effective supremacy. That done, he compelled the rulers of Wales also to submit to him. To complete his 'Conquest of Britain', celebrated in Exter in 928, Athelstan effectively annexed

Cornwall and established a refortified base at Exeter, where he forcibly resettled large numbers of supposedly recalcitrant 'Corn-Welsh.'

It was an astonishing position to have achieved, only 50 years since his grandfather Alfred had been penned back in the marshes of Athelney.

Athelstan, King of the English – With his father's and his own accumulated wealth enabling him to reward his supporters handsomely, Athelstan had achieved a remarkable primacy in a very short space of time – and with relatively limited destruction. From being *King of the Saxons or Anglo-Saxons* he smoothly became *Rex Anglorum, King of the English*, later described by scribes and on coinage as king of 'the whole of Britain,' a position to which he claimed to have been elevated by Christ. But social disorder was rife, encouraging the king to become active in regulating the laws and government of the country, a kingly and Christian duty which he took extremely seriously. Royal control of coinage and moneyers became rigorously enforced, helping build a strong economy backed by firm laws and the Church.

Athelstan also initiated huge assemblies and feasts, where a thousand or more people from across the land might be called to be present. Here he could be seen in all his glory, majestically impressive yet able to meet and listen to his people. It was a very early form of parliament, albeit paternalistic and dominated by the king. He also encouraged poetry, the arts and learning generally, again seeking it as part of his duty. And while Athelstan's reputation might have been poor in Ireland and Scotland, it positively glowed on the Continent, attracting to his court rich gifts, acclaimed intellectuals, and heady marriage proposals for his many sisters.[156]

The king's success, however, also attracted envy and dissention at home. In 933 his half-brother Edwin seems to have been drowned

---

156 *Several of whom did join the powerhouses of Continental royalty.*

WESSEX FROM DISASTER TO TRIUMPH

at sea in doubtful circumstances. This may have caused Athelstan to do penance, and also to take more steps to protect his young half-brothers and intended heirs, Edmund and Eadred, then aged 11 and 9 respectively. The other big problem for Athelstan was that Constantin, king of Scotland (increasingly called *Alba* after 900),[157] and *Owain*, king of the Strathclyde Britons, had kept their distance since swearing oaths to him in 927. Unwilling to accept this, Athelstan gathered a huge army and marched swiftly north in 934,[158] with his fleet shadowing up the north-east coast. Constantin, then in his mid-50s with a lifetime of fighting Vikings behind him, came to heel. Athelstan duly took his force back south where he issued another charter which he forced Constantin to witness, expressly as a sub-ruler, before permitting him to return to Scotland.

The next year, 935, Athelstan chose the old Roman amphitheatre at Cirencester, with most of his sub-rulers and senior subjects in attendance, as the setting for a major display of his supreme grandeur. It must have been galling in the extreme for those forced to sit at his feet, many of them Britons from parts of Wales and Scotland who might have preferred an alliance with the Vikings rather than subservience to an English king from Wessex. This sentiment was encapsulated by a priest called Gerald of Wales whose long poem, the *Great Prophesy of Britain*, anticipated a revolt of the Britons to drive the Saxons out of the country. This added fuel to smouldering embers. Would there be a spark to re-ignite it all?

York, Dublin and Brunanburh – One other group had been beaten back, but had not succumbed – the Dublin-led Vikings who had also established themselves in York. With connected Norse families contending for supremacy, a bewildering succession of leaders emerged, any one of whom might elect to take the battle back to the

---

157 Alba by then appears to have included Dalriada and former Pictish lands, but not those parts of the Lowlands occupied by Strathclyde or Northumbria.

158 Stopping off briefly at Chester-Le-Street near Durham to give reverence to St Cuthbert, whose remains were installed there at that time, and affirm his connection with Christian Northumbria.

English. So far as anything in those days was predictable, another change of Viking ruler in Dublin might be expected to set in motion a fresh chain of events. And so it proved.

The new leader was *Olaf Guthfrithson*, son of the Viking chief Guthfrith, whom Athelstan had pre-empted in seizing York in 927. Having established his supremacy in Dublin, some years later Olaf set sail with a massive fleet to join dissident Welsh factions and the Scottish discontents, Constantin of Alba and Owain of Strathclyde. Their combined forces jointly proceeded to lay waste to swathes of northern England. Athelstan, whether taking time to assemble his forces, or perhaps focused on international affairs and alliances, seemed wrong-footed and initially hesitant to act as the insurgents desecrated the countryside.

Finally, he assembled a massive army, which met with the insurgents at a place called *Brunanburh* in late 937. This location is uncertain and much disputed. It could have been Bromborough on the Wirral, a favoured Norse Viking landing point, further north-west, or even somewhere south of York. Wherever it was, the contest was fierce and bloody. Athelstan's troops gradually gained the ascendancy, driving back the battered Vikings to their ships and Constantin to Scotland. There was enormous loss of life all round, including two of the king's cousins, but the Vikings and Scots lost even more. Inevitably Anglo-Saxon chroniclers hailed the victory in epic terms as secured by God's favour.

In many ways Brunanburh was to be the high point of English fortunes for some time. The retention of Northumbria especially, even if it was later to be lost and found again, was vital in establishing both the northern reaches of England and the southern reaches of Scotland without an intervening, predominantly Scandinavian, state.

There is, nevertheless, a marked difference between conquering a land and coalescing its people into a viable nation state. Athelstan had made major improvements to his country's administration, laws and money supply. Aware that a king's role included doing good for his people, he had encouraged greater fairness in law, empowered the church as a seat of learning and piety, coordinated the Angelcynn as a people, and set out the possible shape of England. Even so, the English ascendancy was fragile. And of the three main combatants who survived Brunanburh, it was Athelstan who would be the first to die – two years later in 839, about 44 years old. Although his achievements were many, the ground on which they were built was yet to be fully tested.

Overall, however, perhaps the most extraordinary thing about Athelstan is that we really know so little about him. In the words of Tom Holland: 'The King who founded England has largely been forgotten even by the English.'[159]

A short timeline for chapters 11 and 12 – Vikings to Athelstan

745-815	*Charlemagne*
750s	*Initial Viking raids*
789-793	*Raids on Weymouth (south coast) and Lindisfarne (NE coast)*
795-806	*Raids on Iona*
830s	*Raids down North Sea coasts including Dorestad*
840s	*Viking fleets round northern French coasts and rivers and southern Britain*
841/2	*Vikings overwinter on Dublin*
851	*Vikings overwinter on Isle of Sheppey, Kent*
865	*The Great (Viking/ Danish) Army lands in Britain*

---

159 Holland (2016) p 92.

866/7	*Fall of York and East Anglia*
871	*Enter Alfred – Battle of Ashdown near Reading*
874	*Vikings overwinter at Repton and take over Mercia*
878	*Battle of Edington (Ethandune) – Viking surrender at Chippenham*
885-6	*Battle for Paris*
899	*Death of Alfred – accession of Edward 'the Elder'*
911	*Treaty of St-Clair-sur-Epte – Creation of Normandy*
918	*Death of Æthelflaed – Mercia subsumed into Wessex*
919	*Irish Scandinavians seize York and land to the south*
924	*Death of Edward – accession of Athelstan*
925	*Athelstan crowned at Kingston-on-Thames*
934	*Scottish campaign*
935	*Cirencester convocation*
937	*Battle of Brunanburh – Athelstan defeats combined opposing forces*
939	*Death of Athelstan*

POSTSCRIPT

The EMERGENCE OF ENGLAND

Rewind

If we go back to Pulpit Hill, to the time and place this story started, what major changes might we see in a fast-forward of the 10,000 years of this account? We'd see the barren landscape change colour, from grey tundra to flowing water and green shoots. Over time we'd see woods and forests grow up and then be reduced by clearings and meadows; pasture and arable fields emerge and change colour with the seasons; and open land become marked by ditches, hedges and fences. On the neighbouring hillsides, some of the lower slopes and higher valleys might be furrowed with barrows or marked by earthworks and causeways. We'd have heard less crashing through the undergrowth by wild beasts and seen more animals herded in fields, pulling ploughs or waiting for the butcher's knife. We'd have smelled the smoke from fires lit for land clearance, warmth, or ironworking, and heard the sound of tree-felling and flint knapping. Around us, hollowed out pits would show where cartloads of clay or chalk had been dug out and brought down to be made into pottery or Roman bricks, or burned and converted into lime for mortar, whitewash or fertiliser.

With people and animals regularly on the move, the landscape would have become marked by tracks, muddied by groups, and occasionally trampled by armies. At some point we might have detected clashes between Atrebates to the south-east, Dobunni to the north-west and Catuvellauni to the north-east. At this point in the Chilterns, the centuries of Roman occupation seem to have been mainly peaceful, as the main Roman armies and Boudicca's hordes mostly followed other routes. Some villas might then have appeared on the lower slopes, where a web of streams slowly meandered across the plain to join the silver ribbon of the distant river.

Water was vital, of course. The nearby village of Chinnor, for example, possibly first named for a man called Ceonna, was such a 'spring-line settlement' near the foot of the Chiltern scarp. Further afield at Thame we might have caught sight of a Roman settlement growing up alongside the river, adjacent to a former Neolithic causewayed enclosure. Later, we'd see some scattered houses grow into hamlets or villages, with a few great halls. Even then, the dense woodlands of the Chilterns would have provided a refuge for some of the Britons still evading Saxon clutches. As things settled down, small churches appeared, though flashpoints may have occurred when the border was contested between Wessex and Mercia, or by Viking bands ranging across the land.

Away from the royal entourage or seats of learning, few might then have known or cared that they were living during the creation of a new country or had become part of a people called the English.

Country, Nation and State

So what was this country? What, for example, 'makes' a country, nation or state, or indeed a 'nation state'? Although these are somewhat fluid concepts, we might see a *nation* as a large group of individuals with enough in common to be recognised as a distinctive 'people.' This too begs many questions. In Athelstan's England, with its mix of origins, customs and languages, even a sense of being English would have been secondary to individuals' family relationships, lordship allegiance, position in society, local affiliations, and trade connections. Regional groups might therefore have felt little in common with their more distant neighbours, let alone with faraway areas in the same kingdom. How could a sense of common 'national' identity be generated in such circumstances?

Just across the Channel, after a flying start and the heights of the Holy Roman Empire, nascent France was suffering by this time, not just from a seriously divided patrimony after Charlemagne, but also from years of Viking depredations. In many ways, the 911 Treaty of St. Clair-sur-Epte with the tough old Viking leader, Rollo, was a watershed moment. The resulting Normandy was to become a powerful state within a country, with profound later implications for both England and France. And elsewhere national identities were stirring in Ireland as well as in Scotland and Wales, partly in opposition to an emerging powerful England. But all these countries were some way from being nation states. Likewise in Denmark, riven by a century of division, Harald 'Bluetooth', its future unifying Christian king, had just been born, and battles for control of the future Norway and Sweden were intensifying between rival claimants.

All of these emerging countries needed leaders or kings strong enough to gain and maintain control and exercise authority, ideally with some continuity over generations. Their countries would also need understood, if sometimes provisional and disputed, state borders, with the residents within those borders typically becoming *de facto* subjects of the new state, often with little say in the matter.

How soon 'subjects' of a state thought of themselves as nationals of that state was less certain. In time, however, we can see that former Vikings, Danes, Norse or Swedes who settled in emerging England became English, just as those who settled in Frankia or France became French. Not so far into the future, battles for territory would then become national affairs.

By early medieval times the concept of ownership had developed, with much of early English society determined by ownership of land – and of people. This was underpinned by land units, boundaries and responsibilities: the hide as the family allocation, the parish as a social and ecclesiastical measure with defined boundaries, the lord's domain, and the sovereign's kingdom. Yet the composition of a nation and a state could still fluctuate hugely. This gave the opportunity for new people and ideas to influence development, but carried the risk of fracture if the constituents did not mix and work together.

A state therefore needed *cohesion*, built on sound foundations. In Alfred's early England these foundations were largely provided by a hierarchical social structure, held together by land, duty and money, supported by a rapidly developing Church. Protection was provided in return for varying degrees of control, backed by monarchs imbued with spiritual as well as temporal authority. Another key 'binding agent' (then as now) was a flourishing economy. Blessed with natural resources, entrepreneurial people, active production, valued coinage, and a plethora of ports, the country's trade and exports flourished, and standards of living for many (but not all) with it. Levels of physical and financial security had been increased by sound laws, and the beginnings of an effective administrative and judicial system. And with an entrepreneurial zeal and good communications that have often since been its hallmarks, the emerging England could begin to develop a status as a sound financial marketplace, contributing to the sense of a common identity.

All this was aided by a growing international reputation. In England a powerful unifying royal line had been established and seemed set to continue. This left Athelstan fulsomely acknowledged by many of his fellow rulers in western Europe, enabling him (through his many sisters) to join the international marriage and alliance market that was to be such a feature of succeeding centuries.

Culture, language and leadership

Irrespective of relative numbers, Anglo-Saxon culture and leadership became paramount in the emerging England. We might sense that it was the commonality and strength of this culture that Alfred was able to capture and mould into his vision of a land for the English. This emphasises how much of our history is not just about a record of *events* but about how and when our *culture* changes. But then identifying a culture can be even more elusive than giving a balanced view of events! What we can see is that the concept of culture has broadened from an original, often tribally-led, idea of distinctive artistry, fashion or funeral practices towards a modern societal understanding of culture as 'the attitudes and values which inform a society'.[160]

In fostering a common culture, a common language certainly helps. Take, for example, the Beowulf poem. For centuries Beowulf himself, even if fictional, seems to have embodied the supposed Anglo-Saxon (and very male) ideal. Even more remarkably, the hero seems to have maintained his role long after the world described in the poem had disappeared. We can also see this duality in the mix of pagan and Christian references. Even in later Anglo-Saxon times, Beowulf might have seemed an exercise in nostalgia. Yet the memory of a glorious past certainly was (and still appears to be) part of the essence of a national culture, harking back to the 'creation myth' concept discussed in chapter 7.

Especially in the north and east, Viking inroads were introducing fresh linguistic variants (many of which remain apparent today.)[161] *Even so,*

---

160 Chambers (12th edition.) *There is never a moment when culture is fixed! New ways and waves of behaviour, attitude, dress, action and creativity have swept in and been adopted from the last Ice Age onwards. Today, especially, culture change remains a hot topic in business, and many public services have been accused of having a 'toxic' or other deficient culture requiring redress.*

161 *In Yorkshire, Lincolnshire and the East Midlands words such as gate, meaning street, suffixes such as by (farmstead or town), thwaite (clearing) or thorpe (village), all suggest Scandinavian origins. The same is true of family names, such as those with the suffix 'son' (Johnson, Jackson etc.).*

Alfred saw that a common language, written as well as spoken – and available to all, was another powerful way to bring his people together. Clarity and consistency of language also helped provide the extra certainty that state, manorial and church documents needed as Old English replaced Latin.

The importance of leadership has been stressed, and leadership is not for the faint-hearted, especially as it was then. To be effective, as the battles for supremacy between the Anglo-Saxon kingdoms showed, leaders needed many talents, including the ability to respond and adapt well to external events, sudden changes of fortune, the unpredictability of other leaders, their own egos, and above all the ability to carry their people with them. The old idea of the king as warrior and 'ring-giver' died hard, but had to change. This makes the achievements of Alfred and his family all the greater, turning a litany of defeats into an overwhelming victory, and inspiring regional groups, who might previously have stood apart, to come together as a confident and victorious fighting force. Even though 'his' people would have been desperate for relief against the Vikings, it says much for Alfred's standing that so many answered the call before Edington.

Whatever his faults might have been, Alfred showed himself vigorous in strategy, ruthless in war, and generous in victory. He realised that even defeated opponents needed to be left with some dignity and time to adjust. His grandson, on the other hand, while sharing and extending his vision, may have been more intent on imposing his personal authority on his would-be subjects than creating a newly-defined England.

In many ways the Vikings had provided a common enemy against whom effective leaders like Alfred could coalesce support, helping to unite different tribal, religious, cultural or ethnic groups for mutual protection. But many challenges were yet to come, especially with those parts of the country latterly (and perhaps hastily) absorbed under Edward and Athelstan. The takeover of eastern and northern England had been especially fast and enforced, with no certainty that the mix would hold together. And even if there was a sound geographical context for England's coasts, the borders with Wales and Scotland were inevitably contested by growing national identities in those areas.

Athelstan himself was remarkably successful, but few people like to be beholden to an all-powerful monarch, especially if power is too blatantly paraded. The blending of Wessex and Mercia was crucial to the development of England, but old divisions continued under the surface. Nor were the Scots and Welsh really subdued, any more than the Irish (mainly Norse) Vikings. Was Athelstan therefore presiding over genuine integration, or simply sitting on an only partially suppressed powder keg?

Who were the English?

We've seen that Britain had, of necessity, absorbed disparate migration streams from prehistoric times onwards. The Romans who followed came and went, leaving many former soldiers and their families behind as more British than Roman, but taking many Britons with them to fight their wars. It's apparent that murder and mayhem did occur at times thereafter, notably during Saxon inroads into Kent, Sussex and Wessex.

Although there do appear to have been pockets and periods of violence, the evidence overall suggests waves of incomers into the old Roman Britain rather than overwhelming population replacements. As with any new group, some of those incomers clearly had an influence far greater than their relative numbers, driving cultural and other changes without massive immigration or widespread extermination. Ultimately, progressive integration, strong leadership, intermarriage, and an increasing ability to work together for mutual benefit seem to have become more important than common ancestry.

There is, however, an anomaly here. If we follow Bede in seeing the English purely as Anglo-Saxons, we downplay the relevance of the 'native' Britons. If we assume that as much as 40% of the population of the future England were 'Anglo-Saxon' in Athelstan's time (which is very much higher than many estimates), and also assume that Britons and Anglo-Saxons subsequently reproduced and survived at similar rates (allowing for the complexities of intermarriage), Britons overall, not Anglo-Saxons, would genetically have formed – and continued to form – the major proportion of Athelstan's English.

Even this might be misleading. Those 'native' Britons would themselves inevitably have had 'Continental' ancestry from past generations as Britain was repopulated after the Last Ice Age. We were, and are, a nation of immigrants. So the question is much less *where* we all came from as *when and how* we came, and *what* we did afterwards. This is why we need to be careful about dramatic extrapolations from new DNA research findings.

Robert Tombs has suggested that Alfred's seizure of London in 886 was as good a place as any to select as a birth date for England. Financially that may be apposite, as it was a vital base for what followed. Yet, at that time, the Danelaw remained largely intact, and the core ingredients of Mercia and Wessex – even if allies – still saw one another as separate kingdoms. It was only under Edward and Athelstan that the two kingdoms really came together as the core of a new land of the English.

There is, however, another issue here. Alfred had nurtured his vision of his Angelcynn to the point of his role moving from *King of the Anglo-Saxons* to *King of the English*. But he was not King of *England* because England as such did not then exist! We can see Edward and his sister Æthelflaed adding the rest of Mercia, East Anglia and subsequently the Five Boroughs, but still stopping short of York and Northumbria, vital ingredients of the England of the future. Yet even when Athelstan added these critical regions, he did

The EMERGENCE OF ENGLAND

not pause and claim to have founded England. His ambition seems to have been both more basic and more ambitious. More basic because he wanted all other rulers in the island of Britain to acknowledge his personal supremacy and overlordship. More ambitious because his objective seems to have seen – as he was latterly styled – to be *Ruler of the Whole of Britain*.

However unrealistic it may appear to us now, Athelstan seemed unable to rest easy unless and until he was *accepted* as overlord of the entire island. He may have thought that his power and achievement spoke for themselves, but if so he gravely underestimated the politics of cross-border relationships. When all his (apparently former) enemies combined against him at the peak of his power, the shock might even have delayed his normally immediate response. But when he did finally set out for Brunanburh, he was well prepared.

We can only guess, but might sense that his grandfather Alfred, wary of imperial overstretch, would have wanted to consolidate before moving forward. And certainly after Brunanburh there was a more powerful and acknowledged English nation. But even then there was still no England as such. It was to be many more decades before Angle-land, Engla-land or Engla londe fully came into being. And the shortened version, *England*, appears only to have come into general usage very much later, perhaps as late as the 14th century.

The irony then might be that, while Alfred created the genesis of the English nation when he identified 'his Angelcynn' as 'Englisc', this was long before even a proto-England existed. His grandson Athelstan, on the other hand largely created England before its new, wider, and much greater, population were fully English – and before acknowledging it as England!

This history should show that there was nothing inevitable in the creation of England or its borders. Nor was there any certainty that the new state would hold together, especially with a pattern of premature royal deaths starting to become a feature of the House of Wessex. The Wessex kings had, nevertheless, brought together under central royal control a diffuse land of many peoples whom they could now think of as 'English'. Once its boundaries were substantially settled, and even if they had not named it as such, we might therefore fairly conclude that, by 939, *England* and *the English* had *emerged* – but were yet to *evolve*. That evolution, however, is another story!

ADDENDUM

References are to page numbers in the text.

18 The heat of lava flows from widespread volcanic fissures is regarded as having been exacerbated by escaping carbon dioxide operating as an enveloping greenhouse gas, trapping the rising heat in the earth's atmosphere.

20 Although the reasons for the Neanderthals' disappearance remain uncertain, some recent research suggests an earlier date for this, possibly closer to 40,000 BCE.

33 DNA research has also led to suggestions that the Bronze Age and Bell Beaker culture from the Rhine area might have led to up to 90% of Britons being replaced by new waves of incomers in those periods. The debate will doubtless continue.

41 To add to the complexity, a report released in mid-2024 indicates that the massive central altar stone at Stonehenge probably originated from the Orcadian basin of what is now north-east Scotland. This accentuates the sense of a neolithic culture that was far wider and more connected than had been thought. It is perhaps an extra irony that the discovery by a Welsh PhD student of a key stone from an area now within Scotland has evoked nationalist sentiment dating back long before Scotland, Wales and England existed as such!

SELECTED READING AND REFERENCES

Ice to Romans and General

Ackroyd, Peter – *The History of England Part 1: Foundation (2001) Macmillan*

Ackroyd, Peter – *London: The Biography (2000) Chatto & Windus/ Vintage*

Braudel, Fernand – *A History of Civilisations (1987) Editions Arthaud*

Carr, EH – *What is History? (new ed and intro 2001) Palgrave Macmillan*

Chadwick, Nora K – *Celtic Britain (1963) Thames & Hudson*

Churchill, W S – *A History of the English-Speaking Peoples: Vol 1 (1956) Cassell*

Crane, Nicholas – *The Making of the British Landscape (2016) Weidenfeld & Nicholson*

Crystal, David – *The Stories of English (2004) Allen Lane/Penguin*

Cunliffe, Barry – *Europe Between the Oceans : 9000 BC to AD 1000 (2008) Yale*

Davies, Norman – *The Isles (1999) Macmillan*

Garrow, Duncan and Wilkin, Neil – *The world of Stonehenge (2022) British Museum Press*

Hannigan, Des and McBride, Simon – *Ancient Tracks (1994) Pavilion Books*

Hawes, James – *The Shortest History of England (2020) Old Street Publishing*

Miles, David – *The Tribes of Britain (2005) Weidenfeld & Nicholson*

Oliver, Neil – *A History of Ancient Britain (2012) Weidenfeld & Nicholson*

Oppenheimer, Stephen – *The Origins of the British (2006) Constable & Robinson*
Pryor, Francis – *Britain BC (2003) Harper Collins*
Pryor, Francis – *Scenes from a Prehistoric Life (2022) Head of Zeus*
Roberts, Alice – *Ancestors (2021) Simon & Shuster*
Roberts, Alice – *Buried (2022) Simon & Shuster*
Schama, Simon – *A History of Britain Part 1 – At the Edge of the World (2000) BBC*
Stringer, Chris – *Homo Brittanicus (2006) Penguin*
Tombs, Robert– *The English and their History (2014) Allen Lane/ Penguin*
Whitelock, Dorothy – *Beginnings of English Society (1952) Penguin*

Anglo-Saxons and Vikings

Ashe, Geoffrey (ed) – *The quest for Arthur's Britain (1971) Paladin*
Ashe, Geoffrey – *Mythology of the British Isles (1990) Canelo*
Bede, the Venerable (trans. 1955) – *The Ecclesiastical History of the English People – Penguin*
Beresford-Ellis, Peter – *Celt and Saxon (1993) Constable*
Bond, Penn & Rogerson – *The North Folk, Angles, Saxons & Danes (1990) Poppyland*
Brooke, Christopher *The Saxon and Norman Kings (1963) Fontana*
Carroll, Harrison, and Williams – *The Vikings in Britain and Ireland* (2014) British Museum Press
Clarkson, Tim– *Aethelflaed* (2018) *Birlinn*
Clarkson, Tim – *The Picts (2008) Birlinn*
Derry, T K and Blakeway, M G – *The Making of Britain (1968) John Murray*
Derry, T K– *A History of Scandinavia* (1979) *University of Minnesota Press*
Evans, Bryan – *The Origins and Early History of the English (2019) Anglo-Saxon Books*
Fields, Nic – *Rome's Northern Frontier (2005) Osprey*

SELECTED READING AND REFERENCES

Fisher, D.J.V – *The Anglo-Saxon Age* c 400 to 1042 *(1973) Longman*

Grainge, Gerald – *The Roman Invasions of Britain* (2005) Tempus

Harl, Kenneth – *The Vikings – CD course (2005) The Great Courses*

Haywood, John – *The Penguin Historical Atlas of the Vikings (1995) Penguin*

Hill, David – *An Atlas of Anglo-Saxon England (1981) Blackwell*

Hills, Catherine – *The Origins of the English (2003) Bloomsbury*

Hindley, Geoffrey – *The Anglo-Saxons (2006) Constable & Robinson*

Holland, Tom – *Athelstan The Making of England* (2016*) Penguin Monarchs*

James, Edward – *Britain in the First Millennium* (2001) Arnold/ Hodder Headline

Morris, Marc – *The Anglo-Saxons* (2021) Penguin

Newton, Sam – *The Reckoning of King Raedwald (2003) Red Bird Press*

Pollington, Stephen – *Anglo-Saxon FAQs (2008) Anglo-Saxon books*

Randsborg, Klaus– *The Anatomy of Denmark (2009) Gerald Duckworth*

Richards, Julian D – *Viking Age England* (2007*) Tempus*

Townend, Matthew – *Viking Age Yorkshire* (2014) *Blackthorn Press*

Williams, Thomas – *Viking Britain (2017) William Collins*

Williams, Pentz & Wemhoff – *Vikings, Life and Legend (2014) British Museum Press*

Wood, Michael – *In Search of the Dark Ages (2023) Penguin*

Other Viking sources include: *Vikings!* – Magnus Magnusson (Bodley Head) (1980); Yves Cohat – *The Vikings, Lords of the Seas*; David M Wilson; *The Vikings and their origins* (1970) Thames & Hudson; *The Viking Achievement* – PG Foote and DM Wilson, (Sidgwick & Jackson, 1980); *Viking Hersir, 793-1066 CE* by M Harrison (Osprey, 1993); *The Viking Art of War* by P Griffith (Greenhill Books, 1995); *Viking Weapons and Warfare* by JK Siddom (Tempus, 2000)

Plus many articles, heritage books and research references

INDEX

(Note: This Index covers most (but not all) page references, including footnotes. Bold numbers indicate main sections on the relevant topic.)

Aesc, K of Kent 118, 123
Aella, K of Deira 128, 155
Ælle, K of N'umbria 213-5
Æthelflaed, Lady of the Mercians 216, **226-7**, 229, **230-4**, 240, 248, 252
Aethelfrith of Bernicia 128,**155**,181
Æthelred, K of Wessex (Alfred's brother) * 217-8
Aethelred, K of Mercia * 170, 182
Aethelred, K of Mercia * 227, 231 (NB: None of these marked * is the much later Aethelred 'the Unready'!)
Æthelwold (Alfred's nephew) 230
Aethelwulf, K of Wessex (Alfred's father) 217
Agricola (Roman general) 76, 78
Alfred ('the Great'), K of Wessex 109, 138, 145, 191, **217-230**, 236, 240, **245-6**
Alcuin of York 179, 205
Allectus 88-9, 103
Amesbury 42
Amesbury Archer 45, 47
Angelcynn 131, 226, 229, 239, 248-9
Anglesey 75, 157, 208, 217

Angles 108,113, 116, 120, 124-7, 127, 134, 163, 168, 171-2
Anna, K of E Anglia 159, 173, 182
Arras/ Arras Culture 56
Arian (Christianity) 91, 147
Arthur, 'King' **138-142**
Ashdown, Battle of 214, 218, 240
Asser, Bishop 179, 220, 219, 222, 226, 229
Athelney (Somerset) 221
Athelstan, K of 'England' **234-9**, 240, 244, **247-9**
Atrebates **63**, 68, 70, 84, 242
Augustine of Canterbury 149-50, 165
Augustine of Hippo 111
Augustus, Emperor 67, 69, 103
Aurelianus, Ambrosius 139
Avebury 36, 43, 47

Bamburgh 127, 154, 165, 235
Bath 82, 92, 119
Beaker/ Bell Beaker Culture 45, 47, 55, 251
Bede, Venerable 109, 112, 116, 118, 123, 131, 152, 154, **156-8**, 160, 163, 166, 169, 181, 248
Belgae 58, 63, 70, 117

257

Beowulf 132, **141-4**, 201, 245
Bernicia (prev. Bryneich) 128, 154-5, 181, 210
Boudicca, Queen 75
Bretwalda (over-king) 167
Brigantes 83
Brittany 39, 64, 109
Bronze/ Bronze Age 8, 28, 33, 45, **48-51**, 55, **62-3**, 114, 129, 202, 251
Brunanburh, Battle of 237-8, 240, 249
Burhs 228, 231, 233
Burgred, K of Mercia 217
Buxton 83
Byzantium/ Constantinople 91, 147, 150

Caedwalla, K of Wessex 162, 171
Caesar, Julius **65-69**, 71-2
Cadwallon, K of Gwynedd 157, 162, 169, 176, 181, 183
Caledonians 77-8, 89
Calleva (Silchester) 63, 68, 85, 89
Canterbury 70, 81, 111, **149-50**, 153, 178
Caratacus/ Caractacus **71-4**, 83, 100, 103
Carausius, 'Emperor' **88-90**, 93, 103
Camulodunum/ Colchester 71
Cantiaci/ Cantii 70, 84, 117
Cartimandua, Queen 74, 83
Cassivellaunus 68
Catuvellauni 63, 68, 70-1, 84, 242
Causewayed enclosures 40, 43, 47, 73, 242
Celts/ Celtic/ Celtiberian 55, **57-8**, 61, 64, 65, 139

Cerdic/ Cynric (Wessex) 119, 123, 138
Chalk 7, 22, **28-9**, 36, 84, 126, 208, 241
Channel/ Channel River 7, 19, 22, **24-5**, 27, 67, **71-2**, 80, **88-9**, 93, 117, 118, 134, 136-7, 183
Charlemagne 193, 204, 219, 239
Cheddar Man 38
Chester 73, 81, 234
Chichester 72, 85, 118
Chilterns 1, 242
Chippenham 221-3, 240
Chronicle (The Anglo-Saxon) 107, 109, **118-9**, 131, 205, 219, 222, 229, 232
Churchill, Winston 130, 252
Cirencester 70, 81, 85, 94, 119, 182, 237, 240
Civitates 78
Claudius, Emperor 66, 69, 71-4, 103
Coins/ coinage 2, 53-5, 65, 88, 103, 107, 110, 135, 150, 152, 178, 184, 188, 192, 216, 225, 227, 236, 244
Commius 68, 73
Constantin(e), K of Scotland 235, 237-8
Constantine I (the Great) **89-93**, 100, 103, 110, 146, 149
Constantine III (usurper) 98-9, 104, 122
Constantius II (emperor) 92
Constantius Chlorus (emperor) 79, 89, 103
Constantius (author) 109
Corieltauvi 53, 70
Cornovii 70
Cornwall 49, 64, 125, 132, 149, 182, 209, 236

INDEX

Cresswell Crags 37
Culture 34, 45-8, 55-6, 61, 63-4, 202, 229, 245, 251
Cunobelinus/ Cymbeline 71

Dalriada/ Dal Riada 94, 127, 155, 181
Danebury (fort) 54, 65
Danelaw 2, 216, 223, **228-9**, 230, 248
Danes/ Danish 132, 197, 204-5, **207-11**, 217, **220-24**, 227-8, 231, 233
Dark Ages 105, 122, 190
Deira 127-8, 155-6, 181
Dendrochronology 35
Denmark (see also Danes *above*) 7, 23, 113-4, 116, 213, 243
Diocletian, Emperor **88-90**, 103
DNA 9, 20, 33, 38, 56, 63, **195-6**, 248, 251
Dobunni 70-1, 242
Doggerland 23-4, 26-7, 62
Dorchester-on-Thames 54, 70, 81
Dorney Reach 54
Dover 29, 81, 85, 118
Druids 56, 67, 71, 75
Dublin 199, 209, **214-5**, 224, 230, 231, **237-9**
Dumnonii 70, 71, 125, 182
Durrington 42
Dyfed (Wales) 97, 125, 219

East Anglia 2, 19, 36, 79, 108, 113, 116, 120, **125**, 134, 141, 143, 150, 226, 228, **230-1**, 233, 240, 248
Eboracum (see also York) 84, 85, 126

Ecgbert, K of Wessex 179
Edinburgh 77-8, 155
Edington (Ethandune), Battle of **222-4**, 226, 240
Edmund (St), King of E Anglia 141, 172, **213-5**
Edward 'the Elder' – K of 'England' – 216, 227, **229-31**, **233-4**, 240, **247-8**
Edwin, K of N'umbria 156-8, 168, 173, 175, 181
Essex 68, 70, 108, 116, 124, 150, 152, 177, 182, 238

Farming **30-33**, **45-6**, 48, 50, 59, 103, 132, 135, 150, 185, 195-6
Flag Fen 36, 51
Flint 2, **28-30**, 47, 51
Foederati 106, 120, 136
Francia/ Franks 113, **193-4**, 196, 204, 243
Frisia/ Frisians 106, 113, 116, 136, 208

Gaul/ Gallic 55, 58, **61-2,65-68**, 70, 88, 101, 117, 136, 149
Geoffrey of Monmouth 139
Germanic 7, 59, 92, 101, 106, 120, 127, **132-4**, 156, 187
Germanus 109, **111**, 122, 165
Gewisse 119
Gildas **129-131**, 134, 137
Godrey, Danish King **204-5**, 207
Gododdin 127, 155
Goths 95-7, 104
Gough's Cave 38
Great (Heathen) Army **210**, 214, 218, 220, 224
Grimes Graves **30**, 47

259

Guthfrith **215**, 235, 238
Guthrum 2, **214**, **220**, 223, 228
Gwynedd (Wales) **125**, 156-7, 181-2, 217

Hadrian, Emperor 77
Hadrian of Libya 153, 166
Hadrian's Wall 66, 69, **76-7**, 94-5, 103, 219
Hallstatt ('Celts') **60**, 62, 65
Happisburgh 19, 26
Heavenfield, battle 157, 164
Heidelberg man 19, 26
Henge **39**, 43-4, 46-7
Hengest & Horsa **112**, 118, 122, 127, 136, 138, 149
Henry of Huntingdon 131, 154
Hide (measure of land) 168, 184-5, 190
Holocene (period) 3, 18, 21 26
Holy Roman Empire 193, 204, 243
Homo sapiens 19, 26
Homoousian 147
Honorius, Emperor 87, **96-8**, 104, 107, 122
Humber (Estuary) 83-4, **125-6**, 155, 167, 170, 231, 235
Hwicce 170

Ice Age 5, 7, 18-21, 26, 28, 31, 37, 248
Icel, K of Mercia **168**, 172
Iceni 2, **70-1**, 74, 76
Icknield Way 2
Iona, Isle 146, 158, 162, 164-5, 181
Ireland 5, 7, 94-5, 97, 145-6, 196, 199, 206-7, **209**, **214-5**, 231, 243
Iron Age 1, 28, 52, 55-6, 59, 62, 73
Ivar (the Boneless) 212, 214-5

Julian, Emperor 92-3
Jutes/ Jutland 106-7, **112-6**, 118, 122-4, 127, 168, 172, 204

Knapping (flint) 30, 241
Kraki, Hrolf 141

Langdale Pikes 30
Language **58-9**, 62, 101, **131-3**, 142, 153, 177, 191, 216, 226, **245-6**
Latin 7, 58-9, 79, 81, **101**, 191, 226, 246
Law 58, 146, 151, 185, **189**, 218, **225**, 236, 244
Leadership 44, 142, 201, 216, **245-6**
Legend 122, 129, **137-8**, 140-1, 161, 195, 212
Leicester/shire 70, 81, 224, 231
Lincoln/shire **53**, 70, 84,-5, 94, 126, 156, 224, 233
Lindisfarne 127, 154, 158, 161, **164-5**, 195, **205-6**, 239
Lindsey 126
London/ Lundenwic 74, **84-6**, 94, 103, 117, 151, 167, 177, **192**, 227, 248
Longship(s) 115, 197, 199, 200, 210
Lothbrok, Ragnar **212-3**, 215

Marsalia (Marseilles) 60
Maximus, Magnus 97, 104, 110, 122
Mellitus (Bishop) 192
Mercia **125**, 157, **167-73**, **177-8**, 181-3, 192, 214, **216-7**, 226-8, **231-4**, 240, 248
Mersey, River 224, 231, 233

INDEX

Mesolithic 27, 46, 59
Middle Anglia 125, 171, 173
Migration 5, 14, 33-4, 62-3, 99-100, 108, 113, 124, **133-4**, 137, 247
Mons Graupius (Battle of) 77
Mount Badon (Battle of) 108, 120, 123, 136, **139-40**
Myth 112, 122, 129, 138-40, 212, 245

Nation, national 5, 129, 196, 216, **229**, 235, 238, **242-3**, 245
Neanderthal 20, 26, 251
Nennius 110, 126, 140
Neolithic 27-8, 30, 33, 40, 46-7, 73, 251
Normandy / Normans / Northmen 2, 131, 195, 197, **211**, 224, 240, 243
Northumbria 69, 109, **126-7**, **154-158**, 163-5, 169-70, 181, 214-5, 238, 248
Nydam (ship) 115

Offa, K of Mercia **177-9**, 216
Offa's Dyke 179-80
Oppida 53, 65, 81
Orkney (Islands) 39, 47, 206-7
Oswald/ Oswy, K of Northumbria **157-8**, 162, **169-70**, 181
Ouse, River 84, **125-6**

Paris 199, 211, 240
Parisii 56, 70, 83
Paviland (Red lady of) 20, 26, 38
Pelagius/ Pelagianism 111, 122, 158
Penda, K of Mercia 153, 157, 164, **168-70**, 173, 177, 182

Pennines 23, 70, 76, 84, 127
Picts 77, **94-5**, 107, 122, 146, 157, 181
Plague 86, 121, 123
Pope **147-50**, 153, 162, 179, 225
Powys (Wales) 125, 182
Pulpit Hill 1, 241

Rheged (kingdom) 127, 155, 181
Rhine, River 22, 24, 63, 113, 208
Ridgeway 29, **36**, **43**, 55, 218
Rock Route (Scotland) 17
Rome 61, 65-7, 73-4, 78, 86, 90-1, 93, **95-8**, 103-4, 111, 139, **148-9**, 158, 225
Rouen (France) 199, 211

Saxon shore 93, 106
Scotland 5, 7, 17-8, 24, 52, 77, 95, 127, 146, 196, 199, 207, 216, 237-8, 243, 247, 251
Scotti/ Scots (see also Picts) **87**, **94-5**, 103, 122, 155, 181, 195, 215
Seine, River 29, 63, 89, 199, 208, 211
Severn, River 54, 70-1, 82, 124-5, 168, 180, 208
Severus, Septimius, Emperor 77, 86, 103
Sheppey, Isle of 117, 159, 210, 239
Silbury Hill 43
Skald 139, 143
Snettisham 53
Southampton 119, 123, 135, 178
St Albans/ Verulamium 74, 81, 85
St Columba 146, 165
St Cuthbert **161**, 164-5, 181, 206, 215

261

St Frideswide **160-1**, 166
St George 141-2
St Patrick 145-6
St Seaxburh **159**, 165
St Wilfred **162**, 165, 171
Staffordshire Hoard 169
Stonehenge **39-42**, 45, 47, 251
Strathclyde 127, 155, 214, 216, 235, 237-8
Storegga Slides 24
Sutton Hoo 142, **171-4**, 182, 203

Tacitus 74, 79-80, 99, 187
Tamworth 178, 231, 232
Tène, la ('Celts') 60, 62, 65
Thames, River 22, 24, 36, 50, 68, 70-1, 84, 120, 125, 167, 192, 208, 210, 228
Thanet, Isle of 52, 112, **118**, 149, 206
Theodore of Tarsus 153
Theodosius, Emperor 96-7, 104
Tin 45, 49, 52, 80
Trent, River 125-6, 170, 181, 227, 233
Trinovantes 68, 70-1, 74, 84
Tsunami 24-5, 27

Uffington White Horse 55, 65
United Kingdom 7
Urnfield Culture 46, 55, 62

Venutius 83
Verica 69, 73
Vespasian 73, 83, 86, 103
Vikings 2, 109, 126, 145, 165, **194-211**, 214, 217, 219, 227, 229-31, 237-40, 243, 246

Volcanic eruptions 25-6, 65, **121**, 123, 136, 143, 251
Vortigern 112, 122
Votadini 69, 78
Votive offerings 49, 54

Wales/ Welsh 23, 41, 49, 55, 69-70, 80, 82, 85, 97, 112, 119, 124-5, 132-3, 139-40, 157, 167-8, 180-3, 216, 219, 227, 235, 237, 243, 247, 251
Watling Street 81-2, 85
Watlington (Hoard) 2, 227
Waylands Smithy 43
Weald (of Kent) 80, 117
Wessex 2, **117-9**, **123-5**, 138, 153, 171, 179, 182-3, 209, 214, **216-23**, 225-7, **232-5**, 247, 250
Whitby, Synod of 158, 161-2, 166, 181
Winchester 63, 70, 81, 119
Windmill Hill 43, 47
Witham, River 53, 126
Witan 217
Wolds, the 29, 56, 70, **84**, 126-7
Wroxeter 81-2
Wuffingas, dynasty 168, **172-3**, 175
Wulfhere, K of Mercia 159, 170, 183

Yngling, dynasty 144, 173
York (see also Eboracum) 77, 81, **83-5**, 89, 94, 103, 126, **149**, 197, 210, 213-6, 231-3, **235**, **237-8**, 240, 248
Yorkshire 23, 27, 29, 54, 56, 62, 65, 70, 76, 120, **125-7**, 154, 245
Younger Dryas (Interlude) 3, 21, 26, 38

ACKNOWLEDGEMENTS

Because this has been mainly a solo work, my acknowledgments are limited, but to those who have supported and contributed I am immensely grateful. These include the various groups of family and friends with whom I've walked much of the length and breadth of England (and beyond) over many years; my tutors and colleagues on the MPhil 'Critical Management' course at Lancaster University Management School, who opened my eyes to other ways of thinking and seeing; the tutors on the various stimulating Oxford University Continuing Education courses I've attended; and my friends and colleagues in Thame Green Living, with whom I've shared a different kind of journey. Individual thanks are due to Isobel, poet and agent extraordinaire, who gave me the faith to write and publish; to Sylvia, who took time out from her doctorate to give me editorial and text support; to Sam and Gareth for their contributions; and overall to Hazel for her understanding and insights, and for living with the Celts, Romans, Anglo-Saxons, Vikings for longer than she might have wished! And thanks too to Paul Futcher for preparing the maps, Carolina for taking me through the initial stages, and the rest of the Troubador team for their open and professional approach in bringing this book into being.

For further reference or feedback
please visit www.charlesboundy.com